# The Evil Twins of Technocracy and Transhumanism

by Patrick M. Wood

*Technocracy is transforming the world. Transhumanism is transforming people who will live there.*

*Printed in the United States of America*

*First Printing 2022*

*ISBN 978-0-9863739-4-7*
*Coherent Publishing, LLC*
*P.O. Box 52247*
*Mesa, AZ 85208*
*www.CoherentPress.com*

*Additional information & Updates*
*www.Technocracy.news*

# Dedication

To the cherished youth of the world, many of whom are lost in ignorance or denial: May they gain understanding and courage to choose a future that elevates freedom and liberty as essential values of culture and civilization. I especially dedicate this book to my grandchildren who may be the first generation to grow up in a thoroughly technocratic and transhuman world.

# Table of Contents

# Acknowledgments

This book is the cumulative result of several presentations delivered to prominent groups as well as many conversations with colleagues and researchers. My editor, a seasoned professional who wishes to remain anonymous, brought fresh eyes to the topics of technocracy and transhumanism and pushed me to clarify text until it made sense to her. Her work kept me on schedule, making an otherwise monumental challenge manageable. My wife, who followed along with every paragraph, supported me every day that I disappeared into my "writing room" to avoid distractions. My supporters, who subscribed to my Substack blog, gave valuable feedback as I released each chapter. They also helped to finance the research and time it took to complete the work. To all of you, a humble "Thank you!"

# PREFACE

*All around me are familiar faces*
*Worn-out places, worn-out faces*
*Bright and early for their daily races*
*Going nowhere, going nowhere*
*And their tears are filling up their glasses*
*No expression, no expression*
*Hide my head, I want to drown my sorrow*
*No tomorrow, no tomorrow*
*— Roland Orzabal, "Mad World"*

The song "Mad World," written by Roland Orzabal and originally recorded in 1983 by Tears with Fears in England, has become increasingly popular as the modern world seemingly spins out of control. At the beginning of COVID lockdowns in early 2020, Tears with Fears lead singer Curt Smith and his daughter, Diva, created a simple rendition of "Mad World" at home and posted it on YouTube. In the two years since, it has scored over 9 million views and is still climbing.

Why?

As art reflects culture, "Mad World" surfaces inexpressible sentiments buried deep in the hearts and minds of man in today's mad world. In less than fifty words, the lyrics draw out emotions that have likely been lurking for years, looking for ways to escape the lips, but for lack of words could not.

In short, "Mad World" is a realistic mirror of the hopelessness felt by many who know something is desperately wrong but just cannot put their finger on it. Fed a steady diet of ubiquitous propaganda, their scrambled thoughts and ginned-up emotions cannot produce any coherent explanation of what is happening, who is making it happen, how are they doing it and, most importantly, *why*.

If this is you, dear reader, please take some hope from these pages as I attempt to lay out the necessary elements that will give you a unified view of the world as it is today and where it is headed. True, the picture I paint isn't pleasant, so you may be tempted to turn away—to ignore what I say. But solutions can never come out of ignorance. It has been self-evident throughout history that you cannot fight an unseen or unrecognized enemy. As you will discover, today's enemies of humanity have been hiding in plain sight. Once you see them, you will not be able to unsee them.

This is the third book I have penned on technocracy and the first to formally introduce the topic of transhumanism. You will soon learn why and how they are intertwined. I often refer to them as Siamese twins joined at the hip, and indeed, they are. They are necessary and essential to each other's advancement. One is useless without the other, but together they intend to transform the entire world into something humans have never seen before.

Technocracy is a replacement economic system for free market economics, originally designed by scientists and engineers in the 1930s at the most progressive educational institution of that era, Columbia University. Today technocracy is known by multiple names, among them sustainable development, stakeholder capitalism, green economy, smart growth, and so on. Early technocrats defined technocracy in 1938 as:

> *[. . .] the science of social engineering, the scientific operation of the entire social mechanism to produce and distribute goods and services to the entire population. [. . .] For the first time in human history it will be done as a scientific, technical, engineering problem. [. . .] There will be no place for Politics, Politicians, Finance or Financiers, Rackets or Racketeers. [. . .] Technocracy will distribute by means of a certificate of distribution available to every citizen from birth to death.* — The

Technocrat, 1938

Technocracy proposes to eliminate private property by putting all resources into a common trust managed by unelected, unaccountable scientists, engineers, and technicians (i.e., the technocrats), who would control all aspects of human existence.

It is no coincidence that the elitist World Economic Forum's (WEF) so-called Great Reset of the world is identical in scope and purpose: "You will own nothing and be happy."

In June 2020, WEF Chairman Klaus Schwab laid out the rationale for the Great Reset:

> *COVID-19 lockdowns may be gradually easing, but anxiety about the world's social and economic prospects is only intensifying. There is good reason to worry: a sharp economic downturn has already begun, and we could be facing the worst depression since the 1930s. But, while this outcome is likely, it is not unavoidable.*
>
> *To achieve a better outcome, the world must act jointly and swiftly to revamp all aspects of our societies and economies, from education to social contracts and working conditions. Every country, from the United States to China, must participate, and every industry, from oil and gas to tech, must be transformed.* **In short, we need a "Great Reset" of capitalism.**[1] *[Emphasis added.]*

Schwab went on to write, "There are many reasons to pursue a Great Reset, but the most urgent is COVID-19." Here, he was clearly tying the stimulus to the solution. Then he further emphasized his point:

> *The pandemic represents a rare but narrow window of opportunity to reflect, reimagine, and reset our world to create a healthier, more equitable, and more prosperous future.*[2]

The term "reimagine" is frightening. It evokes images of the children's game 52 Card Pickup, in which the whole deck of cards

---

*1 World Economic Forum website. June 3, 2020. https://www.weforum.org/agenda/2020/06/now-is-the-time-for-a-great-reset*
*2 WEF website. June 3, 2020. https://www.weforum.org/agenda/2020/06/now-is-the-time-for-a-great-reset*

is thrown into the air, lands helter-skelter on the floor, and is picked up randomly by the opponent. "Reimagine" also provokes many obvious questions, such as: Who decides who will do this reimagining? What are the ground rules? Is the reimagining pure speculation or is it informed by other factors? What factors? How will we know the outcome will truly be good for mankind in general and individuals in particular?

Note the subtle broadening between the phrases "great reset of capitalism" in the first Schwab quote cited above and "reset our world" in the last. The direction he is heading points us toward the rest of his Great Reset ideology—the reset of humanity itself.

Elsewhere, the WEF writes pointedly about transhumanism:

*Biological evolution takes place over generations. But imagine if it could be expedited beyond the incremental change envisaged by Darwin to a matter of individual experience. Such things are dreamt of by so-called "transhumanists". Transhumanism has come to connote different things to different people, from a belief system to a cultural movement, a field of study to a technological fantasy. You can't get a degree in transhumanism, but you can subscribe to it, invest in it, research its actors, and act on its tenets.*

*So what is it? The term "transhumanism" gained widespread currency in 1990, following its formal inauguration by Max More, the CEO of Alcor Life Extension Foundation. It refers to an optimistic belief in the enhancement of the human condition through technology in all its forms. Its advocates believe in fundamentally enhancing the human condition through applied reason and a corporeal embrace of new technologies.*

*It is rooted in the belief that humans can and will be enhanced by the genetic engineering and information technology of today, as well as anticipated advances, such as bioengineering, artificial intelligence, and molecular nanotechnology. The result is an iteration of Homo sapiens enhanced or augmented,*

> *but still fundamentally human.*[3]

Since the WEF is promoting both technocracy and transhumanism, this has led me to observe, "Technocracy is to the structure and operation of society as transhumanism is to the people who live there."

Ever since a bioengineered virus was used to create what I call the Great Panic of 2020 in January of 2020, the world has experienced the cunning, cold-hearted candor of an unelected and unaccountable technocratic/transhumanist cabal telling us what we must think, feel, say, and do. In short, how we must live.

As I said in the Conclusion of my book, *Technocracy Rising: The Trojan Horse of Global Transformation*:

> *[. . .] if today's technocrats are meticulously working toward a scientific dictatorship and applying a specific strategy to get there, wouldn't you think that they have a specific list of criteria that must be met before "game over" can be called? Wouldn't you think that they are comparing such a list to the actual progress they are making in the world? Wouldn't you think that they are monitoring their progress and will recognize when the list has been fulfilled? If you can see my point here, then there are only two questions left: When that day comes, will the Technocrats have the guts to shut the old world order down and simply declare the "system" as dictator? If so, how long will it take them to act?* [4]

When I wrote those words in 2015, the technocrats were perilously close to calling "game over." After the 2018 release of my second book, *Technocracy: The Hard Road to World Order*, they were closer still. By the beginning of 2020, with the release of the COVID-19 virus, they were indeed demonstrating "the guts to

---

*3 "What is transhumanism and how does it affect you." World Economic Forum website. April 10, 2018. https://www.weforum.org/agenda/2018/04/transhumanism-advances-in-technology-could-already-put-evolution-into-hyperdrive-but-should-they*

*4 Wood, Patrick, Technocracy Rising: The Trojan Horse of Global Transformation, (Coherent Publishing, 2015), p. 206.*

shut the old world order down and simply declare the 'system' as dictator."

Once fear of the virus dominated the global psyche, public health authorities began launching economic, political, and social shredding policies in nearly every nation on earth. They ordered face masks, social distancing, the closing of schools and businesses and churches, lockdowns, quarantines, incessant testing, temperature checks, and more. The global economic impact was tectonic, wrecking supply chains, driving small business into oblivion, and causing massive unemployment.

Economic destruction didn't just play *into* technocrat hands. It *was* the hand they played!

When technocracy was originally codified by scientists and engineers at Columbia University in 1932, the Great Depression was believed to represent the death of capitalism and free market economics. Furthermore, as an economic system, technocracy was so radically different from capitalism that even a casual observer would have concluded that the two systems could not possibly occupy the same space at the same time. If the former were to be developed and ultimately dominate, the later would first have to die.

With the declaration of the death sentence on capitalism, a huge moral hazard was created that lured other economic actors to jump on the bandwagon to support technocracy.

The end result of this moral hazard was seen perfectly in the Great Panic of 2020. At the same time that mortal blows were being delivered to the global economy, the WEF and its globalist cronies were setting in motion a massive propaganda campaign designed to convince the world that a Great Reset is not only desirable, but required.

There is a two-word clue hidden in the WEF quote above: genetic engineering. That phrase should give us pause, should cause us to question the new class of experimental injections that are being offered to "cure" COVID-19. These are not traditional vaccines in any sense of the term, but rather are based on mRNA (Messenger RNA) and DNA.

I have written extensively, in books and articles, about technocracy and transhumanism and about how technology is being used to force both upon an unsuspecting world. This book will fill in the details of the deep transformations taking place and will explain how these deep transformations affect normal people. At the end of the book, we will discuss solutions—some possible ways to reject the evil twins of technocracy and transhumanism.

There is no doubt that the time to deal with these life-changing issues is now. Right now! Your future should belong to you and you alone. Does it? Will it? Consider these questions as we examine the future they are "reimagining" for us!

# INTRODUCTION

Between 1955 and 1990, numerous esteemed scholars wrote extensively and authoritatively about technocracy. In many ways, they settled the debate about what technocracy is, about what its intentions are, about how it operates, and about why it should be completely rejected as the model of a future world. In light of that decisive conclusion, one scholar warned in 1977 that technocracy was ascending in power relative to politics.

How unfortunate it is that so few people today care so little about history. If they were willing to take the road less traveled and pause along the way to make even the slightest inquiry, they would quickly discover why we ended up where we are, who led us here, and how we can exit. In their ignorance, they defiantly proclaim, "It's not technocracy!" and instead insist, "This is socialism!" or "This is communism!" or "This is fascism!"

As the old worn-out saw goes, "You cannot possibly know what you do not know." So, let's get busy and uncover the truth.

## What is technocracy?

Instead of answering off the bat, I want to first discuss technocracy's practitioners, who are referred to as "technocrats." You may have already heard this term mentioned in the news or in your social circle. Learning how to recognize a technocrat will help you understand technocracy much faster, because it's easier to understand people than it is an esoteric ideology.

The most thorough empirical study on technocracy was published in 1977 by Professor Robert Putnam from the University of Michigan. Titled "Elite Transformation in Advanced Industrial Societies: An Empirical Assessment of the Theory of Technocracy," Putnam's paper presented his analysis based on approximately 100 interviews of high-ranking national civil servants from several nations in Europe. "Data from this study," he wrote, "are particularly useful for assessing propositions about the technocratic mentality."[1] His interviews revealed six stereotypical personality traits, attitudes, and world views, all of which I have personally verified during my own fifteen-year study of technocracy and technocrats. In other words, these observations are just as valid today as they were in 1977.

Putnam summarized:

*1. Above all, the technocrat believes that techies must replace politics and defines his own role in apolitical terms. He has great confidence in the possibility of solving the problems of society by a scientific approach. He is free from all political attachments.*

*2. The technocrat is skeptical and even hostile toward politicians and political institutions. [. . .] [T]echnocrats are anti-political and anti-democratic.*

*3. The technocrat is fundamentally unsympathetic to the openness and equality of political democracy. Convinced of his infallibility, the technocrat is a skilled hand at closed politics. [. . .] He tends toward authoritarianism and absolutism (the "technocratic dictatorship").*

*4. The technocrat believes that social and political conflict is, at best, misguided and, at worst, contrived. The technician who believes that he has arrived at a full understanding of a question is always surprised and often grieved when he encounters opposition to his theories; inevitably, he is tempted to attribute this to ignorance or ill will.*

*5. The technocrat rejects ideological or moralistic criteria, preferring to debate policy in practical, "pragmatic terms." He is a pragmatist, hostile to political ideologies. Technocrats treat ideological arguments with condescending indifference, sometimes with impatience and scorn.*

*6. The technocrat is strongly committed to technological progress and material productivity; he is less concerned about distributive questions of social justice. In the techno-*

1 Putnam, Robert. "Elite Transformation in Advanced Industrial Societies." Comparative Political Studies 10. 1977. Pages 285–387.

*cratic mode, the ends have become simply efficiency and output.*[2] *[Emphasis added.]*

Note that four of the six characteristics express hostility toward political systems and structures, toward politicians and political theory. Modern technocrats have no use for politics and politicians unless they can use either or both to achieve their own agenda. Historic technocrats felt the same way, but they went a step further, thoroughly baking their anti-politics into the ideology of technocracy.

When technocracy was originally codified at Columbia University in 1932, America was suffering the heat of the Great Depression. History does not remember Henry A. Porter, an early technocrat who wrote the 1932 book *Roosevelt and Technocracy.* Incidentally, though Porter claimed on the introductory page that he was a "Nationally known Economist and Financial Analyst," I could find no significant historical accolade to him other than in his book, which I personally acquired from a rare book store. Porter's biggest concern was whether Franklin D. Roosevelt would be elected and would turn his proposed New Deal into a technocracy. Thus, he closes the book with a forceful admonition:

> *That we shall have to pass through a period of chaos is inevitable. The extent and severity of such a period is wholly within control of the people. Radical and immediate changes in both our political and economic systems will be necessary. This can best be accomplished by vesting supreme and emergency power in some one man who has the confidence and respect of a majority of the American people.*
>
> *That man is FRANKLIN D. ROOSEVELT – to whom should be given dictatorial powers in the approaching crisis.*[3]

Needless to say, Roosevelt didn't take Porter's challenge. And no wonder: The new President would have been thrown under the bus before the end of his first year in office. Why? Because he was a politician, not a technocrat!

---

2 Putnam. Pages 285–387.

3 Porter, Henry A. *Roosevelt and Technocracy*. (Los Angeles: Wetzel Publishing Company, Inc. 1932). Page 72.

In his book, Porter was certainly schmoozing Roosevelt, but, to his own detriment, he allowed the radical nature of technocracy to leak from its pages. In his conclusion he wrote,

> *In any national crisis, **individualism must be submerged**; we must all unite on a basis of equality. Surely we are not too hidebound to move forward courageously to an effective and unconventional **reconstruction of our wealth and resources.**[4] [Emphasis added.]*

This language sounds suspiciously similar to the recent call by the World Economic Forum for a "Great Reset" of the global economic system, in which "you will own nothing and be happy" if only you submerge your individuality for the greater good. No thanks!

Porter believed so strongly that technocracy could deliver the world from its Great Depression ills that he laid on the propaganda with religious zeal:

> *The gospel of Technocracy is spreading through our schools, universities and churches. Wall Street is exhibiting an intense but worried interest, and it is whispered [that] even the Vatican is closely following the progress of this new brain-child of our engineer-scientists.*[5]

Technocracy a "gospel"? Even the Vatican follows it?[6] It must be divine, right?

But oh, how Porter and his technocrat cronies hated politicians. They were certain that technocracy would prevail over politics. Even if success were slow, they had an excuse at the ready: "It is plain that its coming will be delayed by political maneuvering and financial chicanery."

Why, you ask, am I making such a big deal about technocracy and technocrats, politics and politicians? Because we must estab-

4 Porter. Page 72.

5 Porter. Page 72.

6 Note: Today, the Vatican and Pope Francis are openly and forcefully supporting sustainable development, green economy, natural capitalism, the Great Reset, etc., all of which are equivalent to historic "Technocracy" (the "T" was capitalized for many years, based on the name of the non-profit organization "Technocracy, Inc.," which was founded in 1933).

lish, from the start, that modern technocrats are currently in an all-out world war with nation-states—specifically with their political structures and with all the people who run the structures.

It was technocrats and not politicians who, in 2020, launched a global health emergency based on what is now recognized as a scientifically engineered virus called SARS-Cov-2. It was technocrats and not politicians who created the policies for PCR testing, universal masking, and social distancing; for shutting down schools and for locking down cities, provinces, states, and countries. It was technocrats and not politicians who railroaded the scientific solution of mRNA-based injections that meddle with human genetics and the immune system.

It was technocrat Dr. Anthony Fauci who stood confidently, with arms crossed and nose lifted high, behind President Donald Trump then behind President Joe Biden, and who, with a nod from each chief executive, orchestrated nationwide emergency measures despite cries of anguish from citizens throughout the U.S. This same scenario played out all around the world, in nation after nation. Who was in charge: technocrats or politicians?

Because this is a global war, national or sub-national blame must be laid aside. In other words, you can't blame Republicans, Democrats, or any other political body in the world. Technocracy in the 1930s was run by scientists and engineers. Technocracy in the 21st century continues to be run by scientists and engineers. Technocrats of any era possess all the personality traits Putnam enumerated above.

The bottom line here is that the future world will not be run by politicians or other representatives of the people. Every Parliament, Congress and Assembly will ultimately be disbanded or neutered so that technocrats can administer a scientific dictatorship, in which everything and everyone is controlled directly by them.

## What is transhumanism?

Just as a technocrat believes in and implements a technocracy, so does a transhumanist believe in and implement transhumanism—or an aspect of it. This book will examine the many variations of transhumanism in a later chapter. One leading transhumanist pioneer, Nick Bostrom, is a professor of philosophy at the University of Oxford. On his website he notes that transhumanism "promotes an interdisciplinary approach to understanding and evaluating the opportunities for enhancing the human condition and the human organism opened up by the advancement of technology."

Bostrom continues,

*Attention is given to both present technologies, like genetic engineering and information technology, and anticipated future ones, such as molecular nanotechnology and artificial intelligence. [. . .]*

*Transhumanists view human nature as a work-in-progress, a half-baked beginning that we can learn to remold in desirable ways. Current humanity need not be the endpoint of evolution. Transhumanists hope that by responsible use of science, technology, and other rational means we shall eventually manage to become posthuman, beings with vastly greater capacities than present human beings have.*[7] *[Emphasis added.]*

In general, transhumanists have in the back of their minds the notion of transhumans becoming posthuman at some point in the future. Thus, becoming a transhuman today is seen as the necessary pathway to becoming posthuman tomorrow. This is a subtle but important point: The word "trans" indicates transition, while the word "post" indicates arrival at the final destination.

What puts a person on the path to becoming transhuman is dissatisfaction with the current state of affairs. Humanity is just a "work in progress, a half-baked beginning," in Bostrom's view. The carrot on a stick, he says, is that "we can learn to remold in desirable ways." He compares the motive to pursue the transhuman condition to a woman who seeks out a plastic surgeon because she is dissatisfied with her body shape or facial features: "I'm not happy the way I am and the doctor says he can fix me."

---

7 Bostrom, Nick. "Transhumanist Values." https://www.nickbostrom.com/ethics/values.html

On his website Bostrom mentions current technologies like "genetic engineering" and "information technology" and anticipated future ones, such as "molecular nanotechnology" and "artificial intelligence." All these words directly reference NBIC, a converging of the scientific disciplines of **N**anotechnology, **B**iotechnology, **I**nformation technology and **C**ognitive science. NBIC is regarded as the scientific playground for human enhancement. Virtually every major university in the world today has an NBIC department or at least a working group of interdisciplinary engineers and scientists. In other words, NBIC is no small deal.

By now you should be noticing some similarities between technocrats and transhumanists. Technocrats see science and technology as the answer to improve and control society; transhumanists see the same science and technology as the answer to improve and control the human condition. They both will be found on the same scientific playground. Technocrats might be more reticent to take the spotlight because they are afraid of public opinion, which has historically stood against them. (Nobody likes to have personal autonomy stripped away or to be micromanaged and controlled by others.) Transhumanists can afford to be much more open and vocal, because hacking the human condition sounds more personal, not to mention alluring and enticing.

## Examples of transhumanists

Elon Musk, currently the richest man on planet Earth, is the chairman of Tesla Motors and SpaceX and a co-founder of Neuralink. His grandfather, Dr. Joshua Haldeman, was the national leader of Technocracy, Inc. in Canada during the 1930s and 1940s. Besides having technocratic roots, Musk is a transhumanist who is quite vocal about his intentions in that field. He launched Neuralink Corporation in 2016 to develop a brain-computer interface and hired leading neuroscientists, biochemists and robotic engineers from the academic community. The near-term goal was to provide treatment for serious brain diseases, but the long-term goal was human enhancement.[8] Why? Because Musk is a transhumanist as well as a technocrat.

8 Urban, Tim. "Neuralink and the Brain's Magical Future." WaitButWhy.com. April 20, 2017. Archived from the original and retrieved on May 4, 2017. https://web.

Peter Thiel intersected with Elon Musk when they created the profitable version of PayPal in 2000. Politically described as a conservative libertarian, Thiel was a major backer of Donald Trump in 2016. One company co-founded by Thiel, Palantir Technologies, was instrumental in creating the highly successful social media campaign for the Trump election committee. In this regard, it is easy to peg Thiel as a technocrat, But, like Musk, he is also a transhumanist. He once told *The Washington Post*, "I've always had this really strong sense that death was a terrible, terrible thing."[9] Thiel has donated to several organizations that promote life extension. He gave millions to the Methuselah Foundation, the Seasteading Institute, the SENS Research Foundation, and other organizations that pursue life extension outcomes.

Other transhumanists include Google founders Sergey Brin and Larry Page, who have invested over $1 billion in Calico Labs—its specific mission is to "solve death"[10]—and Oracle co-founder Larry Ellison, who has donated millions to life-extension research.

Another is Ray Kurzweil, head of engineering at Google and a self-avowed transhumanist who co-founded the Singularity University. In his book *The Singularity is Near: When Humans Transcend Biology*, Kurzweil wrote, "The Singularity will represent the culmination of the merger of our biological thinking and existence with our technology, resulting in a world that is still human but that transcends our biological roots."[11]

And then there's Klaus Schwab, founder and chairman of the World Economic Forum and author of *The Fourth Industrial Rev-*

archive.org/web/20170504070817/https:/waitbutwhy.com/2017/04/neuralink.html

9 Cha, Ariana Eunjung. "Peter Thiel's quest to find the key to eternal life." The Washington Post. April 3, 2015. https://www.washingtonpost.com/business/on-leadership/peter-thiels-life-goal-to-extend-our-time-on-this-earth/2015/04/03/b7a1779c-4814-11e4-891d-713f052086a0_story.html

10 Gabbat, Adam. "Is Silicon Valley's quest for immortality a fate worse than death?" The Guardian. 23 February 2019.
https://www.theguardian.com/technology/2019/feb/22/silicon-valley-immortality-blood-infusion-gene-therapy

11 Sahota, Neil. "Human 2.0 Is Coming Faster Than You Think. Will You Evolve With The Times?" Forbes. October 1, 2018.
https://www.forbes.com/sites/cognitiveworld/2018/10/01/human-2-0-is-coming-faster-than-you-think-will-you-evolve-with-the-times/?sh=5aaa46224284

*olution*, published in 2013. According to the official book review on the WEF's website:

> *Previous industrial revolutions liberated humankind from animal power, made mass production possible and brought digital capabilities to billions of people. This Fourth Industrial Revolution is, however, fundamentally different. It is characterized by a range of new technologies that are fusing the physical, digital and biological worlds, impacting all disciplines, economies and industries, and even challenging ideas about what it means to be human.*

This and other statements by Schwab clearly indicate that humanity's change from human to transhuman is part and parcel of his so-called Great Reset.

## Keep an eye on scientism

This is not the place to dive into the philosophical roots of scientism, but suffice it to say that it is a religious proposition that seeks answers about the universe and the nature of man exclusively through science, at the expense of other belief systems. If science is held by its practitioners as god, then it must be seen to be infallible. Other sources of truth, such as the Bible, philosophy, ethical studies, etc., can take a hike. As we will see in a later chapter, the very dangerous ideology of scientism is the common ground between technocracy and transhumanism: Both worship at the same altar of the god of science.

I must point out, though, that technocrats and transhumanists do not acknowledge that they are followers of scientism. Most call themselves atheists, agnostics, or humanists. Scientism is eerily deceptive in that it is able to convince its followers that they are *not* followers. Thus, it is as important to watch what they *do* as much as it is to listen to what they *say*. Furthermore, largely because scientism is duplicitous, it tends to use science in deceptive ways, conjuring up pseudo-scientific explanations that *sound* like real science but are not.

In this book, I will explore all of these terms in great detail. I aim to demonstrate that the entire world has been hijacked by a narrow group of ideologues and practitioners who are completely out of touch with humanity and indeed, with reality.

## How to read this book

The intention of this book is not to scare you, but rather to awaken you and equip you. I recognize how difficult some of these topics are to grasp, in which case you may need to re-read and stretch your brain a bit. Do not be deterred if this happens, but, rather, press on—and you will get through it!

I want to specifically state right now that I am not anti-technology or anti-science. In fact, I love both. When technology serves us, it can be a wonderful thing. To the extent that it is used to control us, it can be patently evil. Thus, we should not reject all of technology just because the bad actors of technocracy and transhumanism misuse it. When science is done properly, it, too, is a wonderful thing. On the other hand, whenever we encounter pseudoscience, we should not give it serious thought, except to reject it as being false.

Whatever solutions might spring up that enable us to reject technocracy and transhumanism cannot possibly work unless we have a deep understanding of both. Thus, my hope is that I can wade through the tsunami of information deluging us and provide a rock-solid foundation for my readers to stand on. On that foundation we can build our scaffolding to facilitate the process of recognition and understanding.

Our efforts to effect policy changes that snuff out technocracy and transhumanism may not be achievable when we approach these evil twins on a global level, a federal level, or even a state or provincial level. In that case, the actions we take on a local level may be our only viable alternative. Still, I predict the strength of the evil twins may prove insurmountable in some cases.

Yet, dear reader, even if you are unable to reach, reason with, and influence your local politicians, you can reject technocracy and transhumanism in your own personal life and take specific action to buffer yourself and your family against them.

Resistance is never futile.

# Chapter I

# Convergence: Science or Scientism?

*Real science provides tangible benefits to man. Scientism is a road leading to the certain destruction of man.*

Futurist Alvin Toffler coined the phrase "future shock" when he was at IBM in the 1960s. He was describing the phenomenon of "information overload" and anxiety brought on by "too much change in too short a time period."[1] In 1970, he and his wife Heidi published the seminal book on the topic: *Future Shock*.

Because scientific discovery was accelerating at an ever-increasing rate, Toffler predicted a time would come when the mind would get overloaded, would become unable to understand the reality of how things work, and would ultimately view the operation of the technically enhanced world as magic.

In 2019, the British Psychological Society revisited Toffler's work:

> *The psychologically overwhelmed are marked by confusion, anxiety, irritability, and withdrawal into apathy. Today, anxiety disorders are the most common mental illness in the United States, affecting some 40 million adults. Toffler predicted that people will attempt to cope with accelerated change*

1 *Eltringham, Mark. "Future Shock: a message from the past that defines the present." Insight. May 16, 2022. https://workplaceinsight.net/future-shock-message-past-describes-present*

*through denial, specialism, reversion, and simplification.*[2]

If there are four, and only four, adjectives that describe today's psychological manifestations, they would be confusion, anxiety, irritability, and apathy. Furthermore, when we see the coping mechanisms of denial, specialism, reversion, and simplification being played out everywhere, we can understandably conclude that "future shock" has arrived in full force.

Toffler concluded:

*We must search out totally new ways to anchor ourselves, for all the old roots—religion, nation, community, family, or profession—are now shaking under the hurricane impact of the accelerative thrust.*

As a futurist, Toffler had it pegged. What we are experiencing now is the obvious outcome. These days we see large swaths of people in society walking around in a fog, their critical thinking skills obliterated by the shock of "now"—when everything seems to be happening at once—and willingly obeying any suggestive propaganda that enters their brain.

Herein lies the problem: When average people are not able to understand what is going on around them, their ignorance gives "mad scientists" a license to run free—to dream up and carry out whatever technological scheme they want. Guidance from the public is not possible, because how can you guide things that you don't understand? Accountability is not possible, because there is no reliable method to measure cause and effect.

Since the start of the millennium, scientists and their new technological initiatives have operated in this vacuum of non-understanding, further exacerbating the phenomenon of future shock. The result is that a very small percentage of humanity, considered the scientific elite, has achieved a type of intellectual dominance over everyone else. They set the policies for how their inventions and innovations will be used in society. Meanwhile, the uninformed public, increasingly conditioned to blindly

2 *Wilson, Bruce. "Back to Future Shock." The Psychologist. April 2019. https://thepsychologist.bps.org.uk/volume-32/april-2019/back-future-shock.*

believe whatever pretends to be "science," has no option other than to just go along.

If the technological elite were to step outside traditional ethical and moral boundaries in their quest for scientific progress, you can see how a group of them could quickly take on the characteristics of a cult. Its members could be subject to undesired, harmful outcomes that they would *never* have agreed to had they understood the full ramifications.

Could it be that the same technological elite is the source of today's ubiquitous propaganda proclaiming that their version of "science" must be obeyed? That we must follow the data? That "the science is settled"?

As soon as this propaganda is stripped away, we'll discover that we *are* able to understand where we are, how we got here, who the proselytizers are, and what they intend to do to the world and to the billions of humans who occupy it.

## Convergent Science

The term "convergence" normally means the synthesis of two or more unrelated items into a single item. A smart phone, for instance, is a convergence of several different technologies, such as a camera, a mobile phone and an Internet browser.

In the academic and transhumanist communities, convergence refers to a combination of four scientific disciplines—namely, Nanotechnology, Biotechnology, Information Technology, and Cognitive Science, or NBIC, for short. Collectively, they are called "convergence."

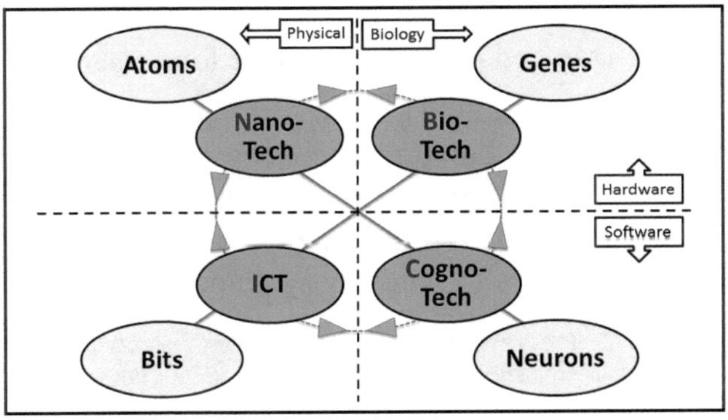

In a university setting, these fields of study were originally separate departments that had only occasional interaction on isolated projects. Each discipline was focused on its respective theoretical science. Starting around 2000, however, universities began to create stand-alone Convergent Science departments and courses. The intent was to go beyond theoretical science and focus on applying the combined disciplines to society at large and to humans in particular.

This move represented a tectonic shift in the philosophy of education. For example, in 2017 the University of North Carolina launched its Institute for Convergent Sciences, an initiative designed to "erase barriers, synthesize information and translate research into impact."

The National Science Foundation, a federal agency, talks about NBIC convergence in terms of five human activity platforms: foundational tools (the four disciplines of convergence), the Earth scale platform, the societal scale platform, the human scale platform, and quality of life. The NSF states that convergence is realized in conjunction with ten theories, which include unity of nature, human interaction ecosystem, economic growth, and response to social problems. Finally, convergence is said to be guided by six general principles:

1. The interdependence in nature and society
2. Evolutionary processes of convergence and divergence
3. System-logic deductions in decisions
4. Higher-level cross-domain languages
5. Confluence of resources leading to system changes (S curve)
6. Vision-inspired basic research for long-term challenges[3]

Convergence is a notable part of a larger trend, in which academic institutions are being transformed from centers of learning into centers of social impact. Arizona State University, for instance, claims to be the pioneer of education on Sustainable Development. It offers degrees in Sustainability up to the PhD

*3 Roco, Mihail C. "Progress in Convergence: Basic Concepts and Applications." National Science Foundation presentation at the RED Convergencia Congress, Mexico City. August 17, 2017.*

level. ASU's transformation began in 2002 with the appointment of Dr. Michael M. Crow as its president. Crow came from Columbia University, one of the oldest and most progressive educational institutions in the United States. His biography on the ASU website reads:

> *As a model "New American University," ASU simultaneously demonstrates comprehensive excellence, inclusivity representative of the ethnic and socioeconomic diversity of the United States, and* **consequential societal impact**.[4] *[Emphasis added.]*

In his public addresses, Crow plainly states that ASU is not measured by academic excellence (as it used to be, prior to 2002) but, rather, by the amount of social impact it has on the world. His 2020 book, *The Fifth Wave: The Evolution of American Higher Education*, speaks of schools that "accelerate social change." The Charter of Crow's New American University states in large print:

> *ASU is a comprehensive public research university, measured not by whom it excludes, but by whom it includes and how they succeed; advancing research and discovery of public value; and* **assuming fundamental responsibility for the economic, social, cultural and overall health of the communities it serves.**[5] *[Emphasis added.]*

Furthermore, Crow and ASU have been exporting their "New American University" concept to other educational institutions around the world, and it has spread like a wildfire. Convergent Science, mentioned above, follows this same theme. Its goal is not to advance theoretical knowledge but to combine and apply technology that can change the world and the people who live in it.

## The Takeover of Evolution

Although NBIC is significantly focused on shaping the physical world, it is even more interested in living things that are shaped by their genetic structure, or DNA. This specific aspect of NBIC

---

*4 Michael Crow biography. Arizona State University website. https://sustainability-innovation.asu.edu/person/michael-crow*

*5 "New American University: Toward 2025 and Beyond." President's Page, Arizona State University website. https://president.asu.edu/sites/default/files/asu_charter_jan_2019_web_0.pdf*

has progressed incrementally over the last thirty years with the genetic modification of bacteria, crop seeds, grasses, insects, fish, and animals. Meddling with nature, with life itself, may look benign, especially when the results are promised to benefit mankind: eliminate hunger, improve human health, save the environment, etc.

The dark side of NBIC "applied science," however, is that its practitioners' goal is to hijack evolution in order to direct and control future life on earth. Although they nearly unanimously deny the intelligent design of life or an intelligent designer (i.e., God), NBIC scientists contend that man can now assume the role of intelligent designer and can create the future according to his own imagination.

Does this sound preposterous? Is it beyond the realm of possibility? Well, let me cite a few quotes from experts on the subject who *don't* think so.

David Pearce, a leading figure in modern transhumanism, puts it bluntly:

> *If we want to live in paradise, we will have to engineer it ourselves. If we want eternal life, then we'll need to rewrite our bug-ridden genetic code and become god-like.*[6]

Singularity Hub's 2016 article *What Happens When Tech Takes Control of Evolution?* says of the future:

> *Over the span of a few billion years, diversity of life has flourished on Earth through the process of natural selection. Then, not long ago (relatively), human intelligence evolved.*
>
> *For the first time one species, Homo sapiens, could consciously control its destiny on this planet. Humans have been shaping ourselves, the environment and other species for thousands of years. Soon, we'll be able to fully control our own biology too, transcending our natural limitations.*
>
> *Genetic engineering and neurotechnology are examples of fields shaping human evolution. Taking control of evolution*

6 Lomeña, Andrés. "Transhumanism: Nick Bostrom and David Pearce Talk to Andrés Lomeña." Literal Magazine, Issue 31. https://literalmagazine.com/transhumanism-nick-bostrom-and-david-pearce-talk-to-andres-lomena

*means what was once a slow, random process will now be exponentially faster. Soon, we'll imagine what kind of a species we want to be and then become what we envision.*

*Genetic engineering, biotechnology and neurotechnology are catalyzing the powerful transition from biological to digital evolution—and the latter will be exponentially faster and more powerful. It'll soon be up to us what direction we choose.*[7]

Another prominent journal gives a name to what Singularity Hub describes above:

*"Transhumanism" is the idea that humans should transcend their current natural state and limitations through the use of technology – that we should embrace self-directed human evolution.*[8]

We cannot leave out the World Economic Forum's contribution to this topic. The WEF has made transhumanism part of its Great Reset doctrine. It envisions that not only will society, the environment, and economic systems be restructured but that a new humanity will enjoy the fruits of that reset:

*The central premise of transhumanism, then, is that biological evolution will eventually be overtaken by advances in genetic, wearable and implantable technologies that artificially expedite the evolutionary process.*[9]

The prestigious European Academy of Religion and Society ties transhumanism to the takeover of evolution:

*Transhumanism is a philosophical movement that promotes the view that the human species should take control of its*

---

*7 Bidshahri, Raya. "What Happens When Tech Takes Control of Evolution?" Singularity Hub. December 20, 2016. https://singularityhub.com/2016/12/20/what-happens-when-tech-takes-control-of-evolution*

*8 Thomas, Alexander. "Super-intelligence and eternal life: transhumanism's faithful follow it blindly into a future for the elite." The Conversation. July 31, 2017. https://theconversation.com/super-intelligence-and-eternal-life-transhumanisms-faithful-follow-it-blindly-into-a-future-for-the-elite-78538*

*9 Trippet, David. "What is transhumanism and how does it affect you?" World Economic Forum. April 20, 2018. https://www.weforum.org/agenda/2018/04/transhumanism-advances-in-technology-could-already-put-evolution-into-hyperdrive-but-should-they own evolution through human-enhancement technologies, such as brain implants and nanotechnology that reverses ageing.*[10]

As the Preface made clear, the topic of transhumanism will be a central theme in this book. Where did the term "transhuman" originate? It was first used in 1957 by Julian Huxley, the brother of Aldous Huxley, who wrote *Brave New World* in 1932. Julian spoke of transitioning from our current form of humanity into another form—hence the prefix "trans." When a transhuman arrives on the other side, Julian believed, he or she will be "posthuman."

## The Abolition of Man

Based on what you have read here thus far, you might be thinking that all of these plans for the future of humanity came into being recently. After all, NBIC convergence is a relatively new concept. The "hijacking of evolution" sounds like a cutting-edge phenomenon, too. And it was only in 2006 that futurist Ray Kurzweil quantified his theory of the singularity. As for the modern iteration of the transhumanist movement, it can be traced to a mere two decades ago—the early 1990s.

Don't be fooled, though. This whole idea of scientific progress is older than the hills. It's been brewing since the beginning of the Scientific Revolution in the seventeenth century. One twenty-first century historian and scholar, William Gilbert, wrote:

*The expression "the scientific revolution," a fairly recent term, is generally employed to describe the great outburst in activity in the investigation of physical nature that took place in the sixteenth, seventeenth, and eighteenth centuries. At the beginning came the important books of Copernicus in astronomy and Vesalius in anatomy, both published in 1543. In 1687 the appearance of Newton's Principia provided a sort of climax for previous achievements in astronomy and physics and became the basis for future developments in those fields. Although there had been much work done in antiquity and in*

---

*10 Peters, Timo. "Coronavirus and the transhuman future." EARS. January 13,2021. https://europeanacademyofreligionandsociety.com/news/coronavirus-and-the-transhuman-future*

> *the Middle Ages to prepare the way for these achievements, the quality and impact of scientific discovery in Europe in this period exceeds anything ever done in any part of the world. Consequently, modern European and western civilization alone can, in fact, be called a scientific civilization. That is to say*, **in no other time or place outside of the modern western world has natural science had so profound and pervasive an impact on the way people live and think. We can even divide the history of western civilization into a prescientific and a scientific phase. If we accept this system of periodization, then the scientific revolution marks the point at which the change took place.**[11] *[Emphasis added.]*

As innocuous as Gilbert's description might sound, there were already warning signs during the Scientific Revolution about what was to come. Writing in the early-1970s, Gilbert presciently pointed out those signs:

> *The scientific revolution, ushering in the modern scientific age, has profoundly influenced patterns of thought.* **By making possible ever increasing control of physical forces, it has helped to instill a confidence that people can master nature for their own purposes.** *By providing rational explanations for phenomena previously unexplained, the scientific revolution has helped to overcome superstitious fear of mysterious supernatural and occult forces. From this point of view, the present day interest in magic and various forms of the occult is a long step backwards.* **The scientific revolution was an important factor in promoting the trust in reason as the most reliable guide for human affairs.** *To some extent, this exaltation of science and reason has led to a downgrading of the claims of sentiment, emotion, art, music, and religion.* **Intentionally or not, the rise of a more scientific consciousness is partly responsible for the secu-**

11 *Gilbert, William. Renaissance and Reformation. (Lawrence, Kansas: Carrie, 1998). https://archive.org/details/RenaissanceAndReformationWilliamGilbert1997*

**larization of the modern world.** *[Emphasis added.]*

The ability to "master nature for their own purposes" did not have an immediate effect on the whole of European society. But by the time French philosopher Henri de Saint-Simon (1760–1825) arrived on the scene, the possibilities seemed endless. He wrote in 1803: "A scientist, my dear friends, is a man who foresees; it is because science provides the means to predict that it is useful, and the scientists are superior to all other men."[12]

Retrospectively, Saint-Simon was considered the ideological "founding father" of scientism, technocracy, and transhumanism. (In his era, these terms were capitalized, but, in keeping with the times, we use lower-case spellings.) He called for a priesthood of scientists and engineers to administer science to the masses. His main disciple, August Comte, became the father of social sciences.

By the early 1900s, the cauldron of philosophical debate was swirling with animated exchanges about Marxism, communism, positivism, progressivism, technocracy, and scientism. As a philosophical proposition, scientism was found to be particularly disturbing, as we shall see in a later chapter. Scientism is the toxic glue that binds the twins, technocracy and transhumanism, which together devise the complete makeover of society.

British scholar C. S. Lewis lectured and wrote extensively on scientism. In his 1948 book, *The Abolition of Man*, Lewis predicted where scientism was headed:

> *Man's conquest of Nature, if the dreams of some scientific planners are realized, means the rule of a few hundreds of men over billions upon billions of men. [. . .] Each new power won by man is a power over man as well.*[13]

Once the process of conquering nature was underway, Lewis reasoned, it would not wander aimlessly for an indefinite period; rather, he concluded, the outcome would be definite and decisive:

> *The final stage is come when Man by eugenics, by pre-natal*

12 *Saint-Simon, Henri de. Letters from an Inhabitant of Geneva to His Contemporaries (1803) in The Political Thought of Saint-Simon (Oxford, England, UK: Oxford University Press, 1976).*

13 *Lewis, C. S. The Abolition of Man. (New York: Macmillan, 1947.) Page 58.*

*conditioning, and by an education and propaganda based on a perfect applied psychology, has obtained full control over himself. Human nature will be the last part of Nature to surrender to Man. The battle will then be won. We shall have 'taken the thread of life out of the hand of Clotho' and be henceforth free to make our species whatever we wish it to be [. . .] the power of Man to make himself what he pleases means, as we have seen, the power of some men to make other men what they please.*[14]

Summarizing his premise, C. S. Lewis noted, "Man's final conquest has proved to be the abolition of man."

He was saying, between the lines: When scientistic planners are motivated merely by their own passions and pleasures and are devoid of moral or ethical constraints, the wind in their sails that sets their course is powered by nothing more than vain imaginations and emotional impulses.

Lewis documented the intentional, premeditated nature of scientism, which can be verified by the purposeful dehumanization of man that is taking place today. He wrote:

*The real objective is that if man chooses to treat himself as raw material, raw material he will be; not raw material to be manipulated, as he fondly imagined, by himself, but by mere appetite, that is, mere nature, in the person of his de-humanized Conditioners. [. . .] [W]e are mere nature to be kneaded and cut into new shapes for the pleasures of masters who must, by hypothesis, have no motive but their own 'natural' impulses.*[15]

It is a fatal error to equate scientism with science. True science explores the natural world using the time-tested scientific method of repeated experimentation and validation. By comparison, scientism is a speculative, metaphysical, upside-down worldview about the nature of the universe and man's relation to it. If left unchecked, scientism, as expressed through technocracy and trans-

14 *Lewis. Page 58.*
15 *Lewis. Page 73.*

humanism, will end with the abolition of man and the civilization it has built.

People today are understandably amazed at the whiz-bang scientific discoveries and advancements being made at jet-speed pace all around them. Meanwhile, though, they have been completely oblivious to the rising religion of scientism with its associated priesthood of scientists and engineers. Relying on modern propaganda designed to deceive and manipulate, scientism promises dignity, food, shelter, health, education, employment, security. It delivers just the opposite: insignificance, starvation, homelessness, sickness, illiteracy, joblessness, danger.

Real science provides tangible benefits to man. Scientism is a road leading to the certain destruction of man.

# CHAPTER 2

# Technocracy: Restructuring Civilization

*HOW CAN WE LIVE THIS SLOW DEMISE?*
*HOW CAN WE LIVE AND DENY IT?*
*ECSTATIC LIES EXPLODE OUR MINDS*
*THE AGE OF TECHNOCRACY - SYBREED, 2008*

I have investigated globalization since 1975 and technocracy since 2007. Still, to my continual amazement, every day I keep unearthing new information, new subtleties, and new insights on these parallel ideologies. Though technocracy is a decades-old tool of societal transformation, in recent years it has been speedily advancing right under our noses, yet escaping detection by all but a few.

Modern globalization and hence, technocracy, started in earnest with the founding of the Trilateral Commission in 1973 by David Rockefeller and Zbigniew Brzezinski. The organization's stated goal was to "foster a New International Economic Order." Membership was initially limited to 289 carefully selected members from North America (109), Japan (74), and Europe (106). They included establishment lawyers, high-ranking politicians, influential journalists, globalist think tank scholars, international bankers, and academics.

The 97 Trilateral members from the US completely dominated the Carter Administration from 1975 to 1979. President Carter and Vice President Walter Mondale were among the original members. So was Zbigniew Brzezinski, Carter's National Security Advisor. In fact, all but one member of Carter's Cabinet belonged to the Commission. Besides Brzezinski, the following sixteen appointments were announced even *before* Carter was inaugurated on January 20, 1977:

Cyrus Vance – Secretary of State

Harold Brown – Secretary of Defense

W. Michael Blumenthal – Secretary of the Treasury

Andrew Young – Ambassador to the United Nations

Warren Christopher – Deputy Secretary of State

Lucy Wilson Benson – Under Secretary of State for Security Affairs

Richard Cooper – Under Secretary of State for Economic Affairs

Richard Holbrooke – Under Secretary of State for Policy Planning

Sol Linowitz – co-negotiator on the Panama Canal Treaty

Gerald Smith – Ambassador-at-large for Nuclear Power Negotiations

Elliot Richardson – Delegate to the Law of the Sea Conference

Richard Gardner – Ambassador to Italy

Anthony Solomon – Under Secretary of the Treasury for Monetary Affairs

C. Fred Bergsten – Assistant Secretary of the Treasury for International Affairs

Paul Warnke – Director, Arms Control and Disarmament Agency

Robert R. Bowie – Deputy Director of Intelligence for National Estimates[1]

By the end of Carter's presidency, no less than one-third of the US Trilateral members had held one or more top positions in his Administration. Such a clean sweep should have raised a lot of eyebrows, but it didn't. Antony Sutton and I blew the whistle and were immediately charged as conspiracy theorists—merely

1 Sutton, Antony C., and Patrick M. Wood. *Trilaterals Over Washington, Vol. I* (The August Corporation, 1978). Page 23.

for stating the obvious. It appeared to be an invisible coup. But why? Although at the time neither Sutton nor I were aware of the historic "Technocracy, Inc." movement, we fully understood what was afoot—namely, the aim "to blur the separation between 'private wealth' and 'public service' for Trilateral advantage: **public wealth is to be oriented to private Trilateral ends.**"[2]

We have co-founder David Rockefeller to thank for the "cone of silence" that covered the Commission's activities for at least the first twenty-five years of its operation. In the late 1970s and early 1980s, Professor Sutton and I began researching the early days of the Commission, which we chronicled in two books. For daring to air our findings, we were branded as not only conspiracy theorists but also left-wing extremists *and* right-wing extremists—plus just plain lunatics. Our accuracy and sanity were vindicated, however, when David Rockefeller admitted in his 2002 autobiography, *Memoirs*:

> *We are grateful to the Washington Post, the New York Times, Time Magazine and other great publications whose directors have attended our meetings and respected their promises of discretion for almost 40 years. . . . It would have been impossible for us to develop our plan for the world if we had been subjected to the lights of publicity during those years.*[3]

The "other great publications" of those early days included the *Chicago Sun Times*, Dow Jones, Media General, and even a TV network, CBS, headed by Arthur R. Taylor.[4] They essentially formed an ad hoc media cartel that decided what would be national news and what would *not* be national news. By extension, their stories radiated out to the rest of the world's print, radio, and television media. They purposely avoided all mention of the Trilateral Commission's existence, membership, and activities. Thus, when historians in another twenty-five years look back at the 1973–1993 period, they will find a dearth of stories on this secretive organization. However, thanks to the in-depth research and out-

---

2 Sutton and Wood. Page 32.

3 Rockefeller, David. *David Rockefeller: Memoirs* (Random House, 2002). Quoted in *The Rockefellers: An American Dynasty,* by Peter Collier and David Horowitz (Holt, Rinehart & Winston, 1976). Page 14.

4 Rockefeller. Page 25.

standing scholarship of the late Professor Antony Sutton, he and I were able to provide that missing documentation in the books we co-authored, *Trilaterals Over Washington, Volumes I and II.*

Today, most in-the-know people accept the suggestion that modern globalization was started by the Trilateral Commission and its notorious co-founder David Rockefeller. Indeed, they not only agree with that proposition but they love to hate him because of it. Rockefeller made himself a convenient target for their animosity: He was secretive, conspiratorial, filthy rich, and super powerful. Worse, he meddled in every part of society he could get his hands on. So did his right-hand minions, the equally despised Henry Kissinger, Robert McNamara, and Zbigniew Brzezinski.

Actually, Rockefeller incriminated himself and demonstrated his dark nature when he confessed in his *Memoirs*:

> *Some even believe we are part of a secret cabal working against the best interests of the United States, characterizing my family and me as "internationalists" and of conspiring with others around the world to build a more integrated global political and economic structure—one world, if you will. If that's the charge, I stand guilty, and I am proud of it.*[5]

These were the exact charges that Sutton and I made against Rockefeller in 1978. As a result, our books were blacklisted by the largest bookstore of the day, B. Dalton Booksellers. Every time we wrote or spoke publicly about the Trilaterals, we were censored and ridiculed. Even Hollywood took a turn beating us up in an episode of the sitcom *Barney Miller*, which featured a man breaking into the offices of the Trilateral Commission with the aim of getting them to "admit" to their One World Order mission.[6] Other characters in the skit ridiculed both the man and his "conspiracy theory"—his insistence that the Trilateral Commission was up to no good.

Likewise, I am ridiculed when I say that modern globalization and technocracy have the mutual goal of remaking the traditional economic order of capitalism and free markets with an entirely

5 Rockefeller. Page 25.

6 "Trilateral Commission — Clips from Barney Miller, Season 7, Episode 8 (1981)." YouTube. https://youtu.be/8q3aa_Q0lus

new economic system that is antithetical to both. When I explain that the technocracy movement of the 1930s is being reborn right now, as we speak, my assertion is immediately dismissed. It's common for people to reject new information that doesn't fit comfortably into their worldview. Nevertheless, understanding the connection between today's globalization and today's technocracy is the only way we can correctly ascertain and interpret modern events.

## What Changed The Global Landscape?

In 1970, David Rockefeller was chairman of Chase Manhattan Bank, then the third-largest bank in the world. With assets of $22.2 billion, it was almost in a tie with the second-largest bank, which had assets of $23.1 billion. By 2010, after it merged and became JPMorgan Chase, his bank moved into second place with $133 billion in assets. In short, David Rockefeller was at the apex of global banking and was acutely aware of all monetary trends.

When President Richard Nixon decoupled gold from the dollar on August 15, 1971, the dollar became a purely fiat currency. In other words, it was no longer redeemable in gold and there was nothing of value backing it up. This was a sea change event for bankers because, while gold could never become worthless, fiat currency certainly could. In fact, it was a mathematical certainty that there would be a point in the future when the fiat currencies of the world would all go up in smoke, potentially engulfing the entire banking system in flames. Thus, accumulating wealth in fiat currencies—money with nothing backing it—was seen to be a futile endeavor.

If you were an international banker and you saw this handwriting on the wall, what would you do? Well, you would start thinking of ways to protect your wealth. But how could you do that when the money your bank held was declining in value? There would be only one logical proposition: directly own and/or control the physical resources of the world. This would require squeezing those assets *out* of private and government hands and moving them *into* the hands of greedy globalists like David Rockefeller.

## The Use of Land

The same year (1973) that the Trilateral Commission was formed, The Rockefellers Brothers Fund released a book called *The Use of Land*. The book was the outcome of the "Task Force on Land Use and Urban Growth"[7] that had been started in the summer of 1972 by the Citizens' Advisory Committee on Environmental Quality. This Committee was originally established by a presidential executive order in May 1969, the year Nixon entered the White House. Nixon, who most observers considered a "Rockefeller man," had no idea that the Rockefellers would soon toss him under the bus when the Watergate incident forced his resignation on August 9, 1974. Vice President Gerald Ford, also known as a "Rockefeller man," assumed the presidency and then proceeded to appoint Nelson Rockefeller (David Rockefeller's older brother) as the new Vice President.

*The Use of Land* was an incredibly important though widely ignored book. It led to massive changes in land use policy in the US. It also paved the way for global land use policies that the United Nations would embed in its Sustainable Development doctrines in the 1990s.

The Rockefellers subsumed[8] the once-legitimate environmental movement because they needed an excuse to promote changes in land use policies. Here are some quotes to that effect from *The Use of Land*:

- Laurance S. Rockefeller [David's older brother], then chairman of the committee, saw the environmental movement as a force of great vigor and excitement which, if it were to broaden its vision and direct its energies to urban growth problems with equal commitment, could achieve impressive results. (Page 1)
- Unlike other movements, the environmental one is here to stay. The beauty of it is, it's the first issue that cuts across all

7 Reilly, William K. *The Use of Land*. (New York: Thomas Y. Crowell Co., 1973).

8 The takeover of the environmental movement by foundations and elitists, such as the members of the Trilateral Commission, is still an open wound to many of the original environmentalists, who were displaced from their respective positions of leadership.

lines – race, religion, class. Land is a very basic thing. (Page 38)

- To protect critical environmental and cultural areas, tough restrictions will have to be placed on the use of privately owned land (Page 23)
- The land market, as it operated today, is the principal obstacle to effective protection of private open space. (Page 21)
- Governments at all levels should actively solicit open space donations and should facilitate the work of responsible private organizations, such as the Nature Conservancy. (Page 20)
- The best regulatory mechanism so far for development review is environmental impact analysis. (Page 25)
- Citizen suits appealing from local regulatory decisions should be permitted by any local resident or civic organization in the public interest, without regard to property ownership or other financial interest. (Page 27)[9]

Modern policies of land use that can be attributed to *The Use of Land* agenda include conservation easements, massive rezoning of urban and rural land, the splintering of property rights, taking private property by eminent domain, endless lawsuits against property owners over environmental "offenses," and much more. All of these policies made it to the global stage when the United Nations produced the Agenda 21 treaty in 1992 at the UN Conference on Economic Development (UNCED) in Rio de Janeiro, Brazil. Agenda 21 also institutionalized the aforementioned doctrine of Sustainable Development, which is predicated on controlling all global resources in a sort of global common trust managed by the United Nations.

The net effect of changing land use policies has been to drive property out of private ownership into institutional ownership or control. This has been happening in the US and around the world for fifty years—and at an especially rapid pace in the past two or three years.

9 Reilly.

## The Use of Technology

In 1970, Zbigniew Brzezinski was a relatively young and obscure professor of political science at Columbia University's School for International and Public Affairs when his new book, *Between Two Ages: America's Role in the Technetronic Era*, caught the eye of David Rockefeller. The book marked out the way for Rockefeller to fulfill his lust to accumulate and exercise control over the physical resources of the world.

Before I elaborate, let me give a brief background on the relationship between Columbia and the Rockefellers. They became bedfellows at least as far back as 1928, when they created a complex real estate arrangement that left Columbia as owner of the Rockefeller Center buildings and of the land upon which the buildings sit. The land rental monies received from the deal funded the school's operating expenses. This permanent endowment was discovered only after the Rockefeller Center applied for a $50 million loan to construct another building on the property. According to *The New York Times*:

> *If Rockefeller Center had not obtained a $50 million mortgage last fall from a consortium of banks headed by the Emigrant Savings Bank, the fact of Columbia's ownership might never have become public knowledge.*
>
> *The 1928 lease containing the language that vests ownership of the buildings in Columbia is not on file at the city's Hall of Records. All that is recorded is a memorandum indicating the existence of such a lease.*
>
> *But the Emigrant Savings Bank had access to the original lease, as well as all the renewals and changes that have been made in the last 48 years, and before granting the center a mortgage it asked the Title Guarantee Company, a title insurance concern, to check the records and report back on who owned what.*[10]

Given that close-knit alliance between the university and the family, it should not be surprising that Brzezinski's book enticed

10 Kaiser, Charles. "The Truth Is, Columbia Owns Rockefeller Center Buildings, Too," The New York Times. March 21, 1976.

David Rockefeller. It should also not be surprising that a book with the word "a" in its title would contain the seeds of modern technocracy, especially considering that Columbia was the historical seedbed of this new type of economic system, which had been planted in the early 1930s by some of the school's top professors of engineering and the sciences. Many of those original collaborators were still around to tell the tales of technocracy's founding to young professors like Brzezinski.

Just when the Columbia-based technocracy movement was flourishing, it was suddenly tainted by a major scandal. In 1932 it was discovered that technocracy's leading spokesman, Howard Scott, had fraudulently claimed that he had an engineering degree. This revelation burned Columbia's flamboyant president, Nicholas Murray Butler, and he summarily banned the whole project and banished it from the campus. Though no Columbia professors who were working on the technocracy project were fired, neither were they allowed to talk about technocracy from that point forward.

Brzezinski cleverly skirted this barrier by substituting the word "technocracy" with his own word, "technetronic."[11] Notice that his book title, *Between Two Ages: America's Role in the Technetronic Era*, actually speaks of *three* ages: the previous age, the current age, and the future age. In 1970, the technetronic era, aka technocracy, had not yet fully blossomed, but the author was clearly predicting that it soon would. Thus, by carefully sanitizing and repackaging a topic that had not been allowed to be openly discussed at Columbia for nearly forty years, Brzezinski managed to grab David Rockefeller's attention. Rockefeller, as we will remember, needed a brand new economic system to carry his monopolistic empire forward, and Brzezinski was providing him with the perfect answer. He wrote, "[C]ontemporary America is in transition from the industrial to the technetronic age,"[12] and later in the book he hinted at his initial plan for how to make that transition:

11 Merriam-Webster Dictionary. https://www.merriam-webster.com/dictionary/technetronic

12 Brzezinski, Zbigniew. *Between Two Ages: America's Role in the Technetronic Era*. (New York: Viking Press, 1970). Page 77.

> *The approaching two-hundredth anniversary of the Declaration of Independence could justify the call for a national constitutional convention to re-examine the nation's formal institutional framework. Either 1976 or 1989 – the two-hundredth anniversary of the Constitution – could serve as a suitable target date for culminating a national dialogue on the relevance of existing arrangements, the workings of the representative process, and the desirability of imitating the various European regionalization reforms and of streamlining the administrative structure.*[13]

In today's setting, Brzezinski's plan to totally rearrange our constitutional structure sounds almost identical to the World Economic Forum's concept of how to achieve the Great Reset: Throw everything up in the air so it can be reassembled after it falls back to the ground. (Build Back Better, anyone?)

So, what did Brzezinski have in mind when he figuratively tossed the US Constitution in the air? After noting that "technological developments make it certain that modern society will require more and more planning," he suggested that "national coordination and local participation could be thus wedded by new systems of coordination" and then added, "This has already been tried successfully by some large businesses."[14]

Again, do we see his ideas in today's setting? Consider the technocratic approach to doing business taken by companies like Amazon, Tesla, Google, Microsoft, Facebook, Twitter, etc. Do employees enjoy personal freedom? Or are they subjected to the most miniscule micro-management possible?

It should be noted that Brzezinski was a proponent of rational humanism, but only if it was headed toward a science-saturated future—toward a "new perspective" that, he observed, "involves growing recognition that man's propensity for scientific innovation cannot be restrained."[15]

Brzezinski's *Between Two Ages* was unquestionably complex. He used constructs and language typical of an ivory tower aca-

13 Brzezinski. Page 258.
14 Brzezinski. Page 260.
15 Brzezinski. Page 271.

demic. Sometimes he seemed lost in irrelevance, but other times he made his vision crystal clear—to wit:

> *More directly linked to the impact of technology, it involves the gradual appearance of a more controlled and directed society.* **Such a society would be dominated by an elite whose claim to political power would rest on allegedly superior scientific know-how.** *Unhindered by the restraints of traditional liberal values,* **this elite would not hesitate to achieve its political ends by using the latest modern techniques for influencing public behavior and keeping society under close surveillance and control.** *Under such circumstances, the scientific and technological momentum of the country would not be reversed but would actually feed on the situation it exploits.*[16] *[Emphasis added.]*

Both Brzezinski and Rockefeller were pragmatists. Judging by their words and their deeds, we know they eyed America as the most powerful economic engine in the world. For this precise reason they targeted the James Earl Carter Administration (1977–1981) for domination. But their purpose was *not* political. Rather, they sought to gain complete control over the United States' economic structure, policy, and activity. This is a crucial point to understand. It underscores the fact that David Rockefeller was using the political systems of the US and other nations as vehicles for restructuring the global economic system in order to transfer physical assets out of the control and ownership of private citizens and national governments and into the control and ownership of the top 1% of the 1%. That is, from the hoi polloi to the elitist Trilateral Commission members and their ilk.

What I am saying is not mere speculation. In 1979 and 1980, Professor Sutton and I engaged in a number of personal debates with certain members of the Trilateral Commission. In every case, when we suggested they were attempting a political coup, the Trilaterals would pointedly remind us that they were interested only in "fostering a new international economic order" and not in politics per se. Their reply confused Tony and me, because Trilateral Commission members had virtually taken over the Executive

16 Brzezinski. Page 253.

Branch of the US government. In hindsight, however, I see that what they were telling us was the literal truth. For, if Rockefeller and Brzezinski were to succeed in creating a new economic order, they *had* to do it from inside the existing system of capitalism and free market economics.

Don't believe me? Well, then, consider what happened starting with the 1973 birth of the Trilateral Commission:

- From 1973 to 2012, all seven presidents of the World Bank were appointed by the President of the United States. The World Bank is arguably one of the largest drivers of economic globalization in history. Out of the seven, six were appointed from the ranks of the Trilateral Commission.
- Since 1974, the US Trade Representative has been the key negotiator and author of foreign trade agreements and treaties. Between 1974 and 2013, only twelve people served in that appointed position, yet no less than nine of them were members of the Trilateral Commission.
- Since 1973, US Secretaries of State have included Trilateral Commission members Henry Kissinger, Cyrus Vance, Alexander Haig, George Schultz, Lawrence Eagleburger, Warren Christopher, Madelyn Albright, Condoleezza Rice, and Anthony Blinken.
- The North American Free Trade Agreement (NAFTA), which was predicted to create a "giant sucking sound going South," was authored by Trilateral Carla A. Hills.
- The credited author of the United Nations' Sustainable Development goals is Gro Harlem Brundtland, a prominent European member of the Trilateral Commission.

Unquestionably, Trilaterals occupying these seats of political power have been instrumental in creating their sought-after New International Economic Order. Indeed, they have marched in precision lockstep to accomplish this objective. Perhaps you can now understand why Rockefeller so cherished his partnership with Brzezinski, the master strategist who knew how to make Rockefeller's dreams come true.

Brzezinski summed up this strategy in several places in his book:

> *[T]he nation-state as a fundamental unit of man's organized life has ceased to be the principal creative force:* **International banks and multinational corporations are acting and planning in terms that are far in advance of the political concepts of the nation-state.**[17] *[Emphasis added]*
>
> *From an American standpoint, the more important and promising changes in the years to come will have to involve Western Europe and Japan.*[18]
>
> *In years to come Chinese development will probably increasingly share the experience of other nations in the process of modernization.*[19]

All these points resonated with Rockefeller and directly led to his inviting Brzezinski to co-found the Trilateral Commission.

The paramount point, to both of them, was that the planning was to be done by "international banks" (i.e., Rockefeller's Chase Manhattan) and "multinational corporations." Their reliance on these global institutions underscores the antipathy *all* Trilateral members felt toward the governments of nation-states, including America. The Trilaterals truly had no interest in the political system but only used it as a necessary means of achieving their preconceived outcome: a total restructuring of civilization.

---

17 Brzezinski. Page 5.
18 Brzezinski. Page 293.
19 Brzezinski. Page 280.

# CHAPTER 3

# Technocracy: Then and Now

*Little boxes on the hillside*
*Little boxes made of ticky tacky*
*Little boxes on the hillside*
*Little boxes all the same*

*There's a pink one and a green one*
*And a blue one and a yellow one*
*And they're all made out of ticky tacky*
*And they all look just the same.*
*"Little Boxes" by Malvina Reynolds*

Remember it was Columbia University where, in 1932, the design for technocracy was originally created by prominent scientists and engineers. The Technocracy Study Group, headed by Howard Scott, was at the time located in the basement of Columbia's Hamilton Hall. Remember, too, it was Scott who brought disgrace and embarrassment to the university when it was discovered he didn't have the engineering degree he had claimed on his resume. By summarily evicting the whole project from its campus in early 1933, Columbia was unwittingly paving the way for the creation of Technocracy, Inc. a year later.

Few surviving documents of the Technocracy Study Group have been found at Columbia. This may be partly due to the angst administrators felt over Howard Scott's deception—they likely tossed the most incriminating papers in the trash—and partly because Scott's one-year stay wasn't enough time to produce a body of scholarly literature to look back on.

However, the documents Scott took with him from the Technocracy Study Group were preserved. Out of them emerged Technocracy, Inc., the organization that Scott and his lone remaining cohort, M. King Hubbert, co-founded in early 1934. Rather than abandoning their earlier research, they carefully documented it in their nearly 300-page *Technocracy Study Course*.[1] [Note: Given my many references to the Study Course, I will insert page numbers in the text instead of creating multiple footnotes.]

This chapter will compare original text from the 1934 *Technocracy Study Course* with modern-day events to demonstrate the shocking continuity of technocracy's ideas, practices, strategies, and techniques over the past ninety years. Although some technocrats have disagreed with me, I believe the Study Course was written primarily by Hubbert, a young geologist and geophysicist who twenty years later found fame as the creator of the so-called peak oil theory (also known as Hubbert's Peak). The peak oil thesis posited the end of new discoveries of oil deposits and hence massive energy shortages. Today some environmentalists consider Hubbert to be a "founding father" of their movement, even though his theory has since been disproved.

The engineering-centric creators of technocracy viewed the whole of society as one giant factory, in which all components must be run with total precision. In their worldwide factory, all the resources, including human labor, were considered equal. The goal was to minimize input and maximize efficiency and output, thus driving out all wastage. Each decision made was based on this sole goal of achieving maximum productivity.

The technocrats knew that gears, belts, and motors were easy to design and control but that unpredictable humans needed social engineering to keep them in line with the grand vision of technocracy. The Preface of their Study Course made it very clear that "technocracy is dealing with social phenomena in the widest sense of the word; this includes not only actions of human beings,

1 Scott, Howard et al. *Technocracy Study Course*. (New York: Technocracy, Inc., 1934). https://technocracyinc.org/wp-content/uploads/2015/07/Study-Course.pdf

but also everything which directly or indirectly affects their actions" (page x).

In the Study Course chapter titled "Lesson 21. The Human Animal," the authors concluded that "practically all social control is effected through the mechanism of the conditioned reflex," which is "no whit different from that of a dog which hears a metronome and secretes saliva." They determined that even humans' inhibitions can be manipulated:

> *If they are taken young enough, human beings can be conditioned not to do almost anything under the sun. They can be conditioned not to use certain language, not to eat certain foods on certain days, not to work on certain days, not to mate in the absence of certain ceremonial words spoken over them, not to break into a grocery store for food even though they may not have eaten for days (page 193).*

"The Human Animal" chapter summarized its theories as follows:

1. *The human animal is composed of chemical atoms which are derived from the ordinary inorganic materials of the earth*
2. *The human being is an engine taking potential energy in the form of chemical combinations contained in food, and converting this potential energy into heat, work, and body tissue*
3. *The human animal responds to its external environment through the mechanism of the conditioned reflex*
4. *There are basic physiological differences [. . .] among various human beings that upset all philosophical theories of equality and hence any governmental theory of democracy*
5. *Human social habits and institutions tend to remain stable or else to undergo change extremely slowly, except in the case of a rapid change of the external environment, especially when this latter affects the basic biological necessities (page 210)*

The chapter ends with an elaboration of the all-important fifth point: Rapid change can be achieved by upending "basic biological necessities" such as food, energy, finances, and health—the withdrawal of which will cause immediate social instability. Social stability "is restored when a new set of social habits and customs are formed that so conform to the dictates of the new environment as to satisfy the basic biological necessities."

From 2020 through the time of this writing in mid-2022, the world has been turned upside down with a parade of social engineering events designed to create conditions for control that will allow the Great Reset to take place: a COVID-19 panic, mRNA "vaccine" injections, energy crisis, soaring gasoline prices, inflation, food and water shortages, a housing crisis, a financial crisis, etc. All of these events were foreshadowed by the original technocrats, who predicted the largest social engineering project in history:

> *Leave the physical environment unaltered, or the industrial rates of operation unchanged, and any effort to alter the fundamental modes of behavior of human beings is doomed largely to failure; alter the immediate physical environment of human beings, and their modes of behavior change automatically (page 243).*

I am emphasizing this point to underscore the incredibly low view of humanity held by technocrats of every era. If the technocrats had their way, humans would be essentially stripped of free will and made to obey the commands and demands of a few autocrats who control the machinery of society.

It isn't hard to appreciate the technocrats' own concise definition of technocracy, which appeared in *The Technocrat* magazine in 1937:

> *Technocracy is the science of social engineering, the scientific operation of the entire social mechanism to produce and distribute goods and services to the entire population. [. . .] For*

> *the first time in human history it will be done as a scientific, technical, engineering problem.*[2]

Their main concern was how to apply the "science of social engineering" to the creation and distribution of "goods and services." Again, belts, pulleys, gears, and motors always obey the design of their creators. The rub: Humans, having minds of their own, do *not* always obey. Hence, control over human behavior was all that stood in their way of making the perfect machine. Today's mad dash to create robots that replace human labor is perfectly logical to modern technocrats: Robots are perfectly controlled and monitored, can work twenty-four hours a day, and don't complain or go on strike.

Technocrats don't try to hide their total disdain for political systems:

> *There will be no place for Politics, Politicians, Finance or Financiers, Rackets or Racketeers. [. . .] Technocracy will distribute by means of a certificate of distribution available to every citizen from birth to death. [Emphasis added.]*

Technocracy would remove the every layer of government from society. Although technocrats hated politicians for being ignorant and obstructionist, there was a deeper reason for their contempt: The technocrat ego was so large that they could not see any reason to engage in public discourse on what was right or wrong—on what was beneficial or harmful to society. They had the "science" and the "science was settled." No other discussion was necessary. Furthermore, they reasoned, it was inefficient to waste time talking about things when implementation could already be underway.

The *Technocracy Study Course* listed just seven requirements that would be essential to create a technocracy. Engineers are typically meticulous about creating a "requirements analysis" before starting a new project. So we need to pay close attention to these seven requirements:

---

2 "What is Technocracy?" The Technocrat, Vol. 3, No. 4. September 1937. https://archive.org/details/TheTechnocrat-September1937/page/n1/mode/2up

1. *Register on a continuous 24-hour-per-day basis the total net conversion of energy*
2. *By means of the registration of energy converted and consumed, make possible a balanced load*
3. *Provide a continuous inventory of all production and consumption*
4. *Provide a specific registration of the type, kind, etc., of all goods and services, where produced and where used*
5. *Provide specific registration of the consumption of each individual, plus a record and description of the individual*
6. *Allow the citizen the widest latitude of choice in consuming his individual share of Continental physical wealth*
7. *Distribute goods and services to every member of the population (page 232)*

As we'll soon see in this chapter and beyond, the modern globalization movement—today's implementation of Technocracy, Inc.—is following this prescriptive formula to the letter.

Now let's discuss each of the requirements in greater detail:

**1. Register on a continuous 24-hour-per-day basis the total net conversion of energy**

Control over energy took center stage in the technocracy of the 1930s and still does today. "Conversion of energy" means creating usable energy from stored energy like coal, oil, or natural gas; when these resources are burned, electricity is generated. Hydroelectric and nuclear power also convert energy. Technocrats had two reasons for keeping track of usable energy: First, it was the basis for issuing "energy script" to all citizens for buying and selling goods and services. Second, it predicted economic activity, which technocracy makes directly dependent upon energy.

An abundance of available energy is anathema to technocracy because it would lead to uncontrollable economic activity and the wastage of natural resources. That's why today's war on the abundant oil, natural gas, coal, nuclear, and hydro-power sources of energy is intended to steer customers to alternative—but insufficient—energy sources such as solar, wind, or total energy generation.

**2. By means of the registration of energy converted and consumed, make possible a balanced load**

Once available energy was quantified, it was to be allocated to consumers and manufacturers so as to limit production and consumption. Technocrats want control of both production and consumption so they can manage everything according to their scientific formulas. This was true then and remains true today.

The modern smart grid, with its ubiquitous WiFi-enabled smart meters on homes and businesses, is the exact fulfillment of these first two requirements. The concept of "energy web" was first revitalized in 1999 by the Bonneville Power Authority (BPA) in Portland, Oregon. This federal government agency had a history of employing technocrats dating back to its creation in 1937. The "energy web" was renamed "Smart Grid" in 2009—during the Obama Administration—when the mass installation of smart meters on homes and businesses began. Smart Grid went beyond the United States; it was a global initiative intended to blanket the entire world with this new energy control technology. [Note: Today, both smart grid and smart meter, being universally known, are spelled with lower-case letters.]

The original justification for wirelessly connected smart meters was to make it easier for power companies to read electricity usage remotely. This was a completely disingenuous rationale, however. The unstated reason, we now know, is that the meters are able to identify, connect with, monitor, and report the usage of each energy-consuming device inside a building. And not only that, but the meters can literally *control* each device through the manufacturer's installation of a special circuit board designed for such purposes. Today, it is well nigh impossible for consumers to buy a new major appliance—air conditioner, heater, washing machine, clothes dryer, refrigerator—that cannot be controlled (and thus temporarily or permanent shut off) by a smart meter.

Earlier this year, a British journalist reported that, due to energy shortages in Europe, Spain had "issued a new government decree, which applies to a whole host of public buildings as well as shops, hotels and other venues, [that] will [. . .] stop heating from being raised above 19°C during the winter."[3] Violators could be fined up to €600,000 ($610,000 USD) for "serious violations." Italy, Britain, Germany, and Ukraine have taken similar steps to mandate energy restrictions. None of these "power grabs," so to speak, would be possible without the widespread installation of smart meters throughout Europe.

**3. Provide a continuous inventory of all production and consumption**

From the start, technocrats have been obsessed with aggregating inventory quantities in the economic system from beginning to end. They have envisioned storing inventory in production facilities until it is ready to be delivered to consumers and producers. In their ideal system, only actual consumption by end-users would shrink inventory.

Voila, that ideal system has come to pass. It is termed Supply Chain Management (SCM) and is used extensively by today's corporations. Their goal is to minimize stored inventory (squeezing out the inefficiencies) and make for "just-in-time" manufacturing and consumption.

**4. Provide a specific registration of the type, kind, etc., of all goods and services, where produced and where used**

This granular level of data tracking drills down to specific items and would ostensibly assign a trackable serial number to every item manufactured, shipped, and ultimately consumed by individuals or by other manufacturing processes. Such detailed item tracking is a core value of SCM theory and practice.

The greatest enabler of technocracy is the Internet of Things (IoT), where all connected devices are networked together via the latest 5G wireless technology. Speaking at a 2016 press conference, Tom Wheeler, then-chairman of the Federal Communications Commission, said of the Internet of Everything (his name for the IoT) : "If something can be connected, it will be connected

3 Watson, Paul Joseph. "Spain Bans Air Conditioning Dropping Below 27°C." Summit News. August 3, 2022. https://summit.news/2022/08/03/spain-bans-air-conditioning-dropping-below-27c

in a 5G world."[4] The harvesting of data from billions of sensors embedded in the IoT will, for the first time in history, provide real-time data collection. In turn, this data flow will put wind in the sails of Artificial Intelligence algorithms designed to control society and the people in it.

**5. Provide specific registration of the consumption of each individual, plus a record and description of the individual**

This requirement entails a cross-check of inventory against actual consumption by each verified individual consumer. The idea is that if an identified person buys a product but does not consume it immediately, the technocrat overlords could act to prevent that individual's wasteful behavior in the future. Once we fathom that technocracy is intended to completely eliminate private property, savings, inheritances, and all personal assets, then we understand that the so-called hoarding of consumable items is viewed as unauthorized savings.

But how do the technocrat busybodies go about collecting the details of each consumer's spending and consumption? Through continuous monitoring and total surveillance—not just of smart meters, as we mentioned above, but of every move made by every living, breathing body on the planet.

Indeed, surveillance and data collection are ubiquitous today. According to meddling technocrats, there is no such thing as "enough" data. US intelligence agencies (the National Security Agency, the Central Intelligence Agency, the Department of Homeland Security, etc.) are creating massive national databases that harvest real-time data from every conceivable source. Surveillance includes biometric data (i.e., facial scans, iris, and voice scans), communications (email, phone calls, texts), financial transactions, location tracking (geospatial intel), social media (posts, shares, likes, connections), psychographic data (predispositions), and much more.

---

4 Prepared Remarks of FCC Chairman Tom Wheeler: "The Future of Wireless: A Vision for U.S. Leadership in a 5G World." June 20, 2016. https://transition.fcc.gov/Daily_Releases/Daily_Business/2016/db0620/DOC-339920A1.pdf

**6. Allow the citizen the widest latitude of choice in consuming his individual share of Continental physical wealth**

We must understand this requirement from the perspective of a technocrat. If technocrats had their druthers, there would not be a wide selection of goods and services because there would be no competition between manufacturers. Products would be designed and manufactured by technocrats and at their sole discretion. The real issue here is the aggregate amount of "Continental physical wealth" and how much of it a regular Joe or Jane deserves to consume. Technocrats view all humans—themselves excepted—like cattle in a feed lot, existing only to be fattened up with a managed diet from birth to death, shielded from inclement weather, medically treated for maximum efficiency, and eventually turned into a source of protein and profits for their superiors.

**7. Distribute goods and services to every member of the population**

The key to this last requirement is the technocrats' demand that *every single person* in society be forced to participate in their system. Outliers were not to be allowed then, nor are they to be allowed today. Want proof? Look for the motto "Ensuring that no one is left behind" throughout the United Nations' literature on sustainable development.[5] Another word for "ensure" is "guarantee." Globalists' guarantees take the form of "mandates." (By the way, the "no one . . . left behind" phrase is eerily reminiscent of the US Department of Education's No Child Left Behind Act of 2001.)

Since private property and, hence, competition, would not be allowed, there would be only *one* source for the universally distributed goods and services. This point references the fifth and sixth requirements.

But how, exactly, would this sweeping system work? Well, technocrats would design and operate the factories. Technocrats would also control all the resources used in the factories. Technocrats would force you to work in their factories. Technocrats

5 "Ensuring that no one is left behind: How do we protect the poorest and most vulnerable from the crisis and empower them to realize the SDGs?" United Nations' High-Level Political Forum on Sustainable Development. 6 July 2021. https://sustainabledevelopment.un.org/content/documents/27871BN_HLPF_2021_LNOB.pdf

would also force you to consume the output of their factories—their food, for example, if you want to stay alive. Technocrats would assume total control of your health. Technocrats would not permit you to own a house or land. Instead, you would rent a unit in an apartment building constructed and owned by them. Technocrats would give you a Universal Basic Income that would expire at the end of the allocation period, making it impossible for you to save for the future. In reality, this is the exact fulfillment of the World Economic Forum's proclamation that "By 2030, you will own nothing and be happy."[6] Do you see it?

Those early technocrats were so sure that a utopia was within their grasp that they wrote,

> *So today, with the operation of our technological mechanism, the control measures that must and will be adopted are those that most nearly conform to the technological operating requirements of that mechanism (page 219).*

Taken together, these seven requirements describe a feudalistic, scientific dictatorship (which is actually pseudoscientific) in which people are essentially owned and managed from cradle to grave by technocrat overlords.

But do not confuse technocracy with Marxism, socialism, communism, or fascism: It is none of those. Technocracy is unprecedented in human history. It defies comparison with any other system. Take it from the horse's mouth:

> *Such an organization has no precedence in any of the political forms. It is neither a democracy, an aristocracy, a plutocracy, a dictatorship, nor any of the other familiar political forms, all of which are completely inadequate and incompetent to handle the job. It is, instead, a Technocracy, being built along with the technological lines of the job in hand (page 241). [Emphasis added.]*

## The Predicted Outcomes

According to the *Technocracy Study Course*, the anticipated and promised "end products" of technocracy would be:

6 "8 Predictions for the World in 2030." World Economic Forum. YouTube. https://youtu.be/Hx3DhoLFO4s

1. *A high physical standard of living*
2. *A high standard of public health*
3. *A minimum of unnecessary labor*
4. *A minimum of wastage of non-replaceable resources*
5. *An educational system to train the entire younger generation indiscriminately as regards all considerations other than inherent ability – a Continental system of human conditioning (page 240)*

Not surprisingly, these outcomes overlap perfectly with some of the UN's Sustainable Development Goals (SDGs) adopted at its 2030 Agenda for Sustainable Development conference in September 2015:

a. *Goal #1— No poverty*
b. *Goal #3 — Good health and well-being (note that the banner on Goal #3 states: "Vaccinate your family to protect them and improve public health")*
c. *Goal #8 — Decent work and economic growth*
d. *Goal #12 — Responsible consumption and production*
e. *Goal #4 — Quality education*[7]

When the UN's 1992 Earth Summit in Rio de Janeiro produced the "Agenda for the 21st Century," few people realized that Agenda 21, as it was called, was firmly rooted in technocracy. Nor did anyone suspect that technocracy's name would continue to be changed—that is, concealed—numerous times between then and now.

In 1970, Zbigniew Brzezinski called technocracy the "Technetronic Era." In 1973, the Trilateral Commission referred to technocracy as the "New International Economic Order." In 2015, the UN General Assembly whitewashed technocracy with its aforementioned "2030 Agenda for Sustainable Development." By 2022, the UN-allied World Economic Forum had buried the term "technocracy" under a mountain of clever catchphrases: "Green New Deal," "Smart Growth," "Build Back Better," "Great Reset," "Green Economy." All of this rebranding has definitely made it more dif-

7 "Do you know all 17 SDGs?" United Nations Department of Economic and Social Affairs. Sustainable Development. https://sdgs.un.org/goals

ficult to follow the technocracy trail. But now that the big picture is in full view, thanks to the worldwide awakening engendered by the fake pandemic, it is no longer possible for technocracy to hide under attractive, even urgent-sounding names.

What we've been talking about here is more than remarketing a moniker its adherents want to keep covered up. What we've been exploring is how humans are being "conditioned" to accept technocracy—to welcome it. We've been fleshing out the fifth "end product" described in the *Technocracy Study Course*—to repeat, "a Continental system of human conditioning." This ties back to study course concept we quoted much earlier in this chapter: "If they are taken young enough, human beings can be conditioned not to do almost anything under the sun." Indeed, it is not surprising that modern schooling is the practice of non-stop conditioning—indoctrination, brainwashing—rather than true education.

## On Transportation

The *Technocracy Study Course* viewed the existing transportation system as horribly inefficient because hordes of drivers either owned or aspired to own a vehicle. So, after technocrats declared that "[n]o automobiles would be privately owned" (page 254), they instead authorized the Automotive Branch of Transportation to "provide a network of garages at convenient places all over the country from which automobiles could be had at any hour of the night or day" (page 254). Of course, for data-hungry technocrats, "the exact energy cost per mile for the automotive transportation of the entire country is known at all times" (page 254).

The technocratic lust for efficiency was to be taken out on the people who simply needed to get from point A to point B:

> *If while the automobile is out of its operation it has been maintained at a rate equal to or greater than the national load factor for all automobiles, charge is made on a mileage basis only.*
>
> *If the load factor of the car while out is made on the basis of the number of miles that the car would have travelled during that time had it operated a rate equal to the average load*

*factor, the charge is made on the basis of the number of miles that the car would have travelled during that time had it operated at a rate equal to the average national load factor for automobiles (page 255).*

Thus, you pick up a car, zip to your destination, and, once there, immediately check it back in. If you let the car sit idle, you will be charged for the miles it could have driven in that time.

Agenda 21 and the 2030 Agenda for Sustainable Development likewise call for the elimination of private automobiles, opting instead for foot power, bicycles, buses, trains, scooters, and shared rides like Uber and Lyft. Even traffic policies like "street calming" and "traffic calming," both of which the UN embraces, are geared to push people out of private vehicles.

## On Agriculture

Technocrats held an equally dim view of traditional agriculture. The soil, they claimed, "is of no importance except as a container of plant foods and as a support for the growing plant." They believed that agriculture was "the most primitive and backward industry." The technocrats' answer to this perceived dismal state of affairs was science—or, rather, their twisted version of science. They observed that "any other container for properly proportioned plant foods, used in conjunction with a suitable support for the growing plant, would constitute an alternative to an agriculture based upon tilling of the soil" (page 257).

Alas, they also had the temerity to write: "[T]he fact remains that the application of the technological methods will revolutionize [agriculture] to where present methods are truly primitive in comparison" (page 260). If that statement shocks you, consider their final solution:

*All present farms and land divisions would be eliminated. Agriculture would be only one division of a fast chemical industry which would convert the raw materials of the land into use products and in turn supply to the land its requirements in fertilizers and plant food. Tracts of probably tens of miles square would be worked at a unit. [Emphasis added.]*

This obsessive need to control nature and consolidate industries explains the technocrats' war on family farms over the last eighty years as well as the massive accumulation of farmland by multinational corporations in the US and elsewhere.

In fact, an abrupt about-face in agricultural policy is what caused China to morph from a communist state into a technocracy. China's communist scheme had created a system of food production based on rural, locally operated agriculture. That changed in 2016, when it was announced that "the Chinese government said it plans to relocate 100 million farmers, or about 12 percent of the rural population, mainly into smaller cities with a large stockpile of unsold homes, and turn the farmers' small holdings into larger farms." It was reiterated that "small plots of land left behind by city-bound villagers could be turned into larger farms that use modern methods to make the agricultural sector more competitive."[8] There was no mention made of compensating the generational farmers who had known nothing but agriculture all their lives.

## On Housing

Housing was yet another established industry that early technocrats found inefficient and wasteful. "[S]o great is the effect of habit on the human animal," they fretted, "that it becomes almost impossible for one to detach himself sufficiently to take an objective view of the subject of housing." Even architects didn't escape the technocrats' censure. "[T]he problem of designing building in accordance with the functions they are to perform," they complained, "seems rarely to have occurred to architects" (page 261).

The technocrat solution was to design houses that met basic needs yet incurred minimal expense and used the fewest possible resources. One way to achieve those ends was to offer only a few house designs to the entire population. (They focused on the US populace but their formula could be applied globally.) The most efficient solution quickly became clear to them:

---

8 "China to Relocate 100 Million Farmers in Urbanisation Push." Today Online. October 22, 2016. https://www.todayonline.com/chinaindia/china/china-relocate-100-million-farmers-urbanisation-push

*The requirements of low cost construction would necessitate that the housing be of factory fabricated types, where the individual units can be turned out on a quantity production schedule ready for assembly. [. . .] [T]here would be a limited number of models (page 262).*

They also planned every detail of house interiors. Furniture would be designed into the house. Indirect and dimmable lighting would be designed for optimum physiological effects. In effect, the entire US continent would live in tiny cookie-cutter-like homes constructed with cheap materials. There would be no beauty or artistic expression and no freedom of choice. One cannot help but conclude that the outcome of such a crackpot scheme would be a continent-wide—if not worldwide—ghetto slum within twenty years.

## On Christianity

Technocracy was heavily dependent on the evolutionary theories of Darwin and reflected the general criticism of the Bible that was in full swing during the early 1900s. As the *Technocracy Study Course* put it, "the picture of the supernaturalism of man and the special creations received a final thrust when, in 1859, Charles Darwin issued his book *Origin of Species*" (page 184).

Technocrats specifically excluded biblical Christianity as a source of truth. Viewing Darwin as inerrant, they mockingly wrote that Christian principles were "handed down from a primitive and ignorant people of the past" (page 182). They reasoned that Christianity had been defeated, that Christians were "far removed from the pedestal upon which they had originally imagined themselves to be," and that "at last they were obliged to admit blood kinship with other members of the animal kingdom" (page 185).

The Study Course expanded on this anti-Christian sentiment a few paragraphs later:

*It might be remarked that the most minute anatomical dissection had never revealed anything that corresponded to a 'mind' or a 'conscience' or a 'will.' The reason for this is not difficult to find when one considers that all of these terms were inherited from an ignorant, barbarian past, and had never been subjected to scientific scrutiny. Let us remember that real scientific progress is at all times based upon the correlation of objectively observable (see, feel, hear, taste, smell, etc.) phenomena (page 186).*

Technocrats presented their dark view of humans in this coup de grace:

*When we observe a human being we merely perceive an object which makes a certain variety of motions and noises. The same is true, however, when we observe a dog or a Ford car (page 186).*

There we have it. To the authors of the *Technocracy Study Course*, Christians were primitive, ignorant, mindless, soulless entities without a conscience, without free will—were merely material objects that made meaningless motions and noises.

Why this harsh assessment? Because the founders of technocracy had zero tolerance for any system of thinking that was not in accordance with their own.

## The Way Forward

You can see why Columbia University ran technocracy off its campus in 1933 and why most Americans who had heard of Technocracy, Inc. rejected it during its heyday in the 1930s and 1940s. Indeed, anyone who saw through the entire dystopian plan realized it would eliminate all private property and the ability to accumulate wealth, would cripple human ambition, creativity, and ingenuity, would deny human dignity and worth—would, in a word, destroy human civilization.

Today, though, Americans by and large are still unaware of the existence, much less the danger, of technocracy. Thankfully, a growing number of Europeans are waking up to its encroaching threat. Though the phenomenon is not yet widely understood, the 2018 article "Technocratic Government and Economic Policy," written by an associate professor at a university in Glasgow and published by Oxford University Press, at least asks the right questions:

> The surge in the appointments of technocrats to the top economic portfolios of finance since the 2009 Great Recession, and even the formation of fully technocratic governments in Europe, raises questions regarding the role of technocrats and technocratic governments in economic policy in democracies. **Who are the technocrats? Why are they appointed in the first place? What is their impact on economic policy, and finally what are their sources of policy influence?**[9] [Emphasis added.]

Anyone asking these questions would do well to read this book.

---

9 Alexiadou, Despina. "Technocratic Government and Economic Policy." Oxford University Press. 24 May 2018. https://oxfordre.com/politics/view/10.1093/acrefore/9780190228637.001.0001/acrefore-9780190228637-e-614

# CHAPTER 4

# The Genesis and Progress of Transhumanism

*We are actually hacking the software of life. We think about it as an operating system. So if you could actually change that, if you could introduce a line of code, or change a line of code, it turns out it has profound implications for everything. — Tal Zaks, former Chief Medical Officer, Moderna*

When I titled this book *The Evil Twins of Technocracy and Transhumanism,* I was *not* thinking of that pair of famous brothers who are, ironically, closely associated with these intertwined ideologies. I'm referring, of course, to Aldous Huxley, who dramatically pictured technocracy in his 1932 book *Brave New World*, and Julian Huxley, who twenty-five years later introduced the word "transhumanism" to the English lexicon.

In his 1957 book *New Bottles for New Wine*, younger brother Julian wrote:

> *The human species can, if it wishes, transcend itself — now just sporadically, an individual here in one way, an individual there in another way, but in its entirety, as humanity. We need a name for this new belief. Perhaps transhumanism will serve: man remaining man, but transcending himself, by realizing new possibilities of and for his human nature.*[1]

1 Huxley, Julian. "Transhumanism." *New Bottles for New Wine*. (London: Chatto & Windus, 1957). Page 17.

Another twenty-five years would elapse before transhumanism became a viable movement. The first modern transhumanists met formally in the early 1980s at the University of California, Los Angeles, and "quickly became the centre of transhumanist thinking." Not surprisingly, transhumanism has since become one of the de facto ideologies of Silicon Valley.[2]

Futurist Max More is considered the philosophical father of modern humanism. In a 1994 essay, More refined the tenets of modern transhumanism in urgent, if not stark, terms:

> *No more gods, no more faith, no more timid holding back. Let us blast out of our old forms, our ignorance, our weaknesses and our mortality. The future belongs to posthumanity.*[3]

In all of their speeches and literature, transhumanists have made it clear that they regard transhumanism as merely an interim state—a state that ultimately leads to posthumanism. They call transhumanism the process and posthumanism the target. They envision machines, computers, and artificial intelligence eventually merging with man. They predict that death will be eliminated when man's immortal state is achieved by uploading the content of the human brain into the "cloud." There, they say, man will be reanimated either into another body or into an avatar or into the nose of a spaceship to travel the universe.

More, who holds a PhD in philosophy, has obviously rubbed shoulders with other academics and with scientists and computer engineers, which has allowed him to gain futuristic insights into newly emerging technologies. In the aforementioned 1994 essay—yes, it was written nearly *two decades* ago—he anticipated:

> *The dawn of the new millennium will see the ability to use engineered viruses to alter the genetic structure of any cell, even adult, differentiated cells. This will give us pervasive*

---

2 https://archive.org/details/NewBottlesForNewWine/page/n5/mode/2up

3 Piesing, Mark. "Silicon Valley's 'suicide pill' for mankind." UnHerd. August 20, 2018. https://unherd.com/2018/08/silicon-valleys-suicide-pill-mankind.

3 More, Max. "On Becoming Posthuman." Free Inquiry. The Free Library. September 22, 1994. Accessed August 20, 2022. https://www.thefreelibrary.com/On+becoming+posthuman.-a016378926

*control over our physiology and morphology. Molecular nanotechnology, an emerging and increasingly funded technology, should eventually give us practically complete control over the structure of matter, allowing us to build anything, perfectly, atom-by-atom. We will be able to program the construction of physical objects (including our bodies) just as we now do with software. The abolition of aging and most involuntary death will be one result. We have achieved two of the three alchemists' dreams: we have transmuted the elements and learned to fly. Immortality is next.*[4] *[Emphasis added.]*

Engineered viruses to alter genetic structure? Complete control over the structure of matter? Immortality? Was this an early vision of the blending of Nanotechnology, Biotechnology, Information science and Cognitive science (NBIC)—the moon-shot rocket that would launch Humanity 2.0?

When this passage was written, its resemblance to science fiction novels and films caused most observers to laugh at early transhumanists like Max More.

Few are laughing now. In the intervening years, the transhumanist philosophy and the applied science of NBIC have been spreading like wildfire throughout the world's top academic institutions and emerging biotech companies.

Big Pharma has been visibly involved in transhumanism and NBIC since at least 1992, when the UN Convention on Biodiversity met in Rio de Janeiro. By early 2020, enough progress had been made to spring the transhuman trap on all of humanity.

The trap took the form of the SARS-CoV-2 virus, which Big Pharma and the biotech industry used as an opportunity to launch a revolutionary new "vaccine" technology based on messenger ribonucleic acid, or mRNA.

A little explanation is in order. We are more familiar with DNA than with RNA, so let's start with DNA. Spelled out, DNA is deoxyribonucleic acid, a substance found in all living organisms. It is a double-stranded set of base pairs (adenine, thymine, guanine, and cytosine), which is arranged in the shape of a twisted helix.

4 More.

The ordering of base pairs is called a gene, and a collection of genes is called a chromosome. Human DNA consists of 23 pairs of chromosomes.

RNA is shorthand for ribonucleic acid, which is a single strand of DNA that contains the instructions needed to make proteins. mRNA, or messenger RNA, delivers those blueprints to the ribosome for the construction and arrangement of the amino acid building blocks of each protein. Once the protein is successfully created, the original mRNA strand simply dissolves. This is a never-ending process in the body. It generates the proteins necessary to sustain life.

This is obviously a very complex subject, and my description is not intended to be complete.

The new mRNA "vaccine" is created synthetically in a laboratory. When injected, this man-made mRNA bypasses your normal genetic processes and spoofs your normal cells into producing a different kind of protein called a "spike protein." Since spike proteins do not belong in your body, the idea is that your body will see them as foreign invaders and will build antibodies to attack, repel, and destroy them. Theoretically, the antibodies are supposed to stick around until you are struck by a real virus—at which point they provide a defense against infection.

To quell growing public fear that mRNA injections might somehow affect our DNA, the mRNA injection manufacturers, scientists, the CDC, the FDA, and other health authorities all united in a vehement denial that any such thing could ever happen. However, their denials were proven unfounded when, on February 22, 2022, a study was released by Lund University in Sweden, describing a process of "reverse transcription," whereby foreign mRNA can indeed find its way back into one's DNA. According to the researchers:

> *Our study is the first in vitro study on the effect of COVID-19 mRNA vaccine BNT162b2 on human liver cell line. We present evidence on fast entry of BNT162b2 into the cells and*

*subsequent intracellular reverse transcription of BNT162b2 mRNA into DNA.*[5]

## When Transhumanism Met Technocracy

The 1992 UN Convention on Biological Diversity, which we mentioned above, was conducted simultaneously with the Agenda 21 Conference, whose full name was the UN Conference on Economic Development (UNCED). Both were held in Rio de Janeiro, and both were sponsored by the United Nations Environmental Programme (UNEP), the United Nations Educational, Scientific and Cultural Organization (UNESCO), and the International Union for the Conservation of Nature (IUCN).

"Agenda 21" was shorthand for "the agenda for the 21st century." Its raison d'être was sustainable development, a resource-based economic system virtually indistinguishable from the historic Technocracy, Inc. movement.[6] Both then and now, the UN has acted as the global agent spreading this contagious ideology around the world.

According to the International Institute for Sustainable Development (IISD):

*Sustainable development has been defined in many ways, but the most frequently quoted definition is from Our Common Future, also known as the Brundtland Report:*

*"Sustainable development is development that meets the needs of the present without compromising the ability of future generations to meet their own needs."*[7]

The book the IISD mentioned, *Our Common Future*, was published in 1987 by the United Nations. It became the blueprint for the Rio conference that the UN sponsored five years later. Its author was Gro Harlem Brundtland. Hence its handle, the Brun-

5 Aldén, Markus et al. "Intracellular Reverse Transcription of Pfizer BioNTech COVID-19 mRNA Vaccine BNT162b2 In Vitro in Human Liver Cell Line." Current Issues in Molecular Biology. MDPI. (Lund, Sweden: Lund University, 2022). https://www.mdpi.com/1467-3045/44/3/73/pdf?version=1645805899

6 Wood, Patrick M. *Technocracy Rising: The Trojan Horse of Global Transformation*. (Coherent Publishing, 2015).

7 International Institute for Sustainable Development (IISD). https://www.iisd.org/mission-and-goals/sustainable-development

tlandt Report. It was produced by the World Commission on Environment and Development (renamed the Brundtland Commission), which she chaired.

Lest you think Gro Brundtland a forgettable, bit-part player in this real-life drama, consider some of the other notable posts she has held: Norway's Minister of the Environment (1974–1981); first female, youngest, and three-term Prime Minister of Norway (1981, 1986–89, and 1990–96); Director-General of the World Health Organization (1998–2003); and UN Special Envoy on Climate Change (2007–2010). Throughout her career—first as a medical doctor, then as a politician, and finally as a so-called environmentalist, Brundtland has been a member of the Trilateral Commission. Considering her cachet, it is fitting that the UN has hailed her as the "mother of sustainable development." Nonetheless, given the fatal flaws in sustainable development, it is no wonder that her ideology has been turning the world upside down ever since it was adopted.

At the Rio conference, a question was proposed: What can be done to save the earth from the excessive development that has caused pollution, [supposed] global warming, rainforest depletion, and other harms [real or imagined], to the environment?

The answer proffered by the Brundtland Report? *More development*! Yes, more development will surely solve the problems that more development has already created. Huh? How so? Apparently by erasing the destructive effects of the earlier development! Notably, this further development can and must be accomplished *only* by the earlier developers—that is, by the very same actors whose greed has already wrecked habitats and plundered nations.

Believe it or not, Brundtland convinced the UN membership that this line of reasoning somehow made sense, and it was adopted as "the agenda for the 21st century" in 1992.

However, two genuine environmentalists who participated in the Agenda 21 conference, Pratap Chatterjee and Matthias Finger, saw through the smoke and mirrors. In their book, *The Earth Brokers*, published two years later, they noted that "free trade and its promoters came to be seen as the solution to the global ecological crisis."[8]

*The Earth Brokers* co-authors were explicit:

> *We argue that UNCED has boosted precisely the type of industrial development that is destructive for the environment, the planet, and its inhabitants. We see how, as a result of UNCED, the rich will get richer, the poor poorer, while more and more of the planet is destroyed in the process.*[9]

Their prognostication could not have been more spot-on. Today, the rich are raking in new billions, the poor are literally living in tents, if not the gutter, and the entire planet—from its ecosystems to its social systems to its economic systems—is in tatters.

How did we get here? asked Chatterjee and Finger. They concluded:

> *Neither Brundtland, nor the secretariat, nor the governments drafted plans to examine the pitfalls of free trade and industrial development. Instead, they wrote up a convention on how to 'develop' the use of biodiversity through patents and biotechnology.*[10] *[Emphasis added.]*

Despite what UNCED purported to be, its *true mission* was to capture and capitalize on biodiversity for the sole sake of the biotechnology industry. This fact was largely overlooked between 1992 and the Great Panic—misnamed pandemic—of 2020. In the past two years, though, it has become impossible to ignore the fact that the global takeover has been, from the Rio conference on, orchestrated by elements of that very same biotechnology industry.

## What Biodiversity Really Means

Transhumanism has been hiding in the shadows, coming to light in fits and starts, in both preaching and practice, ever since Julian Huxley first penned the word in his 1957 collection of es-

---

8 Chatterjee, Prabat and Matthias Finger. *The Earth Brokers: Power, Politics and World Development* (London and New York: Routledge, Taylor & Francis Group, 1994). Page 40.

9 Chatterjee and Finger. Page 40.

10 Chatterjee and Finger. Ibid.

says. As with anything new and especially anything occult, transhumanism is not easy to spot until we learn what to look for. At least that's how it was for me when I first heard of transhumanism several years ago. After that, I began to see the transhumanist hand everywhere, starting with Brundtland's 1987 report, *Our Common Future*:

> *The diversity of species is necessary for the normal functioning of ecosystems and the biosphere as a whole. The genetic material in wild species contributes billions of dollars yearly to the world economy in the form of improved crop species, new drugs and medicines, and raw materials for industry.*[11]

The specific development of biodiversity can be found in her Chapter 6, Species and Ecosystems: Resources for Development, where she writes:

> *Species and their genetic materials promise to play an expanding role in development, and a powerful economic rationale is emerging to bolster the ethical, aesthetic, and scientific case for preserving them. The genetic variability and germplasm material of species make contributions to agriculture, medicine, and industry worth many billions of dollars per year. [. . .] If nations can ensure the survival of species, the world can look forward to new and improved foods, new drugs and medicines, and new raw materials for industry.*[12]

Further on, Brundtland opines:

> *Vast stocks of biological diversity are in danger of disappearing* ***just as science is learning how to exploit genetic variability through the advances of genetic engineering.*** *[. . .] It would be grim irony indeed if just as new genetic engineering techniques begin to let us peer into life's diversity and use genes more efficiently to better human conditions, we looked and found this treasure sadly depleted.*[13] *[Emphasis added.]*

---

11 The World Commission on Environment and Development (WCED): Chairman Gro Harlem Brundtland, Vice-Chairman Mansour Khalid et al. *Our Common Future*. (Oxford, England, UK: Oxford University Press, 1987). Page 13.

12 WCED. Page 147.

13 WCED. Pages 149–150.

Sure enough, *The Earth Brokers* authors found that Brundtland's written statements perfectly align with what they observed during the UNCED and Biodiversity Convention summit. In their eyewitness testimony, they noted:

> *The convention implicitly equates the diversity of life — animals and plants — to the diversity of genetic codes, for which read genetic resources. By doing so, diversity becomes something that modern science can manipulate. Finally, the convention promotes biotechnology as being 'essential for the conservation and sustainable use of biodiversity.'*[14]

Leaving no room for doubt as to the UN's goal, they made this mind-blowing statement:

> *The* **main stake raised** *by the Biodiversity Convention is the issue of ownership and control over biological diversity. [. . .] [T]***he major concern was protecting the pharmaceutical and emerging biotechnology industries.**[15] *[Emphasis added.]*

To further reinforce their bold claim, the authors added, "[T]hey wrote up a convention on how to 'develop' the use of biodiversity through patents and biotechnology."[16]

Note carefully—and I underscore this point with bold and italic and capital letters—that ownership and control over genes was not a side issue or a minor stake of the Biodiversity Convention: ***It was the MAIN STAKE!***

Though the UNCED conference was expected to bridge the gaps between the North and South, it was soon apparent that everything was being totally dominated by the developed nations of the North. As *The Earth Brokers* explained, all solutions were provided by "Western science, Western technology, Western information, Western training, Western money and Western institutions."[17]

---

14 WCED. Page 42.

15 WCED. Page 43.

16 WCED. Page 171.

17 WCED. Page 50.

## It Is Consistent Throughout UN Documents

Also in 1992, the same year as the UNCED conference, UNEP and IUCN published a book titled *Global Biodiversity Strategy* and subtitled *Guidelines for Action to Save, Study, and Use Earth's Biotic Wealth Sustainably and Equitably.*[18] Its themes, which matched the goals of the UNCED conference, were presented carefully in order to win the Third World's approval, cooperation, and participation.

For example, a royalty stream from all new anticipated revenue generated by the biotech companies was promised to the originating countries. This point was clarified under the subhead, "Promote recognition of the value of local knowledge and genetic resources and affirm local peoples' rights," where concerns over Intellectual Property Rights (IPR) are noted:

> *Any collection agreements should reflect the concepts of just compensation and accountability, and codes of conduct should apply to genetic resource collectors, anthropologists, or other researchers studying local peoples or local resource management. In some cases, contracts may be needed to ensure the return of royalties or other benefits to local communities or individuals.*[19]

*Global Biodiversity Strategy* offered further reassurance to developing countries with this statement: "Since **biotechnology depends on biodiversity for its raw material**, the value of genetic resources will grow with the industry."[20] [Emphasis added.]

Would you be shocked that the sustainability and equity promises made in the UNEP/IUCN book haven't been kept? Just the opposite has happened. Monsanto, for instance, developed and patented genetically modified crop seed then proceeded to force farmers to *pay* royalties for the use of the seeds—instead of *giving* them royalties from the revenues generated. Headlines like "Monsanto Bullies Small Farmers," "Argentine farmers will

18 World Resources Institute (WRI), World Conservation Union (IUCN), United Nations Environment Programme (UNEP). *Global Biodiversity Strategy: Policy-Makers' Guide*. (Washington, D.C.: World Resources Institute, 1992). Page 1.

19 WRI, IUCN, UNEP. Page 94

20 WRI, IUCN, UNEP. Page 43.

pay royalties to seed companies," and "How Monsanto wrote and broke laws to enter India" became common.

Indeed, it is now obvious that publications like *Global Biodiversity Strategy* and UNEP's follow-up series of "Global Biodiversity Assessment" reports, first published in 1995, were written for one cynical purpose only: to snag the signatures of the 196 or so nations of the world. These nations didn't realize they were signing on to a fantasy. The UN and its myriad NGOs have held them hostage to the treaties and agreements they've endorsed, regardless of the harm and pain inflicted by the treaties and agreements on those very same nations.

## Game Change: The Post-2020 Global Biodiversity Framework

In the same way that Agenda 21 was updated by 2030 Agenda in 2015, the Global Biodiversity Convention is currently being refined by the Post-2020 Global Biodiversity Framework. Working groups have been busy since 2020, creating the various elements that will go into the framework, which was expected to be completed sometime in late 2022.

Because biotechnology and genetic science have progressed so rapidly over the last twenty-five years, a previously used phrase, "genetic resources," is now deemed unsuitable and it is being replaced with "digital sequence information on genetic resources" (DSR). According to the National Human Genome Research Institute:

> *Sequencing DNA means determining the order of the four chemical building blocks - called "bases" — that make up the DNA molecule. The sequence tells scientists the kind of genetic information that is carried in a particular DNA segment. For example, scientists can use sequence information to determine which stretches of DNA contain genes and which stretches carry regulatory instructions, turning genes on or off. In addition, and importantly, sequence data can highlight changes in a gene that may cause disease.*
>
> *In the DNA double helix, the four chemical bases always bond with the same partner to form "base pairs." Adenine (A) al-*

*ways pairs with thymine (T); cytosine (C) always pairs with guanine (G). This pairing is the basis for the mechanism by which DNA molecules are copied when cells divide, and the pairing also underlies the methods by which most DNA sequencing experiments are done. The human genome contains about 3 billion base pairs that spell out the instructions for making and maintaining a human being.*[21]

All life forms on earth have DNA that can be sequenced and fed into a computer for storage, retrieval, and analysis. The National Human Genome Research Institute also envisions synthetic biology, where DNA would be re-engineered in ways that do not occur in nature but that would somehow result in the "improvement" and "well-being" of the environment.

According to the "Report of the Open-ended Working Group on the Post-2020 Global Biodiversity Framework on its Third Meeting (Part I)," held August 23–September 3, 2021:

*[The working group] recognizes the intrinsic relation between genetic resources and digital sequence information on genetic resources, as well as the scope of bioinformatic tools in the design and creation of new digital sequence information on genetic resources elements that are created artificially; that digital sequence information on genetic resources are not genetic resources as defined in the Convention on Biological Diversity (1992); that access to and utilization of digital sequence information on genetic resources is useful for research relating to conservation and sustainable use of biodiversity, food security, health and other important sectors, including commercial applications resulting in commercial products.*[22]

21 National Human Genome Research Institute. NIH. "DNA Sequencing Fact Sheet." https://www.genome.gov/about-genomics/fact-sheets/DNA-Sequencing-Fact-Sheet

22 United Nations Environment Programme (UNEP), Convention on Biological Diversity. "Annex V, Report of the Open-ended Working Group on the Post-2020 Global Biodiversity Framework on its Third Meeting (Part I)." Aug. 23–Sept. 3, 2021. Pages 161–162. https://www.cbd.int/doc/c/187e/84cd/fd4f-6bc8f301770a2481b8c8/wg2020-03-05-en.pdf

Interestingly, another item in the same report notes that "any approach to address digital sequence information on genetic resources should provide for **the special status of pathogens of pandemic potential**."[23] [Emphasis added.]

It could be argued that any changes made by the working group—in words, in definitions, in meanings, in approaches taken—are minor in the scheme of things. But such an assertion is easily rebutted. Consider that the phrase "digital sequence information on genetic resources" is used 167 times in all 167 pages of this document. Clearly, the report reflects a sea change. Clearly, it constitutes a major doctrine. Clearly, it affords the biotech industry a superlative opportunity to meddle with all life systems on earth, using the transparent excuse of making them more "sustainable."

You may still be wondering: Why would genetic scientists want digital access to the DNA structure of all living things on earth? The answer: Genetic scientists believe that all DNA has the potential to be transplantable between species and subspecies:

> *A transgenic, or genetically modified, organism is one that has been altered through recombinant DNA technology, which involves either the combining of DNA from different genomes or the insertion of foreign DNA into a genome.*[24]

This cited paper concludes:

> *The entire biotechnology industry is based upon the ability to add new genes to cells, plants, and animals. As scientists discover important new proteins and genes, these technologies will continue to form the foundation of future generations of discoveries and medical advances.*[25]

Vaccine makers like Pfizer, BioNTech, and Moderna use proprietary recombinant "recipes" for creating their respective mRNA "vaccines." They are not about to release the details.

---

23 UNEP. Page 162.

24 Pray, Leslie. "Recombinant DNA technology and transgenic animals." *N ture Education* 1(1):51. 2008.

25https://www.scribd.com/document/329054039/Leslie-Pray-Ph-D-2008-Recombinant-DNA-Technology-and-Transgenic-Animals/Pray.

## Conclusion

NBIC technology has become the Holy Grail of transhumanism. The ability to manipulate the basic building blocks of life means that "the future belongs to posthumanity," to reiterate Max More's point.

The problem is that transhumanists did not ask us if this is the future we want. Had they done so, we would have dismantled their NBIC playground and kicked them back into their metaphysical dream world. Our feelings echo the sentiments of a reputable scholar, who understands transhumanism well enough to suggest that "transhumanists are just about the last group I'd like to see live forever."[26]

Sentiments aside, several conclusions can be drawn from this chapter's discussion of transhumanism.

> #1 Transhumanists regard DNA as something to be exploited and manipulated. Disregarding individual sovereignty and nature's design, they experiment with ways to use DNA more efficiently than it is used in its original state.
>
> #2 When transhumanists refer to "biodiversity," they really mean "genetic resources."
>
> #3 "Genetic resources," in turn, refers to genetic material that is to be owned, exploited, and controlled through genetic engineering performed by the biotech industry.
>
> #4 UNCED and Agenda 21 were largely smokescreens to obscure the reality of conclusions #1 through #3.
>
> #5 The Third World is being set up to be plundered yet again—this time in the name of sustainable development and biodiversity. The plunderers' prize is genetic engineering and ownership of the resulting genetically engineered products.
>
> #6 Biodiversity is not about preserving species but is, rather, using species as the source of raw materials for the biotech industry, whose mission is to sequence the DNA of all living entities on earth.

26 Fukuyama, Francis. "Transhumanism." Foreign Policy. October 23, 2009. https://foreignpolicy.com/2009/10/23/transhumanism

#7 After being digitally sequenced, these living things are placed in a globally accessible database, are recognized as a global common asset, and are made available for "licensing" by biotech firms.

Technocracy was crystallized in 1932 but has philosophical roots as far back as the early 1800s.

Transhumanism came to the fore in the early 1980s but has roots dating back to the recorded beginning of mankind:

> *"You will certainly not die," the serpent said to the woman. "God knows that when you eat fruit from that tree, you will know things you have never known before. Like God, you will be able to tell the difference between good and evil."—Genesis 3:4–5 NIRV*

Neither of these ideologies had actionable strategies until the advent of advanced technology. Now both of them are using that technology to transform the earth and the beings who dare to live on it.

# CHAPTER 5

# The Great Reset

THE PANDEMIC REPRESENTS A RARE BUT NARROW WINDOW OF OPPORTUNITY TO REFLECT, REIMAGINE, AND RESET OUR WORLD. — KLAUS SCHWAB

The Great Reset is a complex and far-reaching topic that has all too often been misunderstood or misrepresented. The globalist narrative claims that a Great Reset is inevitable, given the rapid advances in science, technology, and engineering, and that it is happening, must happen, in spite of human attempts to intervene and prevent it. As a result of the Great Reset, the globalists insist, almost every aspect of society, of the economy, and even of human identity will be disrupted and forever changed.

One frequently hears talk about disruptive technologies having the ability to upend existing products, processes, companies, and markets. Often overlooked, however, is the fact that, as Harvard Business Review notes, disruptive innovations have always originated in low-end or new-market footholds.[1] For instance, when expensive engine-powered buggies first appeared, they were not a threat to the horse and buggy, both of which were plentiful and cheap. The disruption came only when Ford Motor Company mass-produced the Model T at a price people could afford and willingly paid. Thereafter, the entire transportation industry was thoroughly and permanently disrupted.

Today, the original theory of disruptive enterprise has regressed to mean any shocking new thing that can be quickly capitalized while driving large competitors out of business. The tradi-

1 Christensen, Raynor et al. "What Is Disruptive Innovation?" Harvard Business Review. December 2015. https://hbr.org/2015/12/what-is-disruptive-innovation

tional checks and balances that normally operate in a free market economic system have been thrown to the wind. The resulting feeding frenzy has bolstered belief of the Great Reset's inevitability as well as the doctrine behind it.

Although World Economic Forum founder Klaus Schwab had already called for a Great Reset in 2015, the WEF formally launched its Great Reset Initiative in June 2020 in response to the COVID-19 pandemic. The inaugural announcement was delivered by Prince Charles (King Charles as of September 2022). In a short but dramatic video, he declared that the natural world is in a state of crisis and that there is a desperate need to RE:IMAGINE, RE:THINK, RE:INVENT, RE:DESIGN, RE:VIVE, RE:FORM, RE:PRESENT, RE:BALANCE, RE:CREATE, RE:INVEST and RE:START the whole planet. All of these "RE: . . ." needs, the Prince of Wales made clear, call for a RE:SET.[2] He ended his remarks with an urgent appeal: "In order to secure our future and to prosper, we need to evolve our economic model. [. . .] We need to put nature at the heart of how we operate. [. . .] We simply cannot waste any more time."

In less than two minutes, Prince Charles (now King) had described what we recognize today as the Great Reset. Of course, none of his dire predictions or vague-sounding solutions had anything to do with a virus called SARS-CoV-2 or a disease named COVID-19—the supposed cause of the global economic and ecological emergency.

But the absence of a link between the pandemic and the WEF's panic didn't hinder WEF propaganda. Not in the least. As the introductory statement on its Great Reset Initiative page proclaims:

> *There is an* **urgent need** *for global stakeholders to cooperate in simultaneously managing the direct consequences of the Covid-19 crisis. To improve the state of the world, the World Economic Forum is starting The Great Reset initiative. [. . .] The Covid-19 crisis, and the political, economic and social disruptions it has caused, is fundamentally changing the tra-*

2 The Prince of Wales' Sustainable Markets Initiative and the World Economic Forum launch #TheGreatReset. June 2020. YouTube. https://youtu.be/hRPQqfwwuhU

*ditional context for decision-making. The inconsistencies, inadequacies and contradictions of multiple systems — from health and financial to energy and education — are more exposed than ever amidst a global context of concern for lives, livelihoods and the planet. Leaders find themselves at a historic crossroads, managing short-term pressures against medium- and long-term uncertainties.*[3]

The economic model that Prince Charles alluded to in the video can only be understood from the perspective of the United Nations' Sustainable Development Goals (SDGs), which are based on a resource-based economic system designed to replace capitalism and free market economics. On February 3, 2015, the UN's global warming czar, Christiana Figueres, held a press conference in Europe, during which she made an earth-shattering announcement:

*This is the first time in the history of mankind that we are setting ourselves the task of intentionally, within a defined period of time to change [sic] the economic development model that has been reigning for at least 150 years, since the industrial revolution.*[4]

The UN's unambiguous declaration of war on capitalism received very little attention at the time, but it should have—for two reasons.

First, it came at a time when Figueres was in the process of organizing the December 2015 United Nations Climate Change Conference in Paris. The conference would draw 196 nations, whose representatives would sign a treaty agreeing to limit global warming—preferably to **1.5 degrees Celsius (2.7 degrees Fahrenheit)** compared to pre-industrial levels. This so-called Paris Agreement was the first time in history that all the nations of the world were lined up to be force-fed a steady diet of sustainable development dogma. The crux of the dogma was that noth-

3 World Economic Forum. Sustainable Development Impact Summit: The Great Reset. September 21–24, 2020. https://www.weforum.org/great-reset
4 "Figueres: First time the world economy is transformed intentionally." Press release from the United Nations Regional Information Centre for Western Europe. February 3, 2015.

ing short of total economic and social transformation would save the world.[5]

Second, the sustainable development dogma was based on a two-pronged lie—namely, that there was a need to overhaul the entire economic system and that this need was precipitated by global warming (now called "climate change"). In fact, there was no such need and no such causal connection between the two.

In both cases—the 2015 pretense that global warming was a threat and the 2020 pretense that the pandemic was a threat—the objective was to destroy capitalism and replace it with sustainable development, aka technocracy. The UN's self-declared crisis, followed five years later by the WEF's self-declared crisis, pushed a confused and fearful worldwide populace into going along with the globalists' preconceived agenda. There was never any other agenda or "fix" offered. It was their way or the highway.

The world had been conned by two false fears and one false solution.

## Two Wings on the Same Bird

If sustainable development can be represented by a bird, the two wings that allow the bird to fly are the United Nations and the World Economic Forum. Both organizations are tightly aligned at all levels. The UN provides countries with a common legal framework through treaties, agreements, and memorandums of understanding. The WEF, meanwhile, steers the global economic community toward fake solutions to imaginary problems—solutions that choke off capitalism and provide massive financing of climate reduction goals.

Here's an example of how the latter organization operates. In preparation for its May 2022 meeting in Davos, Switzerland, the World Economic Forum interviewed six CEOs of major global corporations and asked them to explain how they are "onboard" with climate reduction goals. The testimony of Christian Mumen-

5 The Paris Agreement." The United Nations Framework Convention on Climate Change. 2016. https://unfccc.int/sites/default/files/resource/parisagreement_publication.pdf

thaler, CEO of insurance giant Swiss Re, shows how one company is achieving these goals:

> *Swiss Re continues to decarbonize its underwriting business. In line with our oil and gas policy,* **we no longer provide individual insurance cover to the most carbon-intensive companies** *and continue to implement the phase-out of thermal coal-related re/insurance in OECD countries by 2030, and in the rest of the world by 2040.*
>
> *But measuring the carbon footprint of insurance contracts remains a challenge for the insurance industry. To address this, we co-founded the United Nations-convened Net-Zero Insurance Alliance (NZIA) in conjunction with several of our industry peers. Together,* **we are advancing a methodology to calculate carbon emissions** *associated with insurance portfolios, which will be essential* **in steering our underwriting business towards less carbon-intensive activities.**[6] *[Emphasis added.]*

So we have Swiss Re refusing to do business with suspected global warming "deniers" who, in its opinion, emit too much carbon. But who decides how much is too much carbon? Why, the United Nations and the Net-Zero Insurance Alliance, of course. Their decision potentially affects thousands of carbon-emitting businesses, which must pay higher premiums to other insurance companies that are not so discriminatory. Meanwhile, carbon-friendly insurers will become harder to find, since Swiss Re has persuaded other giant insurance companies to join the NZIA.

Earlier we spoke of Sustainable Development Goals (SDGs). At the 2030 Agenda Conference in September 2015, a total of 17 SDGs were adopted by 193 nations. Soon thereafter, the WEF created the Global Future Council on SDG Investment. Like the WEF's other Global Future Councils (GFCs), the Council on SDG Investment serves as "a brain trust for leaders from government,

6 Broden, Jesper and Christian Mumenthaler and Gim Huay Neo. "How are companies accelerating their commitments to net-zero? 6 CEOs share their strategies." World Economic Forum. May 19, 2022. https://www.weforum.org/agenda/2022/05/how-are-companies-accelerating-their-commitments-to-net-zero-5-ceos-share-their-strategies-52b79ad93c

businesses and civil society [. . .] to "collaborate in shaping agendas."

When you read the Council on SDG Investment's mission statement, notice how it underscores Swiss Re's role in the decarbonization of the planet:

> **COVID-19 has exacerbated the vulnerabilities of the global economic architecture, worsening social and economic inequalities**. *In a post-pandemic ecosystem, building resilient and sustainable societies will be critical for the stability of our economies, but how can this agenda be pursued in a climate of rising debts and increasing risk aversion? The Global Future Council on SDG Investment will explore how to "reconnect the dots" between countries, private and institutional investors, donors and development finance actors* **to unlock capital at scale towards the Sustainable Development Goals and leverage them as a recovery framework to transition into an inclusive, resilient and sustainable future for all**.[7] *[Emphasis added.]*

How many agendas does that mission statement refer to? Only one agenda, naturally. To no one's surprise, it must be directly compatible with the goals of the United Nations. And how is this single agenda being financed? By massive amounts of unlocked capital redirected solely and wholly towards the UN's Sustainable Development Goals.

The WEF employs fancy language to describe all of its GFCs, calling them collectively the world's foremost "multistakeholder and interdisciplinary knowledge network dedicated to promoting innovative thinking to shape a more resilient, inclusive and sustainable future."

We are supposed to be duly impressed by the exclusive coterie of 1,000 GFC members who serve by invitation-only. And we are meant to be equally dazzled by their high-minded mission:

> *Global Future Council members provide strategic insights, scientific evidence, forward guidance and multidisciplinary*

---

7 Global Future Council on SDG Investment. World Economic Forum. https://www.weforum.org/communities/gfc-on-sdg-investment

*understanding of major issues that* **will shape the post-COVID world** *through:*

— *Identifying and monitoring the latest trends, scientific research and frontier technologies with significant* **potential to transform societies, industries and regions**

— *Contributing their expertise and knowledge, sharing key lessons and developing innovative ideas to* **"building back better" initiatives** *of industry, regional and solution platforms*

— *Providing decision-makers from business and government with a multidisciplinary understanding of the strategic implications*

— *Deepening understanding of the drivers and enablers* **of the Fourth Industrial Revolution** *and how emerging technologies can be leveraged to address global, regional and industry issues*

— **Informing the World Economic Forum's strategic initiatives** *by providing feedback on the direction of existing projects as well as new areas of focus*

— **Increasing public awareness** *of the potential benefits and risks related to major breakthroughs*[8] *[Emphasis added.]*

Is it just me, or do you, too, wonder where this flood of highfalutin rhetoric comes from? If it seems to be out of the blue, that's because it is. Prior to 2019, there were no Great Reset or Build Back Better initiatives.

Then, at the beginning of the pandemic, the floodgates broke. Magically, a pair of heroes, the UN and the WEF, rose up to save the world from drowning in the predicted pandemic-induced destruction of the economy. Predicted by the UN and the WEF, that is! Their declaration that capitalism and the free market were as good as dead was a ruse meant to force sustainable development (technocracy) upon a credulous, panicked public.

Remarkably, their ruse is reminiscent of the plot hatched by the founders of the original technocracy movement in the 1930s.

8 Global Future Councils. World Economic Forum. https://www.weforum.org/communities/global-future-councils

They, too, predicted capitalism's certain and swift demise. And they did their best to make sure it happened.

To explain another similarity between 1930s and 2020s technocracy, I'll refer to the nursery rhyme character Humpty Dumpty. In both the original and modern versions of technocracy, once it was determined that the free market, the economic equivalent of Humpy Dumpty, was doing just fine sitting on the proverbial wall and was in no danger of falling, the technocrats did what came naturally to them: They gave good ole Humpy Dumpty a strong shove. They couldn't wait to watch him break into smithereens on the rocks below.

And that, my friends, is what the technocratic mind is hardwired to do: get rid of whatever obstacles are in its way. Traditional economic, social, and political systems that block the technocratic goal of total control of the planet and its people must go.

## ESG — Environmental, Social, Governance

Now that we understand the acronym SDG, we're going to introduce a related acronym,

ESG, which stands for Environmental, Social, Governance. A Canadian information services company, ESG The Report, says of both acronyms:

> *[T]hese two may actually be the most influential acronyms in the history of our species. And if you have never heard of them before, then don't worry[,] you are not alone. But in less than a generation, if we are lucky, every child will know what they mean. SDG stands for Sustainable Development Goals and ESG refers to quantifiable and measurable factors that represent sustainable practices. In other words, they are the cornerstone of accountability.*[9]

I have a darker view of ESG. I prefer to think of it as the evil stepchild of stakeholder capitalism. Stakeholder capitalism is a business management theory that originated in 1932, was popular in the 1950s and 1960s, and was re-popularized by Klaus Schwab when he founded the WEF in 1971. Since 2019, stake-

9 "What is SDG and ESG?" ESG The Report. https://www.esgthereport.com/what-is-sdg-and-esg

holder capitalism has been enjoying yet another resurgence, thanks to both the Business Roundtable and the WEF. The latter updated its Davos Manifesto in December 2019 "to more clearly state that businesses must be stewards of the environment, uphold human rights throughout their global supply chains, and pursue sustainable shareholder returns that don't sacrifice the future for the present."[10]

Unlike shareholders—institutions or individuals who own part of a public company through its shares of stock—stakeholders may be employees, customers, suppliers, shareholders, local communities, and society as a whole.[11] Though stakeholders may have only a self-declared interest in a company, they are accorded the privilege of telling management what it can or cannot do.

Now, then, why do I call ESG the evil stepchild of stakeholder capitalism? From my intensive research, I have concluded that ESG is essentially a ratings scam. ESG drives a company's stakeholder-approved investments into sustainable development projects to meet the UN's SDGs. And it keeps investments away from everything that does not fall under those SDGs. One large ESG rating agency, MCSI, agrees with my definition, though certainly not with my stance on the subject. ESG, according to MCSI, is "the consideration of environmental, social and governance factors alongside financial factors in the investment decision-making process."[12]

Traditionally, a company is rated on its financial performance—earnings, assets, market share, and the like—all of which are quantifiable, thus objective. ESG, however, rates a company according to subjective criteria, such as carbon emissions, sustainable development policies, and compliance with the UN's SDGs.

This difference applies not only to corporations but also to individuals. Traditionally, an individual receives a financial rating

10 "What is Stakeholder Capitalism? How It Relates to ESG." ESG Enterprise. https://www.esgenterprise.com/governance/what-is-stakeholder-capitalism-relates-to-esg

11 "What is Stakeholder Capitalism? How It Relates to ESG."

12 "ESG 101: What is Environmental, Social and Governance?" MSCI Inc. https://www.msci.com/esg-101-what-is-esg

based on income, assets, debt repayment habits, etc., whereas ESG rates an individual according to lifestyle, type of car driven, trips taken, amount and types of purchases, size of house, and, importantly, energy and water consumption.

Although the concept of ESG, like that of its evil stepmother, stakeholder capitalism, goes back a few decades, it was supercharged and extended by the WEF at the onset of the COVID-19 pandemic. At its Sustainable Development Impact Summit held in September 2020, a virtual meeting called "Implementing ESG for Corporate Governance" included this (poorly worded) statement by Klaus Schwab:

> *This work is part of our Great Reset Initiative. [. . .] We're talking about a substantial shift which is taking place which is the transition of an economy which is more based on shareholder value to an economy which is more based on stakeholder responsibilities.*[13]

There are currently more than 100 so-called ESG rating agencies. They include the aforementioned MCSI Inc. as well as S&P Global Ratings, Bloomberg L.P., Thomson Reuters Corp., and CDP. You can be sure that everything and everyone that can be rated is being rated by these agencies. Every agency has its own criteria and metrics, so ratings from each can be radically different.

ESG is being applied everywhere these days. In the U.S., for instance, the Securities and Exchange Commission (SEC) proposed a new ESG rule, "Enhancement and Standardization of Climate-Related Disclosures for Investors," that would require large upline companies to extract ESG compliance data from their small suppliers. Farmers and ranchers, even though they are not corporations, must be in compliance, because all of their products are sold to larger entities (food manufacturers and distributors) and because they buy equipment from large companies like Deere & Company and Massey Ferguson. If farmers and ranchers were unable to comply with ESG, their contracts could be terminated, leaving them and their crops and cattle out in the cold.

---

13 "Implementing ESG for Corporate Governance l Sustainable Development Summit 2020." World Economic Forum. YouTube. https://youtu.be/f3ONOcZvC4g

Consider a commercial bank with one billion dollars to loan out. To be "socially responsible" and thus receive a high ESG rating, the bank would have to loan money only to companies and individuals who have an equally high ESG rating. Low-scoring individuals need not apply.

To call ESG "transformative," as its supporters are wont to do, is a cruel misappropriation of that word, which generally has a positive connotation. "Malevolent" and "disfiguring" might be more appropriate descriptions of ESG, for it is causing massive amounts of mal-investment and dis-investment and thus badly dislocating the existing economic system.

## Who is Klaus Schwab?

Indeed, who is Klaus Schwab? His name has been mentioned more times in this chapter than that of any other person. Briefly, Klaus Martin Schwab is a German-born engineer and economist who founded and presides over the World Economic Forum as its executive chairman. The WEF gathers hundreds of global elitists in Davos, Switzerland, every year to discuss global economic issues.

For purposes of my book, perhaps the most meaningful statement Schwab has made is contained in his June 3, 2020, article on the WEF website, "Now is the time for a 'great reset.'" Though he was explaining the serious condition of the world economy, his message couldn't have been more exultant:

> *COVID-19 lockdowns may be gradually easing, but anxiety about the world's social and economic prospects is only intensifying.* **There is good reason to worry: a sharp economic downturn has already begun, and we could be facing the worst depression since the 1930s. But, while this outcome is likely, it is not unavoidable.**
>
> *To achieve a better outcome,* **the world must act jointly and swiftly to revamp all aspects of our societies and economies, from education to social contracts and working conditions. Every country, from the United States to China, must participate, and every industry, from oil**

**and gas to tech, must be transformed. In short, we need a "Great Reset" of capitalism.**[14] *[Emphasis added.]*

Okay, we get your point, Klaus. If we want to head off the worst depression since the 1930s, we must take your advice to act "jointly and swiftly" in implementing a "'Great Reset' of capitalism."

For those readers unfamiliar with Klaus Schwab, here he is in a nutshell.

First and foremost, Schwab is a technocrat. His official biography, included in his book, The Fourth Industrial Revolution, implies as much:

*Professor Klaus Schwab (1938, Ravensburg, Germany) is the Founder and Executive Chairman of the World Economic Forum. In 1971, he published Modern Enterprise Management in Mechanical Engineering. He argues in that book that a company must serve not only shareholders but all stakeholders to achieve long-term growth and prosperity. To promote the stakeholder concept, he founded the World Economic Forum the same year.*

*Professor Schwab holds doctorates in Economics (University of Fribourg) and in Engineering (Swiss Federal Institute of Technology) and obtained a master's degree in Public Administration (MPA) from the Kennedy School of Government at Harvard University. In 1972, in addition to his leadership role at the Forum, he became a professor at the University of Geneva. He has since received numerous international and national honours, including 17 honorary doctorates. His latest books are The Fourth Industrial Revolution (2016), a worldwide bestseller translated into 30 languages, and Shaping the Future of the Fourth Industrial Revolution (2018).*[15]

After receiving doctorates in engineering and economics, Schwab entered a Harvard University master's degree program

---

14 Schwab, Klaus. "Now is the time for a 'great reset.'" World Economic Forum. June 3, 2020. https://www.weforum.org/agenda/2020/06/now-is-the-time-for-a-great-reset

15 Schwab, Klaus and Thierry Malleret. *Covid-19: The Great Reset.* (Switzerland: World Economic Forum, 2020).

in 1965 and was taught, as well as mentored, by then-Professor of Government Henry Kissinger. More than fifty years later, in a 2016 interview conducted at the thoroughly technocratic Lee Kuan Yew School of Public Policy in Singapore, Schwab reminisced about the three people in his career who have had a lasting effect on him. The most influential: Henry Kissinger.[16]

Thanks to Kissinger's interest in developing international policies in Europe, his protégé, Schwab, had occasion to meet many U.S. policy experts. By 1971, Kissinger recruited Schwab to start the European Management Forum, renamed the World Economic Forum in 1987. In 1973, Kissinger became a key founding member of the Trilateral Commission along with David Rockefeller and Zbigniew Brzezinski. Though never invited by Kissinger or its other members to join the Trilateral Commission, Schwab nonetheless remains an important ally in the Commission's original and ongoing effort to create a "New International Economic Order."

Another key Trilateral operative who never became a formal member of that august institution was Maurice Strong. Best known for being the organizer of the United Nations Conference on Environment and Development (aka Agenda 21) held in Rio de Janeiro in 1992, Strong also served the UN as Under-Secretary-General and as Secretary-General of its Conference on the Human Environment in Stockholm (1972).

As it turned out, both Strong and Schwab proved more valuable to the Trilateral Commission by having their career paths aligned with it rather than being directly associated with it. How so? I would posit that the intense relationship they each had with the United Nations' sustainable development economic system gave them significant influence over Trilateral policy decisions.

Now, back to Schwab. We said that, first and foremost, he is a technocrat. Secondly, he is a transhumanist. We discussed transhumanism in Chapter 4, but not in relation to Klaus Schwab and his World Economic Forum. Thus, it may be of interest to my read-

16 "[Dialogue Session] Klaus Schwab: Global Leadership needed in the Era of Furth Industrial Revolution." Lee Kuan Yew School of Public Policy. World Economic Forum Annual Meeting 2016. YouTube. https://youtu.be/HTmzbSFNK2c

ers that a 2018 article "What is transhumanism and how does it affect you?" on the WEF website revealed some of Schwab's thoughts on the subject:

> *The central premise of transhumanism, then, is that biological evolution will eventually be overtaken by advances in genetic, wearable and implantable technologies that artificially expedite the evolutionary process.*
>
> *To date, areas to improve on include natural aging (including, for die-hards, the cessation of "involuntary death") as well as physical, intellectual and psychological capacities. Some distinguished scientists, such as Hans Moravec and Raymond Kurzweil, even advocate a posthuman condition: the end of humanity's reliance on our congenital bodies by transforming "our frail version 1.0 human bodies into their far more durable and capable version 2.0 counterparts".*[17]

Two years earlier, in The Fourth Industrial Revolution, Schwab noted that synthetic biology "will provide us with the ability to customize organisms by writing DNA."[18] Furthermore, he wrote in the same book:

> *The ability to edit biology can be applied to practically any cell type, enabling the creation of genetically modified plants or animals, as well as modifying the cells of adult organisms including humans.*[19]

## Conclusion

The Great Reset must be seen as a two-part achievement. The first part is the economic restructuring of the world. The second part is the restructuring of the humans who will live in that economically restructured future world.

Economic restructuring refers to sustainable development—that is, the rebirth of 1930s technocracy. The end result of technocracy/sustainable development is scientific dictatorship. Dictatorship of any sort is hardly the Utopia its fanatical adherents insanely envision and glowingly describe.

17 Trippet, David. "What is transhumanism and how does it affect you?" WEF Forum. April 10, 2018.
18 Trippet. Page 24.
19 Trippet. Page 25.

Human restructuring refers to the genetic takeover of the human genome. The end result of this restructuring is the creation of Humanity 2.0, otherwise known as simply H+.

The WEF presents both outcomes—economic restructuring and human restructuring—as inevitable, inescapable. The WEF reminds me of Star Trek's futuristic Borg, who coldly advised the freedom-seeking Picard: "Resistance is futile."[20]

Since the start of the COVID-19 pandemic in early 2020, the WEF has pulled out all the stops to enact both parts of its Great Reset throughout the world. For Schwab, this has been a matter of great urgency. As he noted in a memorable WEF post: "The pandemic represents a rare but narrow window of opportunity to reflect, reimagine, and reset our world."[21]

Realizing that massive financing is needed to accelerate the Great Reset, Schwab has fast-tracked ESG. Indeed, ESG investments have become a veritable a tsunami of green—green dollars and green, climate-friendly projects. His fast-tracking of ESG is in perfect alignment with UN rhetoric:

> *The SDGs are not being achieved.* **Success is held back by severe financing constraints facing the developing countries***: constraints that have been gravely aggravated by the COVID-19 pandemic and the war in Ukraine. The key to achieving the SDGs, besides preserving peace and lowering geopolitical tensions, is having a plan to finance them. This was emphasized by United Nations Secretary-General António Guterres in his briefing to the General Assembly on major priorities for 2022:* **"[W]e must go into emergency mode to reform global finance."**[22] *[Emphasis added.]*

20 "'Resistance is Futile!' Borg & Picard in Star Trek The Next Generation 'Best of Both Worlds.'" YouTube. https://www.youtube.com/watch?v=TRjMJklb3xU

21 Schwab, Klaus. "Now is the time for a 'great reset.'" World Economic Forum. June 3, 2020. https://www.weforum.org/agenda/2020/06/now-is-the-time-for-a-great-reset

22 United Nations. "A Global Plan to Finance the Sustainable Development Goals." https://dashboards.sdgindex.org/chapters/part-1-a-global-plan-to-finance-the-sdgs

*By July 2021, global ESG data-driven assets hit $35.3 trillion, or more than one-third of the world's largest asset markets.*[23]

But, for all of Schwab's insistence on an immediate, wholesale, tectonic-like transformation of the economy and the human race, the Great Reset cannot be accomplished overnight. It is by necessity a gradual process. Hence its moving target: at one time Agenda 21 (referring to the 21st century) and now the 2030 Agenda (referring to eight years from now).

That said, the Great Reset is not intended to be a future event that will suddenly start when someone pushes a button. No, it is already well underway, as evidenced by the ESG investing that has already sunk trillions of dollars in available capital into sustainable development projects.

23 Jessop, Simon. "Sustainable investments account for more than a third of global assets." Reuters. July 19, 2021. https://www.reuters.com/business/sustainable-business/sustainable-investments-account-more-than-third-global-assets-2021-07-18

# Chapter 6

# The Control Grid

> *. . . Most men and women will grow up to love their servitude and will never dream of revolution.* Aldous Huxley

The late Rosa Koire was a liberal Democrat whose research into local land use programs and redevelopment agencies led to her piercing the veil of the United Nations' Agenda 21 and its 2030 Agenda and its sustainable development economic model. Koire's 2011 book, *Behind the Green Mask: U.N. Agenda 21,* received international acclaim. In the Preface she wrote, "Under the mask of green our civil liberties are being restricted, constricted, and suffocated in every village and hamlet. The plan is imposed locally."[1]

During most of her in-person or video presentations, Koire helped her audience peer behind the green mask of sustainable development, which she defined as follows:

> *It is the inventory and control plan. Inventory and control of all land, all water, all minerals, all plants, all animals, all construction, all means of production, all food, all energy, all information, and all human beings in the world.*[2]

No one has explained sustainable development more succinctly!

In earlier chapters of my book we have equated sustainable development with technocracy. And we have discussed the seven requirements of technocracy listed in the *Technocracy Study*

1 Koire, Rosa. *Behind the Green Mask: UN Agenda 21*. The Post Sustainability Institute. 2011. Page 2.
2 "Rosa Koire interview: UN Agenda 2030 exposed." May 30, 2019. YouTube. https://youtu.be/3PrY7nFbwAY

*Course* published in 1934 (see Chapter 3). But it might be useful to review them again here:

> 1. Register on a continuous 24 hour-per-day basis the total net conversion of energy
>
> 2. By means of the registration of energy converted and consumed, make possible a balanced load
>
> 3. Provide a continuous inventory of all production and consumption
>
> 4. Provide a specific registration of the type, kind, etc., of all goods and services, where produced and where used
>
> 5. Provide specific registration of the consumption of each individual, plus a record and description of the individual
>
> 6. Allow the citizen the widest latitude of choice in consuming his individual share of Continental physical wealth
>
> 7. Distribute goods and services to every member of the population[3]

All seven requirements point to technocrats' micro-management of all inputs, outputs, processes, and assets in the global economy and their micro-management of all people who participate in the economic system.

Even though these requirements were written from a top-down, macro perspective, they are intended to be implemented locally. In fact, they *must* be implemented locally.

Why locally? Because that's where we live, work, and play: locally. Thus, that's where we're controlled. Schools are local. Newspapers and radio stations are local. So are courthouses and city councils. Smart meters and the smart grid are local. So are geospatial surveillance and pre-crime police software. The Internet of Things (IoT) and Internet of Bodies (IoB) are local. So is smart city technology. Health care—better known today as "medical dictatorship"—is local. So are museums, movie theaters, and

---

3 Hubbert, M. King and Howard Scott. *Technocracy Study Course*. (New York: Technocracy, Inc., 1934). Page 232.

libraries. Zoning laws and property valuations are local. We may shop for products on-line and have them delivered from afar, but we cannot avoid living in the local.

It is not surprising, then, that the most widespread application of sustainable development, aka technocracy, has been in local and regional communities. If you are thinking one step ahead of me, you've already figured out that the only effective resistance to technocracy has to be at the local level.

For the balance of this chapter, we will look at some of the new elements of technocratic control that are being arrayed against us in the locales where we live, work, and play.

## Smart Meters

In August 2022, twenty-two thousand residents of Denver, Colorado, received a message on their home thermostat informing them that their electricity provider had locked them out due to an "energy emergency." During the lockout, their thermostats were set remotely—some as high as eighty-eight degrees.[4]

How could it happen that a utility company, Xcel, was able reach into private dwellings and commandeer air conditioner thermostats against the will or knowledge of the residents inside?

The answer is the 115 million[5] so-called "smart meters" that have been installed over the last twelve years on the exterior of houses, apartments, and places of business across America. This is close to seventy percent penetration in a market that continues to grow exponentially.

Smart meters are deemed "smart" for two primary reasons. First, they can establish two-way communication with any device in a building that is equipped with a special Wi-Fi circuit. Second, they maintain a continuous Wi-Fi connection with the utili-

4 Allen, Jaclyn. "Thousands of Xcel customers locked out of thermostats during 'energy emergency.'" ABC News Denver7. August 31, 2022. https://www.thedenverchannel.com/news/contact-denver7/thousands-of-xcel-customers-locked-out-of-thermostats-during-energy-emergency

5 "Number of electric smart meters installed in the United States from 2007 to 2019, with a forecast from 2020 to 2021." Statista. April 2021. https://www.statista.com/statistics/676472/number-of-smart-meter-installations-in-the-united-states

ty company. Thus, the smart meter is a two-way communication pipeline between the utility's data center and every internal device within their service area.

In 2003, the U.S. Department of Energy under the George W. Bush Administration produced "Grid 2030," a report that envisioned a bright future for smart meters:

> *The ability to monitor realtime operations and implement automated control algorithms in response to changing system conditions is just beginning to be used in electricity. Distributed intelligence, including "smart" appliances, could drive the co-development of the future architecture for telecommunications and electric power networks and determine how these systems are operated and controlled.*[6]

The Bush agenda called for "intelligent homes and appliances linked to the grid" by 2010. And, sure enough, the effort to blanket America with smart meters began in earnest on January 8, 2010. As I wrote on March 3rd of that year:

> *On October 27, 2009, the Obama administration unveiled its Smart Grid plan by awarding $3.4 billion awarded to 100 Smart Grid projects. According to the Department of Energy's press release, these awards will result in the installation of:*
>
> - *more than 850 sensors called "Phasor Measurement Units" to monitor the overall power grid nationwide*
> - *200,000 smart transformers*
> - *700 automated substations (about 5 percent of the nation's total)*
> - *1,000,000 in-home displays*
> - *345,000 load control devices in homes*
>
> **This is the "kick-start" of Smart Grid in the U.S. On January 8, 2010,** *President Obama unveiled an additional $2.3 billion federal funding program for the "energy manufacturing sector" as part of the $787 billion American Reinvestment*

6 "Grid 2030: A National Vision for Electricity's Second 100 Years." U.S. Department of Energy. 2003. Page 24.

*and Recovery Act. Funding had already been awarded to 183 projects in 43 states, pending Obama's announcement.*

*One such project in the northwest is headed by Battelle Memorial Institute, covering five states and targeting 60,000 customers. The project was actually developed by the Bonneville Power Administration (BPA), a federal agency underneath the Department of Energy. Since it is pointedly illegal for a federal agency to apply for federal funds, BPA passed the project off to Battelle, a non-profit and non-governmental organization (NGO), which was promptly awarded $178 million.*

*It is interesting to note that BPA takes credit for originating the Smart Grid concept in the early 1990s, which it termed "Energy Web." According to Battelle's August 27, 2009, press release:*

*"The project will involve more than 60,000 metered customers in Idaho, Montana, Oregon, Washington and Wyoming. Using smart grid technologies, the project will engage system assets exceeding 112 megawatts, the equivalent of power to serve 86,000 households.*

*'The proposed demonstration will study smart grid benefits at unprecedented geographic breadth across five states, spanning the electrical system from generation to end-use, and containing many key functions of the future smart grid,' said Mike Davis, a Battelle vice president. 'The intended impact of this project will span well beyond traditional utility service territory boundaries, helping to enable a future grid that meets pressing local, regional and national needs.'"*

*Battelle and BPA intend to work closely together and there is an obvious blurring as to who is really in control of the project's management during the test period.*

*In a "For Internal Use Only" document written in August 2009, BPA offers talking points to its partners. It states that "Smart Grid technology includes everything from* **interactive appli-**

**ances** *in homes to* **smart meters***, substation automation and sensors on transmission lines."*[7] *[Emphasis added.]*

Furthermore, private enterprise had nothing to do with the frenzied launch of the smart meter initiative. As I wrote in the same article:

*The Smart Grid initiative was developed and funded by government agencies and NGOs. It was the Energy Department's Bonneville Power Authority that invented the concept in the 1990s. It was the Department of Energy's Pacific Northwest National Laboratory that invented the Grid Friendly Appliance Controller. It was the Federal Administration that showered billions of dollars over the private sector to jump-start the nationwide initiative to implement Smart Grid in every community.*[8]

Let me connect another dot for you. Pacific Northwest National Laboratory released a short informercial video in 2019 titled "Grid Friendly Appliance Controller Turns Small Loads into Grid Assets." It presents a Grid Friendly Appliance Controller—called GFAC for short—which was to be installed into home appliances and circuits such as electric vehicle chargers. Here is some selected text (key phrases, not full sentences) from the video:

*The GFAC chip is installed in common household appliances – like water heaters, air conditioners* **or electric vehicle chargers** *[. . .] autonomously and immediately reducing demand to allow the grid to stabilize [. . .] enables utility operators to modulate the load to achieve the proper primary frequency.*[9] *[Emphasis added.]*

If the people in Colorado are shocked that the long arm of their utility company can reach into their homes to control their thermostat, just wait until they discover that they cannot charge their electric vehicles!

---

7 Wood, Patrick. "Technocracy, Smart Grid and the Green Economy." Freedom Advocates. March 3, 2010. https://www.freedomadvocates.org/technocracy-smart-grid-green-economy

8 Wood.

9 "Grid Friendly Appliance Controller Turns Small Loads into Grid Assets." Pacific Northwest National Laboratory. March 14, 2019. YouTube. https://youtu.be/2Jl-yRPCp35w

In addition to all the particulars above, one key element that should be further explored is this: Energy usage data is being continuously extracted from our private life and is being sold to the highest bidders, who would want access for various purposes. Why has this extraction of data become a huge market? Because our energy profile reveals an enormous amount of information about us—about our habits, our installed appliances, our coming and going, etc. If you want to understand this point better, read the footnoted 2022 press release, "AI Presents Immense Opportunities to Tap Smart Meter Data."[10]

Another element to consider is the health risk of being exposed to extra amounts of radiation from smart meters. For some, especially those with a low tolerance for radiation, smart meters can pose a serious problem. The talk about health consequences and the resulting health scare grew out of proportion, however, and blotted out the equally grave consequences from the rising technocratic control of all energy. I have consistently warned of this technocratic tyranny since the beginning, but to no avail. Now the world is finding out about smart meters the hard way.

Many utility companies still allow installation of the old-fashioned analog meter with the spinning dials, though most of them charge an extra monthly fee for the privilege. But other utilities have been inflexible, mandating the installation of smart meters with no opt-out allowed.

## Smart Grid

The UN's Sustainable Development Goal 7 aims to "increase substantially the share of renewable energy in the global energy mix" and "expand infrastructure and upgrade technology for supplying modern and sustainable energy services" by 2030.[11]

---

10 Cision PR Newswire. "Global Smart Electricity Meters Market Report 2022: Market to Reach $15.2 Billion by 2026—AI Presents Immense Opportunities to Tap Smart Meter Data." ResearchAndMarkets. April 13, 2022. https://www.prnewswire.com/news-releases/global-smart-electricity-meters-market-report-2022-market-to-reach-15-2-billion-by-2026---ai-presents-immense-opportunities-to-tap-smart-meter-data-301524813.html

11 "Transforming Our World: The 2030 Agenda for Sustainable Development." United Nations. https://sustainabledevelopment.un.org/content/docu-

This goal has led to the concept of developing local, regional, and national smart grids into a fully monitored and controlled *global* smart grid. Though the global smart grid is still a work-in-progress, its growing momentum is plainly evident.

While there are many ways to explain the "smart grid," this definition from Gartner, Inc., one of the largest business research organizations in the world, says it all—in typical technocrat-ese:

> *The smart grid is a vision of the future electricity delivery infrastructure that improves network efficiency and resilience, while empowering consumers and addressing energy sustainability concerns. To make the grid "smarter," and capable of addressing the need to decarbonize generation sources and enable end-user energy efficiency, utilities will have to improve observability and controllability of their networks, while transforming them into geodesic structures that intersperse a variety of distributed energy resources.*[12]

It is obvious that smart meters are a central and key component of the smart grid, but Gartner's definition makes the critical observation that the grid is designed to become "smarter." How? By heeding the sustainable development agenda's need to "decarbonize" the sources of generating electricity and to "intersperse a variety of distributed energy sources."

The real reason behind smart grids and smart meters, we now see, is to accommodate and patch in alternative sources of energy, such as wind and solar. Before alternative power became the playbook to rid the world of carbonized fuels like coal, oil, and natural gas, the energy grid worked just fine. If there was excess demand, utilities would ramp up generation to meet the need. Today, if there is excess demand, the utilities balance the load by taking it out on the consumers of energy—us.

The increase in alternative energy generation coupled with the war on traditional fuels that has taken massive amounts of energy off-line has resulted in energy shortages that simply can-

---

ments/21252030%20Agenda%20for%20Sustainable%20Development%20web.pdf

12 Gartner Information Technology Glossary: Smart Grid. https://www.gartner.com/en/information-technology/glossary/smart-grid

not be overcome or overlooked. At the present trajectory, industrialized nations are headed for a massive train wreck. Hence, we see headlines like this:

- "A summer of blackouts? Wheezing power grid leaves states at risk" (*The Washington Post* 6/2/22)
- "America's Summer of Rolling Blackouts" (*The Wall Street Journal* 5/27/22)
- "Rush toward green energy has left US 'incredibly' vulnerable to summer blackouts" (Fox News 7/4/22)
- "The U.S. Power Grid Can't Support Its Climate Pledges" (Oilprice 9/1/22)
- "Amid Heat Wave, California Asks Electric Vehicle Owners to Limit Charging" (*The New York Times* 9/2/22)

If there were an abundance of energy, there would be no need to control or allocate it. However, if the object of the technocrats is first and foremost to control energy distribution and consumption, then a shortage has to be created to justify that control. The green radicals, following in the footsteps of the United Nations' Sustainable Development Goals (SDGs), have successfully prosecuted a war on traditional sources of energy in favor of alternative energy sources that are unreliable, expensive, and disruptive.

## Surveillance

A panopticon of surveillance surrounds us on every side and is rapidly being integrated into a comprehensive system that some suggest resembles the antagonistic "Skynet" depicted in the *Terminator* movie franchise. This description is in perfect alignment with three of technocracy's aforementioned requirements:

*"3. Provide a continuous inventory of all production and consumption";*

*"4. Provide a specific registration of the type, kind, etc., of all goods and services, where produced and where used"; and*

*"5. Provide specific registration of the consumption of each individual, plus a record and description of the individual."*

Because technocrats view society as a machine, monitoring and surveillance are critical to the maintenance and operation of that machine. While you expect your car to have engine warning lights or your smoke alarm to sound off if fire breaks out, technocrats miss the point that neither individual humans nor society collectively are machines. Conflating us with machines is the false, dangerous thinking that has resulted in ubiquitous surveillance around the world.

To technocrats, there is no such thing as too much surveillance. When they attain one level of monitoring, their next step is to increase the level of magnification and collect even more data. Their addiction to data is unquenchable and unstoppable!

A prime example of such addictive behavior is Rekor Systems. The company initially made a simple license plate reader, which takes a high-resolution photo of a passing car and then uses optical character recognition to record the license plate. It was a foolproof product. However, Rekor CEO Robert Berman wasn't satisfied with reading only plates: "[B]ecause our technology works so well for vehicle recognition, we do more, we identify the vehicle's make, model, color, body type, bumper stickers or window decals, rust, dents and other things like speed of travel and vehicle direction."[13] Rekor now makes the ultimate vehicle panopticon.

Another example of a surveillance addict is Amazon, with its Alexa voice service and its Ring video doorbell. The latter started out as simply a personal security camera. Then microphones were added so Ring devices could pick up local sounds. Amazon's purpose for Ring changed somewhere along the way:

> *Consumer Reports revealed that Ring's audio capabilities are more powerful than anyone anticipated, collecting conversation-level audio from up to 25-feet away. This has disturbing implications for people who walk, bike, or even drive by dozens of these devices every day, not knowing that their conversations may have been captured and recorded. The company*

13 "Rekor Systems on AI-driven Technology for Roadways, Customer Demand and Industry Landscape." Robert Berman, CEO of Rekor Systems, Inc., interviewed by Robert Kraft of SNN Network. July 30, 2020. YouTube. https://youtu.be/ceWhKY-FgvbE

*also refused to commit to eliminating the default setting of automatically recording audio.*[14]

Furthermore, Amazon decided to provide Ring camera audio and video to police departments, in some cases without a warrant or permission from the Ring owner.

## Smart City

In 2012, then-CEO of Ad-Tech Brad Berens proclaimed that "anything that can be digitized will be digitized." In February 2014, the CEO of Deutsche Telekom predicted that "everything that can be connected will be connected." They were both right. Their attitude summarizes the mindset behind the development of smart cities—and behind smart city-derived-and-dependent devices (connected sensors, wearables, medical implants) and terminology (Internet of Things, Internet of Bodies, Big Data, AI algorithms, machine learning, advanced analytics).

The enormity of Internet of Things is difficult to grasp. One cybersecurity threat-prevention specialist, DataProt, reports:

- *In 2021, there were more than 10 billion active IoT devices and it is growing by 21.5% per year.*
- *It's estimated that the number of active IoT devices will surpass 25.4 billion in 2030.*
- *By 2025, there will be 152,200 IoT devices connecting to the Internet per minute.*
- *It's estimated that global IoT spending will total $15 trillion in the six-year period between 2019 and 2025.*
- *The amount of data generated by IoT devices is expected to reach 73.1 ZB (zettabytes) by 2025.*[15]

Currently, only forty-two percent of US cities use some measure of smart city technology, but that percentage is growing. Often the first sign of smart city implementation is installation of

14 Kelley, Jason and Matthew Guariglia. "Ring Reveals They Give Videos to Police Without User Consent or a Warrant." Electronic Frontier Foundation. July 15, 2022. https://www.eff.org/deeplinks/2022/07/ring-reveals-they-give-videos-police-without-user-consent-or-warrant

15 Jovanovic, Bojan. "Internet of Things statistics for 2022." DataProt. May 13, 2022. https://dataprot.net/statistics/iot-statistics

digital light poles with built-in surveillance cameras and microphones. In other smart cities, the pioneering products are license plate readers and street sensors that monitor traffic.

Connecting physical sensor devices is not difficult. It is dealing with the unconnected silos of data that remains a technocrat's greatest challenge. What really makes a smart city "smart" is the fusing of these data silos into a central database that can be analyzed by sophisticated AI algorithms with the goal of facilitating a desired social outcome.

The problem of integration is further exacerbated by the wide mix of public and private devices. For instance, a city might install license plate readers to track individual vehicles—and fine their scofflaw drivers. But what about privately owned smart phones that spin off inordinate amounts of location data in real time? The "smart" answer would be for a municipality to purchase cell phone location data and then integrate that data into its tracking system. Imagine a city building a database of its residents in order to collect all of their online activity, from social media posts to search histories. If that sounds far-fetched to you, you're behind the times. There are, in fact, at least eight companies that can help cities do just that.

It is reported that only 0.06% of devices that could be connected to the Internet are actually hooked up to it. This means that there will ultimately be trillions of connected devices. Is it possible to run wires or cables to all these unconnected devices? Hardly. That stark fact should adequately explain the stampede to 5G wireless connectivity, which offers real-time connections with very large data transmission capacity.

W. Edwards Deming (1900–1993) was a classic technocrat who held advanced degrees in both mathematics and physics. As a sought-after business consultant, he had a huge impact on the reconstruction and success of industrial Japan after WWII. Deming, who famously remarked, "In God we trust; all others bring data," would surely have been an ardent supporter of smart city technology.

## Propaganda

The Oxford English Dictionary defines propaganda as "the systematic dissemination of information, esp. in a biased or misleading way, in order to promote a political cause or point of view."

The man behind that definition is Edward Bernays, who in 1928 invented propaganda as an intentional doctrine and explained it in his seminal treatise, *Propaganda*: "If we understand the mechanism and motives of the group mind, is it not possible to control and regiment the masses according to our will without their knowing it?"[16]

In another chapter of the same book, Bernays wrote, "The invisible government tends to be concentrated in the hands of the few because of the expense of manipulating the social machinery which controls the opinions and habits of the masses."[17]

Was Bernays a closet technocrat? Perhaps even a transhumanist? Neither is implausible, considering that his understanding and use of propaganda paved the way for technocrats and transhumanists to join together to master that art. In so doing, they've commandeered the major engines of news distribution—notably, major media outlets, social media, and search engines.

An entire industry of "fact-checkers" has arisen to challenge any thought contrary to the technocrat/transhumanist narrative. Not surprisingly, much of the censorship associated with their narrative is accomplished automatically with the continuous operation of Artificial Intelligence algorithms. As we have learned during the COVID-19 pandemic, AI algorithms provide no means to appeal or protest their impersonal decisions. Such a human touch would be disastrous to the technocrat mind, which is the epitome of efficiency!

The propaganda machine is meant to deceive, manipulate, and condition its subjects into adopting positions and actions that they would otherwise never adopt. A perfect example: During the heavily propagandized pandemic, half of America got stuck

---

16 Bernays, Edward L. *Propaganda: The Public Mind in the Making*. (New York: Horace Liveright, 1928). Chapter 4.

17 Bernays. Chapter 3.

in the weeds of delusion over mask-wearing, social distancing, lockdowns, and the injection of experimental drugs said to contain mRNA. Their response to the pandemic narrative was proof that propaganda is one of the most frightening tools of control imaginable.

Bernays certainly saw the power of propaganda when he wrote, "Those who manipulate this unseen mechanism of society constitute an invisible government which is the true ruling power of our country."[18]

His conclusion points to who has the real power in America. Politicians would like to think that they are the movers and shakers, but they are not. The technocrats and transhumanists in Silicon Valley and beyond; the Big Pharma executives and the captured regulators they control; the swelling ranks of global elitists, like the members of the World Economic Forum—all are the actual controllers of society. If we believe otherwise, we are entertaining wishful thinking or, more likely, we have been steeped in government-schooling's mass indoctrination.

## Surveillance Capitalism

Retired Harvard Business School Professor Shoshana Zuboff coined the term "surveillance capitalism" and elucidated it in *The Age of Surveillance Capitalism: The Fight for a Human Future at the New Frontier of Power*. In her excellent book, she explains how Google pioneered surveillance capitalism at the start of this century in the same way Ford Motor Co. pioneered the automated assembly line at the start of the last century—in 1913, to be exact. When Google discovered the value in "behavioral surplus"—that is, what is left over after meeting its own users' needs—it tapped into a goldmine of predictive analysis. As a result, it could sell its forecast of users' future behavior to buyers eager to incorporate that data into their own products and offer it for sale. Our human behavior has thus become raw material mined for products and services made and traded by corporations.

18 Bernays. Chapter 1.

Zuboff writes, "[I]t is no longer enough to automate information flows about it, the goal now is to automate us."[19] Of course, Google isn't the only culprit. Other giants, Facebook and Amazon among them, have picked up on Google's success and joined ranks with Google parent Alphabet Inc. in this unchecked exploitation of humanity.

Hence Zuboff's apt definition of them as "surveillance capitalists." She observes that they "know everything about us, whereas their operations are designed to be unknowable to us."[20] Since surveillance capitalism is unprecedented and without legal structure or constraints, its practitioners are "impelled to pursue lawlessness by the logic of their own creation,"[21] she contends.

After Google objectified its clients by selling predictive certainty about future behavior, it soon discovered that it could just as readily manipulate and shape human behavior—both current behavior and future behavior. This is where we really see the element of control being applied.

Zuboff notes:

*It is a form of tyranny that feeds on people but is not of the people. In a surreal paradox, this coup is celebrated as "personalization," although it defiles, ignores, overrides, and displaces everything about you and me that is personal. [. . .] [It is] the obliteration of politics.*[22]

In sum, surveillance capitalism is thoroughly technocratic in nature. As such, it is patently anti-government and anti-democratic, rejecting all forms of political expression and all legislatively enacted, executive-signed, and judicially enforced laws and regulations. Indeed, the power technocracy wields throughout the world is greater than the power of most nation-states combined.

---

19 Zuboff, Shoshana. *The Age of Surveillance Capitalism: The Fight for a Human Future at the New Frontier of Power*. (Perseus Books, 2019). Page 8.
20 Zuboff. Page 11.
21 Zuboff. Page 105.
22 Zuboff. Page 513.

## Conclusion

The technocrats/transhumanists who have been quietly erecting a control grid under the pretense that it is for our convenience and pleasure are not content to apply it only to social entities like countries, states, provinces, or cities. Rather, the only way they are satisfied is if they are controlling the behavior of each and every human being. Personally. Individually. Completely. Continuously.

Actually, that's not quite true. Beyond seeking to control us externally—our day-to-day behavior, movements, activities—technocrats and transhumanists desire to control our thoughts. Personally. Individually. Completely. Continuously.

To them, the final hurdle is not just to monitor our thoughts but to actually *alter* the way we think so that we will come to the right preconceived conclusions (theirs, of course) without requiring any additional external conditioning.

In summary, all that I have described conforms exactly to the original definition of technocracy:

> **Technocracy is the science of social engineering**, *the scientific operation of the entire social mechanism to produce and distribute goods and services to the entire population. [. . .] For the first time in human history it will be done as a scientific, technical, engineering problem. [. . .]* **There will be no place for Politics, Politicians, Finance or Financiers**, *Rackets or Racketeers. [. . .] Technocracy will distribute by means of a certificate of distribution available to every citizen from birth to death. [Emphasis added.]*

Rosa Koire was right about Agenda 21, 2030 Agenda, and sustainable development. She understood that, as I have long argued, the UN's goals to transform the planet are nothing more than warmed-over 1930s-era technocracy:

> *It is the inventory and control plan. Inventory and control of all land, all water, all minerals, all plants, all animals, all construction, all means of production, all food,*

*all energy, all information, and all human beings in the world.*[23]

23 "Rosa Koire interview: UN Agenda 2030 exposed." May 30, 2019. YouTube. https://youtu.be/3PrY7nFbwAY

# CHAPTER 7

# The Science of Social Engineering

*We are governed, our minds are molded, our tastes formed, our ideas suggested, largely by men we have never heard of.* - Edward Bernays

Social engineering is the intentional use of propaganda and other manipulative techniques to influence public attitudes and behavior on a mass scale with the goal of arriving at whatever outcomes have been specified by the social engineers.

Because technocracy originally labeled itself as the "science of social engineering," we should not be surprised that today's technocrats and their allies are still practicing this dark skill for the purpose of achieving their own ends.

During the pandemic, the world has been overtaken by these social engineers, who seem to slither out of the woodwork. Their carefully constructed propaganda, spewed nonstop all day, every day, has convinced many millions of frightened people to wear face masks, practice social distancing, stay locked in their homes, shut down their businesses, close schools, and, finally, obediently submit to being injected with FDA-*un*approved, experimental mRNA shots.

How could this have happened? Has the world gone mad? Let's examine.

In the 1930s, early technocrat dreams of social engineering were emerging. Foundational research had already been conducted by Ivan Pavlov (1849–1936), a Russian neurologist and physiologist who was determined to unravel the cause of human behavior. His experiments on dogs' drooling response to the sight of food enabled him to develop his well-known theory of classical conditioning. He found that a dog can be conditioned to salivate upon simply seeing a food dish, even if there's no food in it. Another of Pavlov's experiments resulted in dogs drooling whenever their dog-feeder walked into the room.

Does the theory of classical conditioning apply to humans, too? Of course, and it works like this: If a dad always dons a certain ball cap just before taking his child to the park to play, eventually the child will anticipate playtime whenever Dad wears the same cap, no matter what the setting or circumstance.

American psychologist and behaviorist B. F. Skinner (1904–1990) came on the scene a bit later than Pavlov. Skinner promoted the idea that human nature is mostly a product of a person's environment. But he also contended that human nature follows certain laws that, if discovered, could be used for the purpose of manipulation and control. In experiments using rats, he developed theories of positive and negative reinforcement, as well as outright punishment, to control behavior. Skinner's theories about rodents jumped the track to humans when he realized that "the species of the organism has made surprisingly little difference."[1] His 1948 book, *Walden Two*, described a utopia in which the free will of the human spirit or soul is rejected and systematic altering of environmental variables controls all human behavior.

Both Skinner and Pavlov held to a mechanistic[2] world view. They attempted to understand human behavior through a process of scientific study. Humans, they reasoned, are accidental beings that have progressed according to Darwin's theories on the survival of the fittest. Their mechanistic philosophy fit perfectly with the mindset of early technocrats and ended up as a

---

1 Skinner, B. F. *Cumulative Record*. (B. F. Skinner Foundation, 1999). Page 182.

2 Britannica's definition of mechanism: "In philosophy, mechanism is the predominant form of Materialism, which holds that natural phenomena can and should be explained by reference to matter and motion and their laws. It rejected the notion of organisms by reducing biological functions to physical and chemical processes, thus putting an end to spirit–body dualism." https://www.britannica.com/topic/mechanism-philosophy

major theme of the *Technocracy Study Course* that was published in 1934.

The danger in this type of thinking is that it reduces humans to having no free will and no spirit or soul that will help them to make moral and ethical life choices. Instead, external conditions and stimuli are necessary to produce better behavior. Of course, technocrats reasoned that they could apply their "science of social engineering" to do just that.

Those early technocrats didn't need to write long expositions about how to operate machines and factories or about how to build roads and cities. Taylorism[3] and systems theory[4] had already done that—and technocrats were steeped in both doctrines. What the technocrats couldn't deal with, though, was human nature. They found people to be far less reliable than physical machines. Nevertheless, they were forced to depend upon unreliable, unpredictable humans in order to actually build the cities and roads and operate the machines and factories.

Can you see the technocrats' dilemma?

Their only solution, as they saw it, was to recast humans in the image of machinery and manage them as such. In fact, people were the one big obstacle technocrats faced whenever they attempted to control *anything* and *everything*—which was *all the time*. Thus, it should be no surprise that when they dreamed up the definition of technocracy in 1937, their ability to control human behavior got top billing: "Technocracy is the science of social engineering."[5]

We can see how the behavioral theories of both Pavlov and Skinner provided salvation to the early technocrats. For if humans can be controlled externally, like physical machines, and if

3 Britannica's definition of Taylorism: A "system of scientific management advocatd by Fred W. Taylor. In Taylor's view, the task of factory management was to determine the best way for the worker to do the job, to provide the proper tools and training, and to provide incentives for good performance." https://www.britannica.com/science/Taylorism

4 Britannica's definition of systems theory (also called social systems theory): "In social science, the study of society as a complex arrangement of elements, including individuals and their beliefs, as they relate to a whole (e.g., a country)." https://www.britannica.com/topic/systems-theory

5 "What is Technocracy." *The Technocrat.* 1938.

that discipline can be recast as a "science," then the "science of social engineering" is legitimately in the technocrats' wheelhouse, isn't it?

Yes, except for the simple fact that the science of engineering human behavior is not a *real* science. It's a pseudoscience. People cannot be "engineered." And even if they could be, the development of the principles of social engineering is a bastardization of the true scientific method that has always served authentic scientists so well, both in the past and in the present.

You may remember that at the end of Chapter 1 we called "scientism" a "speculative, metaphysical, upside-down worldview about the nature of the universe and man's relation to it." The fact that "upside-down" scientism plays such a huge role in technocracy reinforces the fact that social engineering is pseudo-scientific—and should never be equated with the word "science."

All efforts to create a utopia through social engineering (think *Walden Two* by Skinner) have failed miserably. Marxists, communists, and socialists have tried it and failed. So have fascists. Technocrats likewise have failed thus far and will fail in the end as well. However, in the meantime, society is damaged by the hubris of these self-selected social engineers, who practice a warped pseudoscience that will never work because it is . . . not scientific.

The eminent historian Richard G. Olson, author of *Science and Scientism in the Nineteenth-Century Europe*, notes in his Introduction the subtle shift in thinking that preceded the original technocrat movement:

> *I have persistently thought of those early thinkers who sought to bring insights, especially methodological insights, from the natural sciences into the human social domain as engaging in scientism – a term that I intended to indicate the transfer of ideas, practices, attitudes, and methodologies from the context of the study of the natural world (which was assumed to be independent of human needs and expectations) into the study of humans and their social institutions, without impos-*

*ing any judgment on the legitimacy of such an appropriation.*[6]

Scientism is still practiced by today's technocrats, as attested to by the prominent presence of pseudoscience in every walk of life. Instead of improving society along the way, scientism invariably ends up making a bigger mess of everything it touches.

Turning back to the *Technocracy Study Course*, we can now see how the "science of social engineering" has influenced the technocrat mind—both then and now:

*This gives us a clue to the most fundamental social control technique that exists. No other single item exerts more than a small percentage of the influence exerted by the immediate physical environment upon the activities of human beings. Leave the physical environment unaltered, or the industrial rates of operation unchanged, and any effort to alter the fundamental modes of behavior of human beings is doomed largely to failure; alter the immediate physical environment of human beings, and their modes of behavior change automatically.*[7]

Ever since that study course was introduced in 1934, technocrats have been attempting to perfect reliable methods of social control. Below we will cite a few such methods.

## Propaganda

The intellectual father of modern propaganda was Edward L. Bernays (1891–1995), nephew of Sigmund Freud. His seminal book, *Propaganda*, appeared in 1928, just in time for technocrats to integrate it into their science of social engineering toolkit. Bernays was always direct, as evidenced in the opening of his book's Chapter I, Organizing Chaos:

*The conscious and intelligent manipulation of the organized habits and opinions of the masses is an important element in democratic society. Those who manipulate this unseen mech-*

---

6 Olson, Richard C. *Science and Scientism in Nineteenth-Century Europe*. (Univers ty of Illinois Press, 2008). Page 1.
7 Olson. Pages 242–243.

*anism of society constitute an invisible government which is the true ruling power of our country.*[8]

The last statement in his book was just as pointed:

*Propaganda will never die out. Intelligent men must realize that propaganda is the modern instrument by which they can fight for productive ends and help to bring order out of chaos.*[9]

Productive ends? Order out of chaos? This is the stuff technocrat dreams are made of.

Everything between the first page and the last page of *Propaganda* served as a catalyst for what would become an immense industry designed to manipulate and control the masses. Today, the three intertwined but distinct parts of that industry are "public relations" (or publicity), "marketing," and "advertising." Their respective experts spin reality in various directions for the purpose of promoting products that fetch handsome profits. Without PR flacks and marketing gurus and ad copywriters, how would a brewer sell suds successfully? Who'd come up with the perfect scene: a pool party teeming with big-abs blokes and blondes in bikinis?

Bernays had a technocrat's mind and was authoritatively described in those terms. An article in an MIT journal captured his persona perfectly:

*Right up to the end of his life (Bernays died in 1995), he held fast to his belief that the masses needed leadership, and that leadership would come from an elite, technocratic few who would shape the masses' reality and thus produce a better society.*[10]

Propaganda became such an influential tool that academia adopted it and taught it in schools of journalism, social studies, political science, marketing, and other disciplines. Since Bernays'

---

8 Bernays, Edward L. *Propaganda*. (New York: Horace Liveright, 1928). Chapter 1.
9 Bernays. Chapter 11.
10 Gehl, Robert and Sean Lawson. "Masters of Crowds: The Rise of Mass Social Engineering." The MIT Press Reader. https://thereader.mitpress.mit.edu/masters-of-crowds-the-rise-of-mass-social-engineering

seminal work, a bevy of books have been written examining every aspect of what makes propaganda, well, propaganda.

In 2020, I looked at several college textbooks that dealt with propaganda and was surprised to see remarkably similar lists of techniques in each. Below, I've summarized the most common propaganda techniques just to make a point of how the subject has become standardized:

**Fear:** *The most powerful emotion, fear of loss or of physical harm, opens the mind to accept the solutions provided by the propagandist—solutions that would not otherwise have been accepted. The technique of fear has been the foundation of all pandemic-related propaganda.*

**The Bandwagon:** *A claim is made that, because everyone else is doing it, so should you. This assertion is often combined with other propaganda techniques. You'll recognize this all-too-familiar bandwagon entreaty: "Everyone is taking the shot because it is safe and effective; you should take it, too."*

**Card Stacking:** *This technique highlights all the "good" information and leaves out the "bad." In other words, only the facts that support the propagandist's agenda are presented, while everything else is intentionally suppressed. This blatant censorship is rampant in the mainstream media, social media, and search engines these days.*

**Plain Folks:** *The propagandist implies that he's just an ordinary person like you, with the same dreams and desires, and therefore you should believe him.*

**The Testimonial:** *A person unrelated to a product testifies that the propaganda about the product is true and that you can trust his word. Often the ideal testifier is a likeable, credible celebrity. Other times the person giving the testimonial is a "nobody" who is chosen because he comes off as one of the "plain folks" described above.*

**Glittering Generalities:** *Propaganda is sometimes unquestioningly accepted simply because the sweeping statements it makes cannot be defined and often contain vague "virtue* *words." Examples: "This anti-discrimination program will ensure equity for all" and "We will create millions of green jobs with this budget."*

**Name-Calling/Deflection:** *Ad hominem attacks leveled by a propagandist can serve to deflect negative attention away from himself and toward someone else. For example, global warming scaremonger Al Gore once said threateningly, "Deniers deserved to be punished." Today's name-callers claim that America has a "pandemic of the unvaccinated," and they target for ad hominem attacks whoever resists being jabbed.*

**Transfer:** *This technique transfers an organization's prestige to the propagandist's program or product—thus giving that program or product the same degree of prestige. This propaganda tactic takes advantage of an organization's desire to maintain its reputation, to follow the crowd, to obey the rules, to acquiesce to authority. Look at what happened when public health officials and political leaders persuaded the pastors of many US churches to promote pandemic propaganda to their congregations. Of course, church members eagerly complied with whatever "protection measures" pastors urged them to take.*

**False Analogy:** *When two concepts are linked together despite having no actual cause-and-effect relationship, it is called a false analogy or false equivalence. Here's an attempt to do just that: "People who question vaccines are anti-vaxxers. Mary does not want to take the COVID vaccine. Thus, Mary is an anti-vaxxer."*

**Either/or Fallacy:** *"Black-and-white" thinking offers only two choices, even though there might be other admissible answers. The either/or fallacy polarizes people and forces them to accept the outcome desired by the fallacy-promoter. Which of us wants to agree with "You are either for science or against it" when our understanding of "science" is antithetical to the propagandist's?*

**Faulty Cause and Effect:** *This technique suggests that because A follows B, A must cause B. For example, (A) Joe sup-*

*ports gun ownership, and (B) murderers often use guns to kill people; therefore, Joe must be a murderer himself—or at least a fan of murderers.*

**Euphemisms:** *It isn't uncommon for propagandists to use a word or phrase that pretends to communicate truth but in fact does the opposite. One rhetorical device they employ to that end is the euphemism, which "replaces accurate language that may be offensive with language that is more palatable, to instill a positive association," as The Propwatch Project puts it. Thus, the propagandist's euphemistic "alternative facts" really means "outright false or misleading claims." Likewise, the propagandistic UN uses the euphemism "sustainable development" to hide its true technocratic intentions: "social engineering" of the masses.*

**Loaded Words:** *Related to name-calling, loaded words are what the propagandist uses to describe perfectly normal actions and completely ordinary circumstances. You may remember the egregious, extremist language the US government used when it labeled parents who rightfully protest at school board meetings "domestic terrorists" who commit "hate crimes."*

**Scapegoat:** *Quite simply, the age-old scapegoat technique assigns blame to someone who is not a party to something. Two examples of scapegoating will suffice: (1) every presidential administration typically blames current economic woes on the previous administration; (2) after COVID vaccines were offered to the public, only the unvaccinated were blamed for the ongoing pandemic.*

**Logical Disconnect:** *The World Economic Forum is now famous for its ad campaign, "You will own nothing and be happy." What a typical propagandist ploy, to say that happiness is the result of owning nothing, when everyone knows from experience that such a statement is totally illogical and untrue. A corollary to the WEF's absurd claim might as well* *be: "Homeless people own nothing, therefore they must be happy."*[11]

At this point you might be thinking that whoever owns or influences the media would be smart to use these propaganda techniques in various combinations to achieve any conceivable end. You would be correct. The sad truth is, media owners and influencers are already employing this strategy. The sadder truth: It is the technocrats and their transhumanist twins who control Big Media—that is, all the legacy print media and television and radio stations plus all social media (think Facebook and Twitter and YouTube) in America.

Once we know the sources of propaganda and have examined the specific techniques, we can pinpoint the real objectives for promulgating the propaganda.

For instance, throughout 2020, 2021, and 2022, Big Media delivered a non-stop tsunami of propaganda urging everyone to get the COVID-19 mRNA injection to fight the virus. Before long it was discovered that the injections were ineffective and, in many cases, harmful. Turns out the goal of Big Pharma and the complicit captured agencies—in other words, their real objective—was not to prevent contagion but to introduce a new medical therapy. This therapy does something no vaccine ever did: It hacks the human immune system via genetic sequences that are engineered into the mRNA and in doing so ultimately edits the human genome. Not that the propagandists ever came out and said as much!

When we analyze the COVID "vaccine" propaganda, it becomes clear that its source is the pharmaceutical and biotech industries, both of which are heavily influenced, if not dominated, by transhumanists and technocrats. It also becomes obvious that their promises have been at best disingenuous and at worst patently false. Many of its takers have suffered severely and become either permanently injured or a fatal statistic. The cause of their illness or death has been irrefutably determined to be one or more rounds of the COVID shot.

---

11 Wood, Patrick. "Exposing Propaganda: The Vaccine For Liberty, Truth And Reason." Technocracy News & Trends. January 17, 2022. https://www.technocracy.news/exposing-propaganda-the-vaccine-for-liberty-truth-and-reason

Is there a lesson we can take from this dangerous—often fatal—lie and apply it to our future run-ins with propaganda? Yes. Not just one lesson, but many lessons. One I propose we all heed is this: Whenever we detect propaganda at play, our knee-jerk reaction should always be to ask, "What is the product being sold to us by the propagandists?" and "What do those same propagandists say the product will do for us?" Invariably, the product is *actually* designed to do something far different from the propagandists' plug—something far worse.

## The Nudge

In 2008, Richard Thaler, a University of Chicago professor of behavioral economics, co-authored a book titled *The Nudge: Improving Decisions About Health, Wealth, and Happiness.* His "nudge theory" was quickly picked up by many governments, corporations, and non-governmental organizations, which began using it as an influential policy tool to manipulate the behavior of employees, customers, and citizens. Nine years later, Thaler won the 2017 Nobel Prize in Economics for his work on psychological biases in behavioral economics.

Now let's look—through the eyes of Henry Farrell, who teaches political science and international affairs at George Washington University—at the fallout from Thaler's nudge theory, shall we?

In a *Vox* article, Farrell provides a critical analysis of what has become known as "nudgeocracy," or the practice of nudging. He writes:

> *Indeed, there are many circumstances under which nudges are a good idea. But the fad for nudgeocracy has hidden implications. Thaler and [co-author Cass] Sunstein describe the philosophy that underlies nudging as "libertarian paternalism" — libertarian because it lets people make the choices that they want to, paternalist because it provides them with a father's guiding hand. Behind nudgeocracy lies the assumption that daddy knows best.*
>
> *For Thaler and Sunstein, daddy is a "choice architect" — a skilled and intelligent technocrat who uses good data, good*

*social science and his own intelligence to figure out what people would really want to do, if only they were as smart and well informed as the choice architect.*[12]

Farrell concludes that nudging "amounts to a kind of technocracy, which assumes that experts will know which choices are in the interests of ordinary people better than those people know themselves. This may be true under some circumstances," he continues, "but it will not be true all of the time, or even most of the time, if there are no good opportunities for those ordinary people to voice their preferences."

Thaler and Sunstein apparently don't believe that the "ordinary people" Farrell describes know how to "voice their preferences"—or that they even have the ability and the right to *make* their own choices. Hence:

*Our goal, in short, is to help people make the choices that they would have made if they had paid full attention and possessed complete information, unlimited cognitive ability, and complete self-control.*

*A nudge, as we will use the term, is any aspect of the choice architecture that alters people's behavior in a predictable way without forbidding any options or significantly changing their economic incentives.*[13]

The nudging mechanism that controls people's behavior is very subtle. As Thaler and Sunstein explain it, "nudge architects"—who fit my description of technocrats to a T—first determine what the most rational choice or decision should be in a given situation. Then they design a "nudge" to steer the target, without his conscious knowledge, to that outcome.

Fascinating, isn't it, that Thaler and Sunstein believe they and their fellow practitioners always pay full attention, always possess complete information, always have unlimited cognitive abili-

---

12 Farrell, Henry. "This year's economics Nobel winner invented a tool that's both brilliant and undemocratic." Vox. October 16, 2017. https://www.vox.com/the-big-idea/2017/10/16/16481836/nudges-thaler-nobel-economics-prize-undemocratic-tool

13 Thaler, Richard H. and Cass R. Sunstein. *Nudge: Improving Decisions About Health, Wealth, and Happiness*. (Yale University Press, 2021). Page 9.

ty and complete self-control. By contrast, they deem the rest of us perpetually deficient in attention, information, cognitive ability and self-control. Paternalism, indeed.

Similar to the standardized techniques of propaganda we listed above, nudging has developed its own behavior-influencing strategies—among them are social proof, numerical anchors, option restriction, and competition. It's not necessary to know all the details of these nudging techniques, but it *is* important to recognize that nudging has become a highly developed discipline.

Google's search engine provides a good example of nudging in action. When you type in a few letters to begin a new search, a tailored type-ahead list of choices is presented to you, offering one-click suggestions. Google's nudge architects know you are much more likely to pick one of their completed suggestions than you are to type in your original search idea. What you may not realize is that Google very likely had already compiled information about your previous searches, preferences, purchases, etc. The autotype options it presents to you are nuanced by that data to trick you into selecting a certain destination of Google's choosing. While your data can be used to sell you products, it can just as easily be used to nudge you to vote for certain political candidates.

In the hands of technocrats and their transhumanist twins, the practice of nudge theory has exploded since the COVID-19 pandemic began in early 2020. Nudging has caused people to dutifully accept public health policies such as wearing masks, social distancing, working from home, and, ultimately, submitting to experimental mRNA-based injections. In other cases, where nudging alone didn't get the job done, outright mandates were put in place to force compliance.

One journal reported on the effect of nudging in Great Britain during 2020–2022:

> *This politics of behavior has given rise to a new form of technocratic governance. Then prime minister David Cameron gave this technocracy its most explicit form when he helped set up the Nudge Unit in 2010. This was charged with the task of developing policies that could shape people's thoughts,*

*choices and actions. As far as the nudgers were concerned, subliminal psychological techniques were preferable to democratic debate and argument.*[14]

The article goes on to say:

*A government that substitutes its own preferences in place of people's free will is clearly one which does not take freedom seriously. In effect, nudging allows experts to try to colonize people's internal life and attempt to make their decisions for them.*[15]

When the cunning, crafty art of nudging and the devious, deceptive art of propaganda are employed together to achieve specific outcomes, they represent the height of technocracy's "science of social engineering." This is not to say that there are no other tools available, but the combination of nudging and propagandizing is a solid one-two knockout punch.

What, then, is the role of newly popularized "mass formation"?

## Mass Formation

How many times in the past three years have you heard the question, "Why are people so gullible?" They usually go on to describe a driver who is alone in the car with the windows rolled up and a face mask on—for protection from a virus the mask cannot possibly protect against.

One man who has attempted to answer that question is Mattias Desmet, a professor of clinical psychology at Ghent University in Belgium, a practicing psychoanalytic psychotherapist, and one of the world's leading experts on totalitarianism and mass formation.

Desmet published his much-anticipated book, *The Psychology of Totalitarianism*, in June 2022. In it, he lays out his theory of mass formation, a subject he had been interviewed about and had written articles about—bringing him much attention—over the previous twenty-four months. According to Desmet, "mass

14 Furedi, Frank. "'Nudge' has no place in our democracy." spiked. January 14, 2022. https://www.spiked-online.com/2022/01/14/nudge-has-no-place-in-our-democracy

15 Furedi.

formation is, in essence, a kind of group hypnosis that destroys individuals' ethical self-awareness and robs them of their ability to think critically." He points out that today's totalitarianism is led not by iconic dictators like Joseph Stalin or Adolf Hitler but by "dull bureaucrats and technocrats."[16]

To his credit, Desmet accurately explains the "narrative of mechanistic science, in which man is reduced to a biological organism" and becomes an "insignificant by-product of mechanistic processes":[17]

> *Man may not realize it, but his humanity does not really matter, it is nothing essential. His whole existence, his longing and his lust, his romantic lamentations and his most superficial needs, his joy and his sorrow, his doubt and his choices, his anger and unreasonableness, his pleasure and his suffering, his deepest aversion and his most lofty aesthetic appreciations, in short, the entire drama of his existence, can ultimately be reduced to elementary particles that interact according to the laws of mechanics.*[18]

This is, of course, the essence of both technocracy and transhumanism.

Desmet believes there are four simultaneous conditions necessary for a group to form and fall into mass formation. All the individuals in that group must:

1. Experience a lack of social bonds and isolation
2. See life as meaningless or senseless
3. Have free-floating anxiety (be anxious but unable to pinpoint why)
4. Have free-floating frustration and aggression[19]

When these four conditions exist in an individual who is then presented with a narrative that identifies the object of his anxiety, frustration, and aggression, that individual is prone to fall-

16 Desmet, Mattias. *The Psychology of Totalitarianism*. (Chelsea Green Publishing, 2022). Page 2.
17 Desmet. Page 17.
18 Desmet. Page 17.
19 Desmet. Pages 94–96.

ing into mass formation. Doing so enables him to regain both meaning in his life and social bonds with like-minded persons. This temporary psychological state satisfies him but is extremely dangerous, because he has forfeited his ability to think critically, independently.

Desmet's theory of mass formation perfectly explains events like the 1978 Jonestown Massacre in Guyana, where 909 followers were led by Peoples Temple cult leader Jim Jones to drink a poison-laced suicide concoction that sent them all to an instant and early death.

Basically, Desmet seems to be expanding on the simple concept of delusion: "a persistent false psychotic belief regarding the self or persons or objects outside the self that is maintained despite indisputable evidence to the contrary" (Merriam-Webster). Much has been known about delusion for a very long time, and the reader can decide if Desmet is truly adding anything new to the concept or not. Either way, the phenomenon is not local or regional, but global.

Where Desmet errs, however, is in his answer to the question he pointedly asks, "Should we consider mass formation the result of a conspiracy?" Desmet says no. Instead, he posits, authoritarian leaders are drawn into the mass formation themselves and they then solidify and perpetuate their condition. He further suggests:

> *As such, in a certain sense, conspiracy thinking — the thinking that reduces all world events to one big conspiracy — fulfills the same function as mass formation. As with mass formation, conspiracy theorizing fills humans with a kind of enthusiasm. The anxiety, anger, and discontent that are now associated with a few simple mental images transform a strongly negative state into a (symptomatic) positive one.*[20]

Apparently Desmet has not considered: Who creates and distributes the narrative that causes the mass formation in the first place? Is it possible to use social engineering techniques to artificially create the four conditions that he says are necessary for spontaneous mass formation? Are the social engineers who

20 Desmet. Page 128.

actively set out to deceive and subjugate people more to blame than the victims whom they induce into the condition of mass formation?

As the co-author of two books on the globalist Trilateral Commission and the sole author of three books on the globalist technocratic movement (this book being the third), I have followed the process of globalization and the perpetrators of that process for the past forty-five years. In that time, I have observed many clearly despotic characters who conspired together to lay out and execute strategies that achieved their goals at the expense of anyone who dared to get in their way.

When, for instance, United Nations global warming czar Christiana Figueres stated that the UN intended to overthrow capitalism and free market economics, that it had created a timetable to achieve it, that it had the means to do so, and that it was taking immediate action to start the process—she was defining a classic conspiracy. Could Figueres be called a victim of mass formation? Absolutely not. She was a witting fellow conspirator in a globalist plot, pure and simple.

Another example is taken from David Rockefeller's autobiography, *Memoirs*. His own testimony speaks clearly of a multi-decade conspiracy that he created and then participated in:

> *Some even believe we are part of a secret cabal, working against the best interests of the United States, characterizing my family and me as 'internationalists,' and of conspiring with others around the world to build a more integrated global political and economic structure — one world, if you will. If that's the charge, I stand guilty, and I am proud of it.*[21]
>
> *Was Rockefeller a victim of mass formation? No. Did the public make him do it? No. Was he merely deluded? Absolutely not! In short, Rockefeller was a ruthless conspirator who wanted to dominate the world.*

I will concede that partial blame must be accepted by every adult who has fallen into mass formation. The hundreds of men and women who died in the Jonestown Massacre should never

21 Rockefeller, David. *Memoirs*. (New York: Random House, 2002). Page 405.

have entered the trap in the first place. (Of course the innocent children whose parents brought them into the cult are excused from all blame.) That said, you have to remember that it was their insane, murderous leader alone who conceived and executed the killing.

As a psychoanalyst and researcher, Desmet has suggested the mechanics of creating and perpetuating mass formation, but we should never diminish the culpability of those responsible: technocrats and transhumanists—the very ones who have dedicated their entire careers to implementing and enforcing the "science of social engineering."

Thus, in this writer's opinion, the tools of delusion and/or mass formation in the hands of today's technocrats and transhumanists are as dangerous to civilization as the invention of the atomic bomb.

The evidence since 2020 suggests that those technocrats and transhumanists are deploying the tools of social engineering against the rest of the world to the fullest extent. They are conspiring to bring about the most dangerous period of delusion in human history.

# CHAPTER 8

# The Takeover of All Genetic Material

*WE ARE ACTUALLY HACKING THE SOFTWARE OF LIFE.*
*TAL ZAKS, FORMER CHIEF MEDICAL OFFICER, MODERNA*

When Aldous Huxley penned *Brave New World* in 1932, he portrayed a futuristic society where human embryos were "genetically engineered"[1] and then grown in artificial wombs until full term. In 1932, however, there was no understanding of genetic building blocks or what made the genomic process tick. It took another twenty-one years before scientists James Watson and Francis Crick discovered and described the twisted-ladder structure of deoxyribonucleic acid (DNA), which they described as a double-helix. Prior to this, other scientists had made seemingly unrelated discoveries about DNA, but Watson and Crick unified existing discoveries, added their own, and subsequently launched the scientific world on a historic stampede to learn how to manipulate life itself.[2]

1 When *Brave New World* was written, there was no such thing as genetic engineering. Today, the National Human Genome Research Institute defines genetic engineering (also called genetic modification) as a process that uses laboratory-based technologies to alter the DNA makeup of an organism. This may involve changing a single base pair (A-T or C-G) or deleting a region of DNA or adding a new segment of DNA. For example, a gene from one species could be added to an organism from a different species to produce a desired trait. Used in both research and industry, genetic engineering has been applied to the production of cancer therapies, brewing yeasts, genetically modified plants and livestock, and more. Here is an easy-to-understand glossary of terms used in this field: https://www.genome.gov/genetics-glossary/Genetic-Engineering.

2 Crick, Francis. "The Discovery of the Double Helix, 1951–1953." The Francis Crick Papers. National Library of Medicine. https://profiles.nlm.nih.gov/spotlight/sc/feature/doublehelix

Important events and discoveries by other genetic scientists quickly followed:

- 1958: DNA is made in a test tube for the first time
- 1962: Jellyfish protein turns into a tool to observe invisible cellular processes
- 1968: Discovery of restriction enzymes
- 1971: Type II restriction enzymes used for mapping DNA
- 1971: Gene-splicing experiment paves the way for recombinant DNA
- 1972: First recombinant DNA (rDNA) molecules constructed
- 1981: First transgenic animal created
- 1982: First genetically engineered human drug created – synthetic insulin
- 1983: Development of the Polymerase Chain Reaction (PCR)
- 1986: First recombinant vaccine for humans approved
- 1992: Convention on Biological Diversity in Rio De Janeiro
- 1994: Discovery of the principles of CRISPR
- 1999: First human chromosome sequenced (mapped)
- 2003: Complete human chromosome sequenced (mapped)[3]

Before continuing, it is worthwhile to review the concept of "recombinant DNA" (rDNA), whose creation in 1972 is attributed to Paul Berg—though he credits one of his students.[4] rDNA is created by combining DNA sequences from two or more different species of organisms. Synthetic insulin, for instance, is made by

3 "History of Genetic Engineering and the Rise of Genome Editing Tools." Synthego. https://www.synthego.com/learn/genome-engineering-history

4 "How the first recombinant DNA was created, Paul Berg." Cold Spring Harbor Laboratory. DNA Learning Center. https://dnalc.cshl.edu/view/15022-How-the-first-recombinant-DNA-was-created-Paul-Berg.html

inserting a human gene responsible for creating human insulin into a common bacterium, whereby the resulting micro-organism is tricked into producing human insulin. This key type of manipulation was made possible by the observation that all genetic material across living organisms is very similar in basic structure. Terms related to rDNA, such as cDNA, transgenic, and synthetic, will be important to understand later in this chapter, when we look at the United Nation's program of mapping and digitizing all the DNA structures in the world.

If this is your first exposure to the microworld of genetics, what I've written thus far must surely sound foreign to you. And its significance is probably hard for you to grasp. So let me share another example that might help clarify the importance of genetic engineering—and its far-reaching implications.

In December 2013 it was announced that scientists at South China Agricultural University had inserted a gene from a glow-in-the-dark jellyfish into pig embryos. The surrogate mother pig subsequently gave birth to ten piglets whose bodies glowed in the dark when exposed to a black light.[5] The same article also mentioned recent experiments that had created fluorescent bunnies and wildcats. Creepy, right?

Could the glowing jellyfish gene be inserted into a human embryo? Of course, and easily so. But *should* it? Ah, there's the rub. Genetically modifying humans in this way would be a clear violation of medical ethics. (Not that it isn't amusing to imagine the possibilities. Just think: You could turn off the electric light on your bed stand at night and serve as your own reading light!)

## Patent Law and DNA

In June 2013, six months before the news of the glowing pigs, the U.S. Supreme Court issued a huge decision on the patent eligibility of human DNA. In that ruling, it struck down patents on naturally occurring human genes, calling them a "product of nature" and thus not a human invention. The court held:

---

5 Opam, Kwame. "Scientists create glow-in-the-dark pigs using jellyfish DNA." The Verge. December 30, 2013. https://www.theverge.com/2013/12/30/5256732/scientists-create-glow-in-the-dark-pigs-using-jellyfish-dna

*A naturally occurring DNA segment is a product of nature and not patent eligible merely because it has been isolated, but cDNA is patent eligible because it is not naturally occurring.*[6]

The Justices' rationale for patenting complementary DNA was simple but emphatic: "cDNA cannot be isolated from nature, but instead must be created in the laboratory."[7] While DNA is a double-helix structure, cDNA only has one helix. cDNA is created using the mRNA template, but it includes only those sections of mRNA that can be "coded," or genetically altered; the rest is discarded. The resulting cDNA is so easily modified that biotech firms build cDNA "libraries" for use in future applications.

This SCOTUS case decision is relevant to all other species that have a DNA genome. All the principles and processes of mRNA, cDNA, RNA and DNA apply to them in like manner.

Now, keep in mind that the United Nations has begun to sequence and digitize the DNA of every living species on earth. All of this natural DNA—that is, DNA found only in living organisms—remains in the public domain and cannot be patented. However, as scientists in any part of the world download and analyze these digital sequences, they may find amazing sequences that just might fit into their own cDNA projects and allow them to create new and patentable products in the private domain.

To summarize, naturally occurring DNA cannot be patented. Artificially created DNA can be patented, creating a gold mine for the patent holders. As genetic scientists sequence and catalog ever-more naturally occurring DNA, they are gaining open, free, unfettered access to the mother of all erector sets of life itself.

The big question is: Who set up this lucrative scheme, and who stands to profit most from it? The rest of this chapter will lay the record bare.

---

6 U.S. Supreme Court. Association for Molecular Pathology v. Myriad Genetics, Inc. Syllabus. June 13, 2013. https://www.law.cornell.edu/supremecourt/text/12-398

7 U.S. Supreme Court. Page 10.

## The Trilateral Commission and Sustainable Development

In order to expose that record, though, we first need to return to some details in Chapter 4, "The Genesis and Progress of Transhumanism." As we will remember, the United Nations Conference on Environment and Development (UNCED), commonly referred to as the Earth Summit, was held in Rio de Janeiro, Brazil, from June 3 through June 14, 1992. Its two well-known outcomes were Agenda 21 (shorthand for "the Agenda for the 21st Century") and the doctrine of sustainable development.

We will also recall from Chapter 4 that the UN itself recognized Trilateral Commission member Gro Harlem Brundtland as the "mother" of sustainable development, thanks to the publication of "Our Common Future." The landmark report was the outcome of a UN sub-organization started in 1983 and known as the World Commission on Environment and Development (WCED). Because Brundtland was chairman of the WCED task force, that body became affectionately known as the Brundtland Commission.

It should be noted, however, that Brundtland Commission Secretary-General James MacNeill, a Canadian, is credited with the actual architecture and penning of "Our Common Future."

MacNeill was a close associate of the Trilateral Commission, having authored for it, in 1991, a key policy book titled *Beyond Interdependence: The Meshing of the World's Economy and the Earth's Ecology*. It was in *Beyond Interdependence* that, according to one source, MacNeill "articulated for the Trilateral Commission the policy options for sustainable development in terms of 'shaping global bargains.'"[8]

The Foreword to *Beyond Interdependence* was written by David Rockefeller, who at the time held the post of North American Chairman of the Trilateral Commission. In the opening statement of his Foreword, Rockefeller ties MacNeill's sustainable development dogma to the Trilaterals—and vice versa—in no uncertain terms:

8 Union of International Associations. Encyclopedia of World Problems—Archived Information. https://uia.org/archive/ency-trans-approaches-comm-11-1

> *A prominent theme in reports to the Trilateral Commission, as articulated in one of our very first reports in 1974, has been that "growing interdependence and the inadequacy of present forms of cooperation are the principal features of the contemporary international order." [ . . . ] Given the "growth imperative" evident in the material poverty of much of humankind,* **the only reasonable alternative is "sustainable development" — a concept that Jim MacNeill did so much to advance as Secretary-General of the Brundtland Commission in its landmark 1987 report Our Common Future.**[9] *[Emphasis added.]*

MacNeill's 1991 book anticipated the 1992 Earth Summit in Rio. Thus, it is no surprise that the principal organizer and Secretary-General of the Rio conference, Maurice Strong—a Canadian compatriot of MacNeill and a protégé of Rockefeller—wrote the Introduction to *Beyond Interdependence.* In it, Strong praises the book for providing "the most compelling economic as well as environmental case for such reform that I have read."[10]

It is also no surprise that MacNeill's kinship with Strong went beyond like-mindedness on economic and ecological reform. So compatible were they that MacNeill was appointed the Earth Summit's Special Advisor to Strong. In addition, MacNeill was involved in creating and overseeing Ecofund, a Washington, D.C.-based nonprofit that raised special donations from corporations and foundations for the Strong-led Rio event.

Beyond the inevitable personal ties of Rockefeller and Strong and MacNeill, we have corporate connections and globalist goals everywhere we turn in this sustainable development space. And we see the hand of the Trilateral Commission manipulating the strings of this planet-wide puppet show.

Want one more proof? Okay, here you go: Also sitting on the Brundtland Commission task force was Trilateral Commission member William Ruckelshaus, the first director of the Environ-

9 MacNeill, Jim et al. *Beyond Interdependence: The Meshing of the World's Economy and the Earth's Ecology.* A Trilateral Commission publication. (Oxford University Press, 1991). Back cover of book.
10 MacNeill. Page x.

mental Protection Agency (EPA). Though a Republican, Ruckelshaus was an environmentalist—actually, what one might call an industrialized environmentalist, having served on the boards of directors for companies like Cummins Engine, Monsanto, Nordstrom, and Weyerhaeuser.

My purpose in delineating these tight-knit relationships is to establish that sustainable development and its surrounds did *not* originate in the United Nations but were, instead, the sole creation of the Trilateral Commission. This is no conspiracy theory; it is plainly laid out for all to see, both in my above text and in many other places I haven't time or space to mention.

Why, then, has this fact not been obvious to the world? I would suggest it's because very few people, whether politicians or the press or the general public, have cared to look deeply into the subject. If they did, they would see all the incestuous connections. They would learn, for starters, that MacNeill's *Beyond Interdependence* was published by the Trilateral Commission.

Even the book's back cover makes plain the Trilateralists' intent:

> *Beyond Interdependence shows that the interlocking of the world's economy and the earth's ecology is the new reality of the century. Building on the Brundtland Commission's landmark report Our Common Future, the book extends the [Trilateralist] Commission's analysis of the issues of global change and the changing international politics of environment.*[11]

So, we have MacNeill, Brundtland, and Ruckelshaus dominating the Brundtland Commission and codifying the Trilateral Commission's sustainable development policies into the 1992 UNCED conference, aka the Earth Summit. And we have the Earth Summit subsequently spreading those policies to every nook and cranny of the entire planet.

Mere conspiracy *theory*? Try *actual* conspiracy.

---

11 MacNeill. Back cover of book.

## The Aftermath of Rio

Of 196 nations that comprised the world and the United Nations in 1992, 178 bought the sustainable development propaganda hook, line, and sinker. They compliantly signed the Agenda 21 treaty. And, in true technocrat fashion, all attempts at dissent were erased from the record.

Two years later, two of those dissenting souls co-wrote a book we discussed in Chapter 4: *The Earth Brokers*. One author was journalist Pratap Chatterjee, then the Washington, D.C.-based Global Environmental Editor of worldwide news agency Inter Press Service. The other was Matthias Finger, an associate professor at Columbia University Teachers College in New York.

Finger and Chatterjee had gone to Rio with open minds and good intentions. They hoped that something significant would change existing policies of economic development. Afterward, the disappointed pair admitted that the conference "was flawed in both conception and execution" and that "as a result, the new order that is emerging after the Rio de Janeiro conference is identical to the old one."[12]

I agree with this assessment. And I am totally on board with their book, in which they sought to expose the deception. For starters:

> *Throughout this book we show how UNCED has promoted business and industry, rehabilitated nation-states as relevant agents, and eroded the Green movement. We argue that UNCED has boosted precisely the type of industrial development that is destructive for the environment, the planet, and its inhabitants. We see how, as a result of UNCED, the right will get richer, the poor poorer, while more and more of the planet is destroyed in the process.*[13]

In point of fact, UNCED produced a number of other documents in addition to the Agenda 21 treaty. They included the Framework Convention on Climate Change, the Agreement on

---

12 Chatterjee, Pratap and Matthias Finger. *The Earth Brokers*. (Routledge, 1994). Page 1.

13 Chatterjee and Finger. Page 3.

Forest Principles, the Convention on Desertification, and, most importantly for our discussion here, the Convention on Biological Diversity, aka the Biodiversity Convention. According to Finger and Chatterjee, "the biodiversity conference was generally considered the biggest success of the entire UNCED process."[14]

"Biggest success"? Chatterjee and Finger didn't think so. On the contrary, they pointed out the Earth Summit's sleight of hand by boldly declaring:

> *Neither Brundtland, nor the secretariat, nor the governments drafted plans to examine the pitfalls of free trade and industrial development. Instead*, **they wrote up a convention on how to 'develop' the use of biodiversity through patents and biotechnology.**[15] *[Emphasis added.]*

Patents and biotechnology? That's not your grandmother's definition of biodiversity.

The co-authors continued:

> *The convention implicitly equates the diversity of life — animals and plants — to the diversity of genetic codes, for which read genetic resources. By doing so,* **diversity becomes something that modern science can manipulate.** *Finally, the convention promotes biotechnology as being 'essential for the conservation and sustainable use of biodiversity.'*[16] *[Emphasis added.]*

Then, Chatterjee and Finger let the proverbial cat out of the bag:

> *The main stake raised by the Biodiversity Convention is the issue* **of ownership and control over biological diversity.** *[. . .] [T]he major concern was protecting the* **pharmaceutical and emerging biotechnology industries.**[17] **[Emphasis added.]**

---

14 Chatterjee and Finger. Page 42.
15 Chatterjee and Finger. Page 171.
16 Chatterjee and Finger. Page 43.
17 Chatterjee and Finger. Page 43.

Note carefully that ownership and control over genes was not treated as a side issue or regarded as a minor stake. ***It was THE MAIN ISSUE and THE MAIN STAKE!***

Note also that the main actors were the pharmaceutical and emerging biotechnology industries. These main actors are meant to own, exploit, and control genetic resources through genetic engineering performed by the biotech companies.

For nearly thirty years, the Earth Summit's definition of "biodiversity" was well understood by globalists—and by their two lone dissenters—but was virtually undetected by and even indiscernible to us common folks. That is, until the Great Panic of 2020 hit. Then, all of a sudden, what the Trilateralists and their ilk mean by "biodiversity" became all too apparent to us and impossible for us to ignore.

In hindsight, the globalists' decades-old designs for controlling all life forms are crystal clear.

We no longer have to wonder why Monsanto created a global monopoly on genetically modified seeds, claims ownership over everything it touches, and enforces royalty payments for every seed germinated, everywhere.

We no longer have to wonder why insects are being genetically modified, leading skeptical scientists to write papers like "Genetically modified insects could disrupt international food trade."

We no longer have to wonder why animals are being genetically modified—made into transgenic cattle and swine and goats.

Is it therefore any wonder what pharmaceutical and biotech companies are doing to humans? Indeed, why should we be aghast at Big Pharma's attempt to inject us all with an experimental drug containing synthetic, gene-edited mRNA that causes spike proteins to be manufactured by our bodies? (India has recently released a comparable DNA-based vaccine that leapfrogs the mRNA process.)

What is especially disconcerting is that the genetic engineering of all life forms has been happening right under our noses, and all the while our attention has been focused elsewhere. Whatever we imagined were the key issues[18] of Agenda 21 and the 2030 Agenda and the Biodiversity Convention and the Sustainable Development Goals (SDGs) have been real issues, yes, but they were never *THE MAIN ISSUE.*

Rather, **the main issue was and is the takeover of all genetic material on earth.**

Put another way: Ever since DNA was discovered, the primary aim of technocrats and transhumanists has been the takeover of all genetic material on earth. It took the pandemic for this global blueprint to be finally, completely, appallingly exposed.

It is perfectly understandable why the whole transhumanist movement has jumped all over the genetically modified human meme. Historically, transhumanism was just a "lost-in-space" metaphysical philosophy that sought to take control over man's evolution, escape death, and achieve immortality. Today, transhumanism's holy grail has finally appeared: **Hack the human genome to create Humans 2.0.**

Alas, the holy grail of transhumanism is being sought by the modern-day knights of the World Economic Forum, who see the WEF as the great and only savior of the world. A January 2021 article by the European Academy on Religion and Society described the WEF's transhumanist vision this way:

> *While most of humanity is still in the middle of the coronavirus crisis, the highly influential members of the World Economic Forum have a plan for what should come next. It is called 'The Great Reset', and* **it envisions a truly 'transhumanist' future for us all.**[19] *[Emphasis added.]*

To recap thus far, the term "biodiversity" was redefined in 1992 to mean the manipulation of genetic codes. Starting at UNCED that year, genes became something to be exploited, en-

---

18 Agenda 21 called for egregious land use policies, reduction or elimination of property rights, and environmental programs that conflicted with capitalism and free market economics. Those, we imagined, were the key issues. They turned out to be minor distractions compared to the main issue described on this page.

19 "Coronavirus and the transhuman future." EARS. 13 January 2021. https://europeanacademyofreligionandsociety.com/news/coronavirus-and-the-transhuman-future

gineered, and used more efficiently and profitably than they are used in their natural state.

Once I learned what this adulteration of biodiversity looked like, I began to see it in everything I read, starting with MacNeill and Brundtland's 1987 report-now-book, "Our Common Future":

> *The diversity of species is necessary for the normal functioning of ecosystems and the biosphere as a whole.* **The genetic material in wild species contributes billions of dollars yearly to the world economy** *in the form of improved crop species, new drugs and medicines, and raw materials for industry."*[20] *[Emphasis added.]*

The development of biodiversity in specific ways comes through in their Chapter 6, "Species and Ecosystems: Resources for Development":

> **Species and their genetic materials promise to play an expanding role** *in development, and a powerful economic rationale is emerging to bolster the ethical, aesthetic, and scientific case for preserving them. The genetic variability and germplasm material of species make contributions to agriculture, medicine, and industry worth many billions of dollars per year. [. . .] If nations can ensure the survival of species, the world can look forward to new and improved foods, new drugs and medicines, and new raw materials for industry.*[21] *[Emphasis added.]*

Further on in "Our Common Future," MacNeill reasons:

> *Vast stocks of biological diversity are in danger of disappearing just as* **science is learning how to exploit genetic variability through the advances of genetic engineering**. *[. . .] It would be grim irony indeed if just as new genetic engineering techniques begin to let us peer into life's diversity and* **use genes more efficiently to better human con-**

20 MacNeill, James and Gro Harlem Brundtland et al. "Our Common Future." (Oxford University Press. May 21, 1987). Page 13.
Note: What began as a report by the 1983 Brundtland Commission became a paperback book published by the World Commission on Environment and Development in 1987.
21 MacNeill and Brundtland. Page 147.

> **ditions**, *we looked and found this treasure sadly depleted.*[22] *[Emphasis added.]*

I have also looked at how official UN documents have treated the subject of biodiversity.

In the same year as the 1992 UNCED conference, the World Resources Institute (WRI) and the World Conservation Union (IUCN) and the United Nations Environment Programme (UNEP) published a book for policymakers entitled *Global Biodiversity Strategy: Guidelines for Action to Save, Study, and Use Earth's Biotic Wealth Sustainably and Equitably.*[23]

This book presented the same themes featured in "Our Common Future" but handled them with extra-sensitivity so as to win the Third World's participation. For instance, it promised that all originating countries would receive a royalty revenue stream from the anticipated new revenues generated by the biotech companies.

Similarly, it expressed an interest in ensuring that Intellectual Property Rights (IPR) would be honored. Under the subtitle, "Promote recognition of the value of local knowledge and genetic resources and affirm local peoples' rights," the guidelines note:

> *Any collection agreements should reflect the concepts of just compensation and accountability, and codes of conduct should apply to genetic resource collectors, anthropologists, or other researchers studying local peoples or local resource management. In some cases, contracts may be needed to ensure the return of royalties or other benefits to local communities or individuals.*[24]

Elsewhere it lures resource-rich countries with the inviting statement: "**Since biotechnology depends on biodiversity for**

---

22 MacNeill and Brundtland. Pages 149–150.

23 World Resources Institute (WRI), World Conservation Union (IUCN), United Nations Environment Programme (UNEP). *Global Biodiversity Strategy: Guidelines for Action to Save, Study, and Use Earth's Biotic Wealth Sustainably and Equitably*. World Resources Institute. February 29, 1992. Page 1.

24 WRI, IUCN, UNEP. Page 94.

**its raw material, the value of genetic resources will grow with the industry.**"[25] [Emphasis added.]

## Definition Change: The Post-2020 Global Biodiversity Framework

In the same way that Agenda 21 of 1992 was updated with the 2030 Agenda in 2015, so is the Global Biodiversity Convention of 1992 currently being refined by the Post-2020 Global Biodiversity Framework. Since August 2019, an open-ended working group has been busy creating the various elements of the framework, which is to be finished in December 2022.

Because biotechnology and genetic science have progressed so rapidly over the last twenty-five years, the once-used term "genetic resources" is now deemed unsuitable and is being replaced going forward with the phrase **"digital sequence information on genetic resources."**

The National Human Genome Research Institute describes the concept of "digital sequencing" this way:

> *Sequencing DNA means determining the order of the four chemical building blocks — called "bases" — that make up the DNA molecule. The sequence tells scientists the kind of genetic information that is carried in a particular DNA segment. For example, scientists can use sequence information to determine which stretches of DNA contain genes and which stretches carry regulatory instructions, turning genes on or off. In addition, and importantly, sequence data can highlight changes in a gene that may cause disease.*
>
> *In the DNA double helix, the four chemical bases always bond with the same partner to form "base pairs." Adenine (A) always pairs with thymine (T); cytosine (C) always pairs with guanine (G). This pairing is the basis for the mechanism by which DNA molecules are copied when cells divide, and the pairing also underlies the methods by which most DNA sequencing experiments are done. The human genome contains*

25 WRI, IUCN, UNEP. Page 43.

*about 3 billion base pairs that spell out the instructions for making and maintaining a human being.*[26]

All life forms on earth have DNA that can be sequenced and fed into a computer for storage, retrieval, and analysis. Synthetic biology, too, has DNA that can be sequenced—reengineered in ways that do not occur in nature—supposedly for the sake of the environment's "improvement" and "wellbeing."

Once I became familiar with the terms employed in this field, I was able to understand the dense and arcane but clearly consequential Report of the Open-Ended Working Group on the Post-2020 Global Biodiversity Framework on its Third Meeting (23 August–3 September 2021):

*[The working group] recognizes the intrinsic relation between genetic resources and digital sequence information on genetic resources, as well as the scope of bioinformatic tools in the design and creation of new digital sequence information on genetic resources elements that are created artificially; that digital sequence information on genetic resources are not genetic resources as defined in the Convention on Biological Diversity (1992); that access to and utilization of digital sequence information on genetic resources is useful for research relating to conservation and sustainable use of biodiversity, food security, health and other important sectors, including commercial applications resulting in commercial products.*[27]

An item in the report that especially caught my attention—or, shall I say, raised a red flag—reads: "[A]ny approach to address digital sequence information on genetic resources should provide for **the special status of pathogens of pandemic potential.**"[28] [Emphasis added.]

---

26 National Institutes of Health. National Human Genome Research Institute. https://www.genome.gov/about-genomics/fact-sheets/DNA-Sequencing-Fact-Sheet

27 Annex V, Report of the Open-Ended Working Group on the Post-2020 Global Biodiversity Framework on its Third Meeting (Part I). 23 August–3 September 2021. Page 161. https://www.cbd.int/doc/c/187e/84cd/fd4f6bc8f301770a2481b8c8/wg2020-03-05-en.pdf

28 Annex V. Page 161.

It would be incorrect to say that changing the definitions, meanings, and intent of words is a trivial matter. No, we're not talking minor details here. If, for example, you were to read the entire document, you would notice that the phrase "digital sequence information on genetic resources" is used 167 times in its entire 167 pages. That's a big deal!

So, yes, the Post-2020 Global Biodiversity Framework is a major doctrine and is a sea change that opens wide the opportunity for the biotech industry to meddle with all life systems on earth with the goal of making them more "sustainable." Importantly, it establishes that literally all species of life are to be digitally sequenced, placed in a database, recognized as a global common asset, and made available for "licensing" by biotech companies.

## The National Biotechnology and Biomanufacturing Initiative

On September 12, 2022, President Joe Biden signed a stunning Executive Order called the National Biotechnology and Biomanufacturing Initiative. (Its formal title is "Advancing Biotechnology and Biomanufacturing Innovation for Sustainable, Safe and Secure American Bioeconomy.")

The EO is truly tectonic in that it aligns all federal government agencies and mandates that they "coordinate a whole-of-government approach to advance biotechnology and biomanufacturing [. . .] to help us achieve our societal goals."[29]

"Our societal goals"? What "societal goals," pray tell, Mr. President? That phrase is used no less than *six* times. Section 8 tells us that the "societal goals" are identified in Section 3. But, upon examination, we see in Section 3 only self-referential goals that order agencies to create reports to submit to higher levels. For instance, Section 3(v) states that its purpose is "to address the societal goals identified in this section."[30]

But the only goals mentioned in Section 3(v) have to do with the creation of reports.

---

29 Biden, President Joe. National Biotechnology and Biomanufacturing Initiative. White House. September 12, 2022. Section 1.
30 Biden. Section 3(v).

Section 3(i) is apparently one of those report-creation goals:

> *The Secretary of Health and Human Services (HHS), in consultation with the heads of appropriate agencies as determined by the Secretary,* **shall submit a report** *assessing how to use biotechnology and biomanufacturing to achieve medical breakthroughs, reduce the overall burden of disease, and improve health outcomes.*[31] *[Emphasis added.]*

If "our societal goals" are to submit reports, what kind of reports are we talking about? Well, Section 1 specifies that biotechnology is to be used in areas such as "health, climate change and energy, food and agricultural innovation, resilient supply chains, and cross-cutting scientific advances." Obviously, then, the reports would cover those subjects.

The real goal of Biden's EO is contained in its introduction. In light of what we've been talking about throughout this chapter of my book, the real goal shouldn't be a total surprise to you. It reads:

> **We need to develop genetic engineering technologies and techniques to be able to write circuitry for cells and predictably program biology in the same way in which we write software and program computers;** *unlock the power of biological data, including through computing tools and artificial intelligence; and advance the science of scale-up production while reducing the obstacles for commercialization so that innovative technologies and products can reach markets faster.*[32] *[Emphasis added.]*

The introduction also specifies that federal investment is to flood into "key research and development areas of biotechnology and biomanufacturing."

Does the EO hint at what those "key research and development areas" are? No.

Section 3(v) neatly ties those unknown goals to our societal goals and commands the Director of the National Science Foundation to "submit a report identifying high-priority fundamental

31 Biden. Section 3(i).
32 Biden. Section 1.

and use-inspired basic research goals to advance biotechnology and biomanufacturing and to address the societal goals identified in this section."[33]

Are my fellow Americans getting the idea that all this endless genetic modification will be paid for with truckloads of *your* taxpayer money?

By the way, who is going to be capable of holding the new jobs created in the biotechnology sector? Are there enough highly trained, science-savvy, skilled workers to fill all the positions this EO is opening up? Never fear: Section 7(a), "Biotechnology and Biomanufacturing Workforce," solves this problem:

> *The United States Government shall expand training and education opportunities for all Americans in biotechnology and biomanufacturing.*[34]

Considering the EO is a "whole-of-government" initiative, it's no surprise that several agencies are included in the training and education aspect of the scheme:

> *To support this objective, within 200 days of the date of this order, the Secretary of Commerce, the Secretary of Labor, the Secretary of Education, the APDP, the Director of OSTP, and the Director of NSF shall produce and make publicly available a plan to coordinate and use relevant Federal education and training programs, while also recommending new efforts to promote multi-disciplinary education programs.*[35]

There's something for everyone here—even international entities. Section 12 orders the Department of State to engage "international partners" of all types to "enhance cooperation, including joint research projects and expert exchanges, on biotechnology R&D, especially in genomics" and to "work to promote the open sharing of scientific data, including genetic sequence data."

33 Biden. Section 3(v).
34 Biden. Section 7(a).
35 Biden. Section 7(a).

Now, lest a single U.S. citizen still have an ounce of skepticism about this massive national investment in biotechnology, the EO puts all doubt to rest in its "Definitions" section:

> *The term "key R&D areas" includes fundamental R&D of emerging biotechnologies, including engineering biology; predictive engineering of complex biological systems, including the designing, building, testing, and modeling of entire living cells, cell components, or cellular systems; quantitative and theory-driven multi-disciplinary research to maximize convergence with other enabling technologies; and regulatory science, including the development of new information, criteria, tools, models, and approaches to inform and assist regulatory decision-making. These R&D priorities should be coupled with advances in predictive modeling, data analytics, artificial intelligence, bioinformatics, high-performance and other advanced computing systems, metrology and data-driven standards, and other non-life science enabling technologies. Section 13(i)*[36]

> *The term "life sciences" means all sciences that study or use living organisms, viruses, or their products, including all disciplines of biology and all applications of the biological sciences (including biotechnology, genomics, proteomics, bioinformatics, and pharmaceutical and biomedical research and techniques), but excluding scientific studies associated with radioactive materials or toxic chemicals that are not of biological origin or synthetic analogues of toxins. Section 13(p)*[37]

In sum, Biden's National Biotechnology and Biomanufacturing Initiative is a complete capitulation by the United States federal government to the worldwide forces of transhumanism: Big Pharma, biotech players, and the entire cabal of transhumanists who seek to create Humanity 2.0 by changing humans' genetic structure.

And now for a sobering question: Are today's technocrats and transhumanists determined to spawn a superior "master race"? It would seem so. Adolf Hitler had a similar plan in the 1930s

36 Biden. Section 13(i).
37 Biden. Section 13(p).

but was without the genetic editing tools to execute it peacefully. Thus, he sought to cleanse the gene pool by performing ghastly sterilization and other surgical experiments on whomever he deemed unworthy or unfit to live or to procreate.

Of course, the eugenics movement was flourishing in the United States even before WWII. By 1945, eugenics was routinely practiced in California through sterilization of both men and women. This writer was adopted into the Wood family after my adoptive mother was forcibly sterilized at age 17 because her older brother was supposedly mentally retarded. Later in life, it was discovered that this brother was not genetically retarded at all, but, rather, had been oxygen-deprived when the umbilical cord was wrapped around his neck during his breech birth. The law supporting California's outrageous eugenics movement was not overturned until 1979!

Unfortunately, the modern equivalent of genetic engineering, masked by the euphemism "biodiversity," is nothing more than a continuation and expansion of that old eugenics preaching and practice. It should be recognized as such before being tossed back into the flames of Hades from whence it came and where it deserves to stay.

# CHAPTER 9

# Who's Driving This Train?

*If you board the wrong train, it is no use running along the corridor in the other direction.* — Dietrich Bonhoeffer

There are two common misconceptions held by those who oppose globalism. The first misconception is that there is a tiny, identifiable syndicate of banking families who have for centuries run the world with unchecked, tyrannical power. The second misconception is that there is a large, labyrinth network of secret societies that have been running the world behind the scenes with unchecked, tyrannical power.

"They" are the culprits causing all our troubles. When taxes rise, "they" are solely responsible. When the stock market tanks, "they" are to blame. Of course, no one really knows who "they" are, so a few convenient figureheads, whether individuals or organizations, are often made the scapegoats.

Depending on the accuser's political ideology and philosophical bent, the scapegoats could be the Rothschilds or the Rockefellers, a reigning king or queen, the incumbent Russian or US President, the conservative Koch Family Foundations or the liberal Carnegie Foundation. Regardless of which "they" is being impugned, though, the accuser's finger rarely points to the *real* power structure. Many members of the ruling class who constitute the *real* power structure remain hidden from view, unsought out—or purposely ignored—by the establishment news media and orthodox historians, and thus unexposed and unknown to most of us.

All of these misconceptions are understandable, if only because whenever things go wrong, we humans have a burning need to assign blame! Globalists take advantage of that desire and, through sleight-of-hand tactics and out-and-out lies, keep us focused on false assumptions and looking in all the wrong places.

This writer has never charged all large corporations with being guilty of initiating and perpetuating globalization. There are many big businesses, even some banks and investment firms, led by moral, ethical, good-hearted men and women. Just because a company's operations in some way brush up against globalism doesn't mean its management or employees are evil.

However, every bit of my forty-five years of research has underscored the fact that there exists a relatively small yet diverse group of global players who have been the principle planners and instigators of globalization for many decades. The primary driver of this "clique" is *greed*. The secondary motive is *lust for power*. A third force, which drives many academics—who are the unrecognized key to globalism's success—is thirst for *professional recognition, acceptance,* and *grants*—all subtle forms of egoism and lust for power.

I have also found it important to recognize that most core globalists fully understand that their aims, ambitions, agendas, and actions are self-centered and cruelly destructive to humanity—to all species of life. They are *not* dimwitted, ignorant, misinformed, naïve, or well-intentioned.

May I pause here to make clear that the so-called "elite" are nothing more than elit*ists* who view themselves as vastly superior in every way to the rest of the human race. In fact, they are self-deluded snobs whose actions betray them as the very dregs of the earth, *not* the saviors of the world.

These global elitists, as we will call them, march in three columns: Corporate, Political, Academic. Each column is essential and is dependent upon the other two columns. For the sake of clarity, these three capitalized names will be employed in this chapter to describe and distinguish their respective roles in the push toward globalization and one world government.

Usually Corporate creates the goals for globalization. To achieve them, Corporate invites foundations to give direct grants to Academic, which in turn churns out studies and white papers that are slanted in a way that justifies Corporate's objectives. Next, Political sells Academic's arguments to the public. If necessary, Political changes laws to accommodate Corporate—that is, to facilitate Corporate's ability to get what it wants.

An important ancillary player in the globalization game is the news media, which we'll call Press. The purpose of Press is to create lines of communication and filter information from Corporate, Academic, and Political to the public. Press is not a fourth column. Its role is reflective rather than causative. That said, we will discover that Press is dominated by members of Corporate, Political, and Academic who sit on the various boards of directors of major Press organizations.

Now, imagine two neighboring countries that were once at peace with each other. Russia and Ukraine will do. Next, imagine two pranksters, unknown to each other and living anywhere in today's high-tech world, who simultaneously decide to run ads in local Ukraine newspapers. The ads announce an upcoming flash mob rumble at a certain spot in the Ukraine countryside. It'll be a BYOW (bring your own weapons) blowout, proclaim the two pranksters' ads. There will be no generals, no military strategists, no colonels in charge of brigades and divisions. Everyone is invited to show up and duke it out in a free-for-all until a winner emerges, and then it's winner take all.

This is exactly how global elitists want you to think about the mess the world is in right now. No single entity, whether a nation or an NGO, a political party or a powerful person, is behind the turmoil, they assert. Nor, they insist, is the chaos the result of a conspiracy carried out by combined forces. Rather, it's sheer coincidence. Accidental. Unforeseeable. Unpredictable.

Is that true? Certainly not! It is plain that *someone* must be driving this train to rack and ruin. Or, more logically, *several someones* have banded together to plot the train's collision course.

But here's the rub. Whenever any of us speculates as to who that *someone* or those *someones* might be, we're branded a "conspiracy theorist" even before we finish the first sentence. My, how clever of the would-be power brokers to have put in place a derogatory term that acts as an automatic defense mechanism, shielding their identity.

Whoever "they" are, "they" would have us "conspiracy theorists" believe that the world is spinning out of control with *no one* at the helm. That the world stage is just a giant pinball arcade game with balls bouncing around at random. And that we are ignorant and stupid and crazy for suggesting that anyone has devious designs to take complete control of us.

Well, we aren't ignorant, and we aren't stupid, and we aren't crazy. This chapter will establish our sanity. It will prove, to a degree, that the world is being propelled down the train tracks at the hands of master engineers (the "power elitists") and, in train speak, conductors (the "operators" who implement the engineers' scheme for the train's destination).

Specifically, in this chapter we will show how to ferret out the identities of both the elitists and their operators, how to ascertain their operations, and how to recognize the traits of any and all perpetrators of globalist crimes against humanity.

To this end, I will present two reliable methods of discovery: the narrative and network analysis.

## Behold, the Narrative

Let us now be sleuths in search of the narrative. Before our hunt begins, we need to understand that whoever controls the narrative potentially controls everything and everyone in the world. That's why we must first determine what the narrative is and then discover who concocted it. When we know both, we'll be close to finding the actual controllers.

Merriam-Webster defines "narrative" simply and accurately: "a way of presenting or understanding a situation or series of events that reflects and promotes a particular point of view or set of values."[1]

There are all kinds of narratives. Personal narratives. Fictional narratives. Historical narratives. Narratives can be told in either prose or poetry. We should distinguish between narratives and mere descriptions of events or states of being, for a description is not a narrative. Neither is simple storytelling. A narrative can refer to the past, the present, or the future and in some cases combines points in time.

For our purposes here, a narrative starts with a set of values and a particular point of view. From there, it spins events that might occur or that must occur. These events lead to a desired or anticipated outcome. Various narratives impact us to a lesser or greater degree. Some are of minor import and have little effect on society. Others are of larger import and have bigger repercussions. Still others are giant—literally worldwide—in scope. One narrative may be nothing more than pipe dream that never amounts to anything, while another may prove supremely successful in driving societal outcomes.

Why are narratives so intrinsically powerful? I believe it is because they, like scary stories, are designed to make us afraid and are told to us in our vulnerable moments. Narratives could also be compared to bedtime tales told to children when they're sleepy—not fully awake or alert. It stands to reason, therefore, that we can get easily wrapped up in a narrative when our critical thinking skills are at a low ebb or are otherwise limited.

Providing an example of a successful narrative here might be helpful.

Say you want to purchase a new car. You visit an auto dealership that sells the makes and models you like. You tell the salesman what you're looking for. Having been trained in the art of manipulating your emotions—your desires and dreams, your weaknesses and worries—he expertly crafts a personalized narrative for you. That narrative will ultimately determine whether or not you buy a car from him.

1 Merriam-Webster Dictionary. https://www.merriam-webster.com/dictionary/narrative

From the salesman's embellished, elaborate description of the exact car he steers you to, you conjure up visions of happily driving it on your daily errands or loading its spacious trunk with camping gear for your family vacation. You feel virtuous about the money you'll be saving on gasoline and the carbon emissions you'll be reducing.

Once he has helped you implant those vivid images in your mind, the salesman lays out the steps that need to happen before you can become the proud owner of that perfect car: Take a test drive, secure pre-approved credit, make a small down payment, order personalized plates, and so on. One by one, you tick off each step—first mentally, then physically. Having been hooked by his hypnotic narrative, you leave the lot driving the new car of your dreams. The salesman, propagandist that he is, has earned his commission.

We'll now switch from that personal narrative to a global one. In 2022, the World Economic Forum (WEF) published *The Great Narrative* by Klaus Schwab and Thierry Malleret (both members of Academic). In the Foreword, the authors assure readers, "[O]ur views and convictions are informed by our humanistic values." Then, in the Introduction, they explain the problem their book tackles: "A new world is now emerging, the contours of which will largely be defined by the narratives that evolve to inform and construct the way forward."

Beneath that flowery, unspecific language, the authors seem to be saying: "We're going to present you with an agenda that is designed to transform the world as you know it. In order to make our ideas palatable and persuade the majority of you to embrace them, we will weave one consistent, seamless narrative."

The implication is that their book must eliminate any and all narratives that contradict its "great narrative." Those contra-narratives, say Schwab and Malleret, take the form of "falsehoods, misinformation, disinformation and conspiracies." They elaborate:

> *[N]arratives provide the context in which the facts we observe can be interpreted, understood and acted upon. [. . .]*

> *[Narratives] "shape our perceptions, which in turn form our realities and end up influencing our choices and actions. [. . .] [T]hey are how we find meaning in life.*[2]

One aspect of the "great narrative" that the co-authors single out for comment is man-made global warming. They contend: "It is unequivocal that human influence has warmed the atmosphere, ocean, and land. The data makes this plain." *No! The data in no way "makes this plain"!* Such a statement is factually untrue, thus unprovable. Pretending otherwise, Schwab and Malleret offer up a solution to the false problem they cite—namely, decarbonization of the world:

> *There will never be real incentive to decarbonize without a price being put on carbon dioxide emissions around the world. Without it, governments, companies, and consumers will simply not change their behavior in volume and on a scale that matters.*[3]

The gargantuan undertaking of decarbonization is estimated to cost upwards of $300 trillion, or roughly $38,000 for every man, woman, and child on earth. What could possibly account for, much less justify, such exorbitant spending? Schwab and Malleret present two pretexts:

> *First, the move to a zero-carbon global economy will necessitate the replacement of most parts of the energy infrastructure. Second, this in turn will require the development of new carbon-removal technologies that don't (or barely) exist today.*[4]

Global warming, rebranded "climate change," is only one slice of their Great Narrative. But the WEF will be buttering that slice with layers of lies in coming years, so we had best remember its main elements:

- A dire situation (global warming) exists that demands immediate action

---

2 Schwab, Klaus and Thierry Malleret. *The Great Narrative*. (Forum Publishing. 2022). Preface and Introduction.
3 Schwab and Malleret. Kindle version. 22%.
4 Schwab and Malleret. 22%.

- The authors' applied value system is the religion of humanism[5]
- The event (decarbonization) has a minimum price tag of $300 trillion, and that doesn't count other costly technological moves that must be made
- The outcome is zero-carbon global economy
- A self-actuating defense is established to quash any anti-narrative resistance

Once this or any other globalist narrative is constructed, its job is to claim authority and gain an audience. Because Press is already dominated by Corporate—the instigators of the narrative—attracting the audience is a piece of cake. The message gets blasted out, over and over, until it becomes widely normalized within the public's consciousness. Meanwhile, the message tailored to Corporate's "players," who are part of the $300 trillion spending bonanza, is unambiguous: Do everything to support the narrative and do nothing to harm it. For Corporate and Political, the message is spend, spend, spend. For Press and Big Tech, the message is censor, censor, censor.

The World Economic Forum has roughly 1,000 members who represent the largest corporations in the world. It also has a tight, symbiotic relationship with the United Nations and therefore with the UN's NGOs and massive propaganda machine. As the WEF narrative goes forth, it spontaneously generates dozens if not hundreds or even thousands of localized initiatives. All of them follow the greater narrative toward the stated goal. If anyone deviates from the narrative, their insubordination is easily dealt with on a case-by-case basis.

---

5 According to the American Humanist Association, "Humanism is a progressive philosophy of life that, without theism or other supernatural beliefs, affirms our ability and responsibility to lead ethical lives of personal fulfillment that aspire to the greater good" (https://americanhumanist.org/what-is-humanism/definition-of-humanism). In *Torcasco v. Watkins* (1961), the Supreme Court declared humanism to be a religion. Other court cases reinforce this declaration: *Washington Ethical Society v. District of Columbia,* 101 U.S. Appellate D. C. 371, 249 F 2nd 127 (1957); *Fellowship of Humanity V. County of Alameda,* 153 Cal. App. 2nd 673, 315 P. 2nd 394 (1957); *Jaffree v. Board of School comrs of Mobile County,* 554 F. Supp. 1104, 1129 n. 41 (1983); *Zorach v. Clauson,* 343 U.S. 306, 314 (1952).

I've now summarized how narratives work. A main takeaway is that those who order a narrative to be forged in the first place are the ones responsible for all downline activity. Direct puppet "strings" are not necessary.

## Academic Leads in Creating the Narrative

In the Annex of their book, Schwab and Malleret list fifty individual contributors to *The Great Narrative*. I decided to analyze them based on some simple demographics.

First, I segregated the contributors into six categories: Academic (74%), Press (4%), Finance (4%), Think Tank (14%), Political (2%), and Independent (2%). Academic overwhelmingly generates the narrative, followed by think tanks. At the top of this pyramid are Schwab and Malleret, who both land squarely in Academic. Only one contributor is in any way related to Political, but he comes from the autocratic kingdom of UAE, so he doesn't count. Thus, effectively none of the contributors report to, or have any obligation to, the world populace whose future they are presumptuously deciding.

Next, I considered the geographic distribution of the group. The fifty contributors hail from the US (57%), the UK (12%), China (14%), Russia (2%), Japan (7%), Germany (2%), India (2%), Brazil (2%), and the UAE (2%). As we can see, after the dominant US, China is the biggest contributor to the Great Narrative. Add to this list Schwab from Germany and Malleret from France.

My analysis led me to some interesting insights. Schwab bills himself as the consummate internationalist, I noticed. He claims to have consensus backing from the globe's four corners. Yet the vast majority of influential academics who peddle Schwab's narrative live in only one country: the United States. Furthermore, they represent a paltry nine institutions—namely: University of Pennsylvania; University of California, San Diego; University of California, Berkeley; Hoover Institution at Stanford University; Harvard University; City University of New York; University of Chicago; Princeton University; Columbia University; Dartmouth College; and Georgetown University.

Schwab brags about reimagining the world to secure "the future we want," as if he is such a prepossessing pied piper. But his influence in the real world is as narrow as a blade of grass. How is it, then, that he gets away with telling so many lies and making so many baseless assumptions? It is the power of the narrative Schwab spins so deftly that impels easily hypnotized followers to board his globalist train.

## Hierarchy of Narratives Big and Small

There are many other narratives besides Schwab and Malleret's Great Narrative that are alive and actively at work in the world today. Some are global, others national or regional or local. Certain narratives are for public consumption; others are meant for internal use only, by the elitists themselves. The various purposes of these carefully constructed narratives are never at odds with each other. If anything, they overlap, though each serves a unique purpose. Once we understand how to differentiate between the running narratives, we can separate them, like wheat from chaff. We can save and store the one, bind and burn the other.

As I showed above, Academic is the primary source of narratives. This is the pattern I have personally observed for more than forty-five years. When top members of Corporate determine what they want to enact or accomplish, they immediately turn projects over to Academic's "experts," who will rationalize and justify Corporate's decisions and deeds.

Such was the case when the Trilateral Commission was inaugurated in 1973. Its influential Corporate founders immediately declared that "interdependence" and a "New International Economic Order" were to become worldwide goals. Within weeks, scholarly articles about those subjects started popping up in globalist journals. Trilaterals took that "scholarship"—and the widespread "agreement" and "consensus" among the authors of these articles—as proof that their goals were the way to go. Talk about a self-reinforcing circle! But make no mistake, the decision did *not* come from the Commission's Academic column. It came from the Corporate column.

The same self-reinforcing, self-congratulatory circle has been pumping out narrative after narrative ever since, both in the low-key Trilateral Commission and in the highly visible World Economic Forum. At every annual meeting of the latter, held in Davos, Switzerland, we can observe the same pattern: Once Academic has laid the intellectual groundwork for Corporate-initiated narratives, second-, third- and fourth-tier globalists step in and claim their own justification for creating supplemental narratives. Unsurprisingly, these derivative narratives are always linked to their WEF/UN/Trilateral origins. For instance, Big Pharma and fake environmentalists (those who tout the fake climate crisis) have distinct narratives peculiar to their industry and their movement, respectively, but both support the larger globalization narrative.

## Behold, the Network

Network analysis[6] is a relatively new discipline that first emerged in the 1950s. When Professor Antony Sutton and I penned *Trilaterals Over Washington* from 1978 to 1981, we applied network analysis with great success to the 300 or so members of the Trilateral Commission. During the process, we collected, via old-fashioned snail-mail, hundreds of annual reports produced by corporations, financial firms, foundations, and think tanks. From them we extracted the names of board members, trustees, principal advisors, senior executives, etc., who were *also* members of the Trilateral Commission. Many of these annual reports included short biographical sketches that revealed other direct connections we could easily verify.

We then created a table containing the names of Trilateral members and their respective organizations. We were primarily looking for people who had multiple associations. For instance, if one Trilateral was a director of three or four major corporations, we considered that very significant. Furthermore, if two Trilaterals were serving on one or more of those same boards, it strongly suggested that we had discovered a key node in a larger network.

6 Chiesi, A.M. "Network Analysis." Science Direct's International Encyclopedia of the Social & Behavioral Sciences. 2001. https://www.sciencedirect.com/topics/social-sciences/network-analysis

After completing the initial tabulation of names and their affiliated organizations, we studied and refined our master list. We saved, though sidelined, the names of Trilaterals who were associated with only one organization. After all, we reasoned, their circles of influence were limited, and we were looking for the widest influencers.

As we sorted the names by organization, the big picture started to emerge. We noticed that a small number of Trilaterals sat on multiple boards and a larger number on only one or two boards. Then we applied cross-tab analysis to see which organizations shared multiple Trilateral members. Although tedious and time-consuming, our project produced valuable insights into the power structure of the Trilateral Commission. More than forty years later, those insights still apply.

The next phase of our research looked at the "philanthropic" foundations on our Trilateral list that were issuing large grants to representatives of Academic. We did not require the recipients of these grants to be members of the Trilateral Commission, although some were. This "grant analysis" simply followed the money flowing from the foundations, so we could see where it went and what kind of research papers it was funding and publishing at Corporate's request.

Again, as with our previous analysis, the work was tedious, but it produced key insights into the money-laundering operation that was necessary to persuade Academic to undergird Corporate's desired narrative. This opaque triangle—Academic, Corporate, and foundations—always included an element of plausible deniability. That is, Trilateral members would say that their involvement was coincidental, not causative; that the studies by Academic were a product of independent intellectual pursuit, not done at the behest of the Commission; and that foundation grants were autonomous, not under the control of board members. Of course, these denials were pure nonsense.

The method of network analysis described here is admittedly subjective, but when applied across a broad spectrum of people and organizations, it reveals objective insights. When, for example, Sutton and I used network analysis to research and write our book, *Trilaterals Over Washington*, the results were gratifying. We were able to completely expose the existence of the power machine and describe how it worked. Most importantly, we brought to light the inner sanctum of the Trilateral Commission—the core members who were directing its entire globalization plan.

Remember, that was in the 1970s. Until then no one had ever conducted a network analysis of the Trilateral Commission. Our book made waves. So much so that it was banned from the B. Dalton bookstore chain. Why? "They" hated being discovered in their true depict, I guess.

Now, let's give "them" and their controlled booksellers a reason to ban *this*—my latest and last—book.

## The Modern Trilateral Commission

Currently, 131 of the 300-odd members of the Trilateral Commission are from North America, most of them in the US, with the remainder in Canada and Mexico. Here is a breakdown by the same categories I chose when analyzing the Schwab/Malleret book: Corporate (47%), Academic (22%), Political (28%), and Press (10%). Clearly, Corporate dominates Trilateral membership. Interestingly, though, the executive leadership of the North American group includes one Academic (Meghan O'Sullivan), one Government (Herminio Mendoza), and one Press (Jeffrey Simpson).

Trilateral members serve on many overlapping boards of directors and advisory positions. Two examples suffice: The Peterson Institute, founded by Trilateral Peter G. Peterson, has sixteen members of the Commission on its board, and the Atlantic Council has nine board members who are Trilaterals.

These connections serve to reinforce the fact that Corporate is at the top of the totem pole yet hides in plain sight behind Academic and Press. Corporate's clever subterfuge is meant to distract us and steer our focus elsewhere—an effective magic trick technique.

## How Academic Is Funded

In what country are the bulk of philanthropic assets located? How much of the philanthropic assets in that country are given away annually? The answers will hardly surprise you: US assets and US giving far-and-away exceed that of any other country.

The table below includes all sources and sizes of philanthropic giving. It demonstrates the proportionate influence of grants that come from the US. It also adds significant weight to the previously mentioned discovery that 57 percent of the editorial contributors to Klaus Schwab's *Great Narrative* come from a mere nine universities in the US. In other words, funding that originates in the US tends to stay in the US. The $80 billion of expenditures by US philanthropic foundations represents 58 percent of the total giving by the top nine nations in the world.

**Philanthropic Assets/Expenditures By Country (Billions)**[7]

| Country | Assets | Expenditures |
|---|---|---|
| *United States* | *$890* | *$80* |
| Netherlands | $108 | $8.1 |
| Germany | $93 | $23 |
| Switzerland | $88 | $2.4 |
| Italy | $87 | $1.4 |
| UK | $84 | $6.0 |
| France | $30 | $10 |
| Turkey | $20 | $2.7 |
| China | $14 | $4.7 |

Whether we're talking Trilaterals or contributors to the Schwab/Malleret book, most individuals labeled "Academic" are found within universities. But a few of them work in non-governmental organizations and think tanks instead of academia. The globalist-minded Council on Foreign Relations, for instance, is

7 McCarthy, Niall. "Where Philanthropy Dollars Are Concentrated." Statista. May 7, 2018. https://www.statista.com/chart/13766/where-philanthropy-dollars-are-concentrated

not a university. It receives grants to write papers that justify globalist ends. The same is true for the Brookings Institution, the Atlantic Council, and the Center for Strategic and International Studies.

## Breaking Down Corporate

There are sixty-two Corporate representatives in the North American membership of the Trilateral Commission. Of them, fifteen, or 24 percent, are from the financial industry. They all work in asset management firms—namely, these thirteen:

- Shield Street Capital
- BMO Capital Markets
- International Capital Strategies
- RBC Capital Markets
- BlackRock Investment Institute
- BlackRock, Inc.
- Graham Holding Company
- Ariel Investments
- O-Corp Investments
- Bridgewater Associates
- CFFI Ventures
- The Carlyle Group
- UBS Group

Some perspective: The world's ten largest asset managers control over $44 trillion; a full seven of them are US investment companies.[8]

Within the financial industry, banks, both commercial and investment, are moderately represented on the Trilateral Commission:

- Bank of America (1 member)
- J.P. Morgan (3 members)
- Goldman Sachs (3 members)
- Lazard Frères Bank (1 member)

Their numbers are sparse today compared with 1980. That is because within the Trilateral Commission a dramatic shift has

8 World's Top Asset Management Firms. ADV Ratings. https://www.advratings.com/top-asset-management-firms

taken place: *Central banks* have replaced commercial and investment banks in number of members. Today, no less than sixteen central banks are represented on the Trilateral Commission. Naturally, they include the US Federal Reserve Bank and the Bank for International Settlements (BIS). The latter, headquartered in Basle, Switzerland, is the central bank to all sixty-three central banks.

With the advent of Central Bank Digital Currencies (CBDCs), which threaten to control the financial system throughout the world, it stands to reason that the entire central bank system is more directly asserting its power and influence these days, both in the Trilateral Commission and elsewhere. (Note: Keep in mind that all central banks are private corporations owned by big banks and not owned by the nations they serve.)

## The Power Elitists vs. the Operators

It goes without saying that many powerful people occupy important places in the Corporate, Political, and Academic spheres. Each person in each sphere plays a necessary role in the larger scheme. But if the above discussion reveals nothing else, it is that Corporate is the dominant group that controls Political and Academic and that the white-hot core of Corporate is the central bankers.

Where would we start our search for the engineers who are driving the train? By now, I hope I've made the answer obvious:

- **Central Banks** — The central banks represent the vast concentration of global money and possess the financial technologies (fintech) that will revolutionize the global economic and financial system.
- **Corporate** — Trilateral Commission members are overwhelmingly related to giant global corporations—among them Boeing, Intel, Google, Lockheed Martin, Alibaba, and Xerox, to name a few.

Once we have identified an individual as a person of interest and slotted him in the proper sphere, whether Corporate, Academic, Political, or Press, the next step is to discover who that individual influences and what other organizations he belongs to.

Take, for instance, the current Director of the Bank for International Settlements, Agustín Carstens. He is a virtually unheard-of central banker from Mexico, yet his decisions now influence every central bank—and indeed the financial system worldwide. We could call Carstens the chief engineer of our train. As such, he is the individual most responsible for establishing and coordinating the CBDC system, which is based on blockchain technology and will eventually be a centralized database of all transactions.

Another example of extended influence is Trilateralist Larry Fink, who presides over BlackRock's nearly $10 trillion in assets under management and its 18,000 employees working in 85 offices in 38 countries. To say that Fink has enormous global reach is an understatement.

When seeking out Corporate movers and shakers, one can comfortably look beyond membership in the Trilateral Commission. I will identity a few non-members to get you started in your search. The first five are power elitists whom I consider the "core." That is, they're among the foremost engineers who steer the globalist train. The last three are non-core, but they are the "operators" who one could say act as conductors on the train, influencing people and policy in their own unique way.

**Bill Gates** — Gates has no direct relationship to the Trilateral Commission, but he is an influential member of Corporate. Through massive donations from his Bill & Melinda Gates Foundation, he has gained enormous influence in the biotech and pharmaceuticals industries as well as in green technologies and education.

**Michael Crow** — Crow, perhaps an unfamiliar name to most readers, has dual roles in Corporate and Academic. He is the president of Arizona State University, a post he has held since 2002. Previously, he was a professor of Science and Technology Policy in the School of International and Public Affairs at Columbia University. More importantly, however, Crow is chairman of the board of In-Q-Tel, the Central Intelligence Agency's venture capital firm. While at ASU, Crow has transformed it into a social impact organization focusing on the UN's Sustainable Development Goals and programs. The progressive template Crow built at ASU has been adopted by hundreds of higher education centers around the world. Using Arizona taxpayer funds, he has pioneered high-tech incubator zones in the state that are friendly to startups. These startups ultimately give Crow first dibs on promising ventures for In-Q-Tel investment. In-Q-Tel has a long history of co-opting the best technology inventions for the CIA and other intelligence agencies of the federal government.

**Peter Thiel** — A self-avowed transhumanist and technocrat, Thiel has an outsized influence over a number of globalist themes. He was a co-founder of PayPal, which he since sold, and the first outside investor in Facebook, where he remains as a member of its board of directors. His very successful data mining company, Palantir, received its first injection of capital from the CIA's venture capital company, In-Q-Tel.

**Elon Musk** — A self-described transhumanist and technocrat like Thiel, Musk is a poster child for Corporate. As a serial entrepreneur, he is transforming the world to electric through Tesla, Inc. and Tesla Energy. In 2016, he co-founded Neuralink to create brain-computer interfaces. When he founded space exploration company SpaceX in 2002, Musk had hopes of eventually colonizing Mars. Since then, SpaceX has launched over 3,500 satellites to form the Starlink network of high-speed 5G access to earth dwellers. Starlink ultimately intends to launch as many as 42,000 satellites.

**Jeff Bezos** — Founder of Amazon and owner of *The Washington Post*, Bezos is, like Musk, a poster child for Corporate. And, like Musk and Thiel, Bezos is both a technocrat and a transhumanist. Other shades of Musk: Bezos wants to conquer outer space and colonize Mars with his Blue Origin exploration company. Even more "out there": Through his Altos Labs, Bezos seeks to master death.

Klaus Schwab — Non-core. Schwab is an influential technocrat and transhumanist, but he is also an Academic. He heads the World Economic Forum, which he founded in 1971 at the suggestion of mentor and fellow Academic Henry Kissinger. Although the

WEF has many members who belong to Corporate, their biggest role is to pay Schwab's salary. Predictably, then, all of Schwab's efforts have been at the behest of Corporate and serve Corporate.

Yuval Noah Harari — Non-core. There is no doubt that Harari is both a technocrat and transhumanist, and he is also an Academic like Schwab. As such, Harari's purpose in the WEF is, like that of all Academic globalists, to justify the policies and actions of Corporate globalists.

Justin Trudeau — Non-core. Put simply and starkly, Trudeau belongs to Political but is a total shill, a puppet on a string, for Corporate.

Again, the purpose of listing these individuals is not to build an exhaustive list but rather to show you *how* to pinpoint other engineers who are driving the train and other operators who are helping the train reach its destination, where, we hope, it will crash and burn—and disappear.

## Conclusion

I have unearthed a reliable and proven process to help you answer the question, "Who's driving this train?" Yes, as I said, it is tedious and time-consuming research. But with a little patience, it can be rewarding. If I had the time to analyze the entire spectrum of globalist players, my guess is that I would come up with a defensible list numbering between 300 and 500.

Such a list would be rich with names of bankers, especially central bankers, but would also include a hefty number of top corporate executives who have risen to positions of influence and a fair share of bought Political globalists.

Such a list would also be dynamic, in the sense that some players will always be falling out of it while others are joining it or rising up in it. Death is a factor for older members. Becoming a billionaire by age 30 is a factor for younger members.

As you build your own list of the real controllers of globalization, you should test and retest your conclusions every year or so. Even if you choose not to build your own list, you can still use these principles to do a spot check on any one individual.

Some of my readers may still wonder why it matters whether we correctly identify the parties responsible for globalization and its multi-pronged attacks on humanity. The answer lies in an ancient military treatise, *The Art of War*, in which legendary Chinese General Sun Tzu wrote: "All warfare is based on deception." This means, to me, that we must see through the globalists' disguises just as we would decipher an enemy's deceptive strategies and tactics in war. For, as Sun Tzu predicted, "If you know the enemy and know yourself, your victory will not stand in doubt."

Not recognizing or understanding our globalist enemies will lead to certain defeat. Thus, whenever you have an opportunity to finger one of these scoundrels, do it!

# CHAPTER 10

# The One World Religion Emerges

*Our Constitution was made only for a moral and religious people. It is wholly inadequate to the government of any other.* – John Adams

Do you have an old three-legged stool that's gathering dust? If so, take a saw and cut off two inches from one of its legs. Then cut four inches off a second leg. Now try to sit on it. Whoa! You have just rendered your stool dysfunctional, useless, worthless.

You get where I'm going with this analogy, right? It's intuitive, isn't it, that a well-functioning society is like a proverbial stool with three legs of equal length. The first leg is an economic system that works. The second leg is a political system that engages citizens and supports the economic system. The third leg is the social component of society. It includes the moral and ethical constituents needed to keep the stool upright and sound.

The social leg usually includes faith-based religions. They tend to provide sufficient personal and moral restraint to keep the entire society from falling apart. In that social leg is also found the essential element of trust. If citizens don't trust the political process and players or the economic system they live under, they will push back in the same way the immune system attacks a poisonous substance that has invaded the body.

To the extent these three legs are in balance with each other, society will function in a reasonable, even harmonious, way.

No two societies in the world are identical. Each has a stool whose three legs "function" in their own unique way. In China we find a highly engineered economic system, an authoritarian political system, and an official religion of atheism, though the government also recognizes Buddhism and Taoism. By contrast, India has a market economy, a parliamentary democracy, and a dominant religion; eighty percent of the population practices Hinduism. Saudi Arabia, meanwhile, is a monarchy with heavy government controls over the economy and over religion; only Islam is allowed to be practiced. America, for its part, is a constitutional republic based on free enterprise. Its religious system is not dictated by the state but is heavily weighted toward Christianity. It is also founded on a Judeo/Christian system of values and morality.

So, though these four countries are vastly different from one another, they have all figured out how to make things work with their own version of a three-legged stool. Granted, some of the stools are pretty banged up, and some of their legs are uneven, but each society moves forward, nonetheless.

## America Started Well

John Adams was one of the most important and influential figures among America's founding fathers. He was a co-author of the Declaration of Independence in 1776 and served as vice president under George Washington, then as president from 1797 through 1801. Adams understood the three-legged principle, as evidenced by his third State of the Union address in 1799:

> *The flattering prospects of abundance from the labors of the people by land and by sea; the prosperity of our extended commerce, notwithstanding interruptions occasioned by the belligerent state of a great part of the world; the return of health, industry, and trade to those cities which have lately been afflicted with disease, and the various and inestimable advantages, civil and religious, which, secured under our happy frame of government, are continued to us unimpaired, demand of the whole American people sincere thanks to a*

*benevolent Deity for the merciful dispensations of His providence.*[1] *[Emphasis added.]*

This third leg, often dismissed as inconsequential or irrelevant, was well understood by the great twentieth-century Christian philosopher C. S. Lewis (1898–1963). He chose a word, Tao,[2] to describe "Natural Law or Traditional Morality or the First Principles of Practical Reason or the First Platitudes" that are among a series of possible systems of values. Of Tao he concluded, "It is the sole source of all value judgments" and "if it is rejected, all value is rejected." And he added, "[T]he rebellion of new ideologies against the Tao is a rebellion of the branches against the tree."[3]

Another Christian philosopher, Francis Schaeffer (1912–1984), came to essentially the same conclusion as Lewis when he predicted the result of abandoning the "Christian consensus" in modern society. The moral constraint that was afforded by this consensus but is now lost, Schaeffer said, will result in a vacuum. And that vacuum will be filled, he warned, by an authoritarian, technocratic elite that enforces an external form of constraint to control human and societal behavior.

Was Schaeffer ever right. The societal attack brought on by technocracy and transhumanism is being directed at all three legs of our societal stool: political, economic, and spiritual. It's no wonder that the social fabric in the United States, in particular, is so frayed. Americans' trust in the political system is at an all-time low. The free market economic system is disintegrating as technocracy displaces its core principles. Judeo/Christian morality has been mercilessly attacked, ridiculed, and marginalized. All the moral teachings and constraints associated with the Bible and other philosophical writings have been discarded. The authoritarian, technocratic elite Schaeffer warned about is boldly asserting itself and micromanaging everything on earth.

---

1 John Adams' Third State of the Union Address. Wikisource. https://en.wikisource.org/wiki/John_Adams%27_Third_State_of_the_Union_Address

2 "Tao" is a misleading word in today's language, because the concept no longer pertains to Eastern religions. At the time C. S. Lewis wrote, Tao was a more acceptable word that simply referred to the moral structure of society.

3 Lewis, C. S. *The Abolition of Man*. (Harper Collins, 1944). Pages 43–44.

Just because the objects of traditional worship have been removed from our view does not mean that modern man has nothing to worship. If history shows us anything, it is that mankind has always been resourceful at finding objects to idolize, including rocks, carved statues, images, icons, and even other human beings. In today's scientific revolution, however, all of those physical objects are relics of a bygone era. Keep reading to see what I mean.

## Dataism

The philosophy of Dataism was first propounded in 2013 by David Brooks in a *New York Times* article:

> *If you asked me to describe the rising philosophy of the day, I'd say it is data-ism. We now have the ability to gather huge amounts of data. This ability seems to carry with it certain cultural assumptions — that everything that can be measured should be measured; that data is a transparent and reliable lens that allows us to filter out emotionalism and ideology; that data will help us do remarkable things — like foretell the future.*[4]

The idea apparently incubated for a couple of years until being aggressively picked up by Yuval Noah Harari, an Israeli professor of history and principal advisor to the World Economic Forum.

In his book, *Homo Deus: A Brief History of Tomorrow*—published in Hebrew in 2015 and in English in 2016—Harari presented Dataism as a new form of religion whose doctrine and discipline (my words) give meaning to life. His basic concept is that the material universe is made up of and depends on flows of data. Thus, to know more about the universe, we must tap into that data and examine it, understand it, even modify it when it suits our purposes. The idea, professed by both Brooks and Harari, that data can help us "foretell the future" is purely metaphysical and seems to have sprung from Henri de Saint-Simon's well-known argument that scientists and engineers can "predict the future."

---

4 Brooks, David. "The Philosophy of Data." The New York Times. February 4, 2013. https://www.nytimes.com/2013/02/05/opinion/brooks-the-philosophy-of-data.html

Technocracy and transhumanism are well-fitted for Dataism. Both technocrats and transhumanists lust for data. No level of data is too deep for them to explore. In fact, one of their mutual goals is to gather all the data in the universe in order to understand the place, purpose, principle, and process of everything, from the stars, sun and moon down to the subatomic particles in the human body.

But what's the point of harvesting every last piece of information that exists? Harari's explanation of Dataism's objective is explicit:

> *Now, a fresh shift is taking place. Just as divine authority was legitimised by religious mythologies, and human authority was legitimised by humanist ideologies, so high-tech gurus and Silicon Valley prophets are creating a new universal narrative that legitimises the authority of algorithms and Big Data. This novel creed may be called "Dataism". In its extreme form, proponents of the Dataist worldview perceive the entire universe as a flow of data, see organisms as little more than biochemical algorithms and believe that humanity's cosmic vocation is to create an all-encompassing data-processing system — and then merge into it.*[5] *[Emphasis added.]*

Does he mean we will literally merge our bodies and minds with machines? Yes. In a sense, we already *are* intertwined. For, according to Harari, humans are all connected to data—to "tiny chips inside a giant system that nobody really understands."

And, oh, by the way, "no one needs to understand," Harari hastens to add. No one, that is, *except* the ruling technocrats and transhumanists, whose mission it is to control the world! As for us common folk, we don't have to comprehend how Dataism works. In fact, they'd rather we *not* know.

Regardless, we will surely be sucked into Dataism anyway. As Harari puts it:

> *Just as free-market capitalists believe in the invisible hand of the market, so Dataists believe in the invisible hand of the*

5 Harari, Yuval Noah. "Yuval Noah Harari on Big Data, Google and the end of free will." Financial Times. August 16, 2016. https://www.ft.com/content/50bb4830-6a4c-11e6-ae5b-a7cc5dd5a28c

*dataflow. As the global data-processing system becomes all-knowing and all-powerful, so connecting to the system becomes the source of all meaning.*[6]

Has your life been devoid of meaning? If so, no problem! Just connect your body and mind to the global data processing system, and you'll find fulfillment beyond your wildest dreams.[7]

It sounds crazy, but they're dead serious. And for that reason, none of us can afford to be ignorant of the far-reaching intent and effects of Dataism. So let's find out more from Harari:

*Dataists further believe that given enough biometric data and computing power, this all-encompassing system could understand humans much better than we understand ourselves. Once that happens,* **humans will lose their authority, and humanist practices such as democratic elections will become as obsolete as rain dances and flint knives.**[8] *[Emphasis added.]*

It's worth noting here that just as humanism replaced traditional religion in the twentieth century, so is Dataism replacing humanism in the twenty-first century. Whereas humanism valued human experience, Dataism values raw data.

Where is Dataism leading us? Harari proposes: "Once Big Data systems know me better than I know myself, authority will shift from humans to algorithms. Big Data could then empower Big Brother."

Oh, so *that's* what's been happening the past two years, throughout the so-called pandemic, when public health officials, hospitals, and drug companies fed us false data, including false PCR test results; put us on dangerous protocols and shot us up with toxic, gene-altering therapies, which too often resulted in injuries and deaths; and—complicit with Big Tech—blocked our access to real, scientific data and life-saving medicine. In short, Big Data has *already* empowered Big Brother.

---

6 Harari.

7 Elon Musk has already figured this out, as evidenced by his company Neuralink, which develops brain-computer interfaces.

8 Harari.

Commenting further on the humans-to-algorithms shift in authority, Harari writes:

> *This has already happened in the field of medicine. The most important medical decisions in your life are increasingly based not on your feelings of illness or wellness, or even on the informed predictions of your doctor — but on the calculations of computers who know you better than you know yourself.*[9]

A young millennial blogger and web developer named Reuben Rapose sees this shift as more than just a passing fad. "[F]or scholars and intellectuals," Rapose writes, "Dataism promises to provide the scientific Holy Grail that has eluded us for centuries." He describes that Holy Grail as "a single overarching theory that unifies all the scientific disciplines from musicology through economics, all the way to biology."[10]

## Back to the Three-Legged Stool

If the Tao (recall C.S. Lewis) and Christian consensus (recall Francis Schaeffer) and other systems of moral restraints are superseded by Dataism, what happens to the other two legs of our stool? Well, the political leg would be completely sawed off by technocrats, who intend to remove that layer of society. The economic leg, meanwhile, would rapidly move toward a scientific dictatorship, under which all consumption and production would be micromanaged.

The next question is whether these two remaining legs, economic micromanagement and Dataism, could be made compatible with each other for the purpose of maintaining a society. Perhaps they can be. But does a stool ever have just two legs? If so, it is not a stool at all. Thus, the more realistic scenario is that the political leg will *not* be sawed off—despite technocrats' best efforts—but will remain and be wholly incompatible with the other two legs.

---

9 Harari.

10 Rapose, Reuben. "How Dataism is Revolutionizing the Idea of the Individual." Towards Data Science. March 15, 2021. https://towardsdatascience.com/how-dataism-is-revolutionizing-the-idea-of-the-individual-no-fluff-74bda98ff5f8

Rapose, for his part, thinks that "in the future data is going to dictate our lives unlike any other divine doctrine or man-made religion we've ever known." He observes, "No longer will we study horoscopes [and] astrological signs, consult holy books and holy men, if Dataism has its way." In other words, all future decisions will be made based on cold, hard data alone. Rapose concludes:

> *If humankind is indeed a single data-processing system, what is its output? Dataists would say that its output will be the creation of a new and even more efficient data-processing system, called the Internet-of-All-Things. Once this mission is accomplished, Homo sapiens will vanish. Dataism is neither liberal nor humanist. It should be emphasized, however, that Dataism isn't anti-humanist. It has nothing against human experiences. It just doesn't think they are intrinsically valuable. Like capitalism, Dataism began as a neutral scientific theory, but is now mutating into a religion that claims to determine right and wrong.*
>
> *To Dataism, human experiences are not sacred and Homo sapiens aren't the apex of creation or a precursor of some future Homo Deus. Humans are merely tools for creating the Internet-of-All-Things, which may eventually spread out from planet Earth to cover the whole galaxy and even the whole universe.*[11] *[Emphasis added.]*

An unexpected twist is that the technocracy/transhuman meme, propped up by the new religion of Dataism, is displacing traditional societal structures with a structure that will not—and, indeed, cannot—maintain any semblance of known societies.

Which reminds me. In 2016, just as Harari was signing copies of *Homo Deus*, a strange and creepy nine-minute video titled *The Selfish Ledger* was being written by Google X head of design Nick Foster and Near Future Laboratory co-founder David Murphy. It was meant for Google employees' eyes only, but in 2018 an insider leaked it to The Verge, which in turn made it public. According to The Verge article written in May 2018:

11 Rapose.

*The video, shared internally within Google, imagines a future of total data collection, where Google helps nudge users into alignment with their goals, custom-prints personalized devices to collect more data, and even guides the behavior of entire populations to solve global problems like poverty and disease.*[12]

The gist of *The Selfish Ledger* is that the data of individuals collected and saved in one generation can be passed down to individuals in succeeding generations, about whom even more data is collected and further passed down. At some point, this accumulation of data would ostensibly result in top-down control over all behavior of all species, everywhere. The final section of the video, "Behavioral Sequencing," makes that very point:

*As patterns begin to emerge in the behavioural sequences, they too may be targeted. The ledger could be given a focus, shifting it from a system which not only tracks our behaviour, but offers direction towards a desired result.*

*We are at the very beginning of our journey of understanding in the field of user data. By applying our knowledge of epigenetics, inheritance and mimetics to this field, we may be able to make mental leaps in our understanding, which could offer benefits to this generation, to future generations and the species as a whole.*[13] *[Emphasis added.]*

Ah, Dataism. Each of us will finally find meaning to our lives—just by connecting to the system. The data will tell us what is right and what is wrong. We don't have to make any decisions or choices, because the system does that for us. And it never makes a mistake, for it knows us better than we know ourselves. "What about free will?" you may be asking. "How old-fashioned," is Dataism's response.

---

12 Savov, Vlad. "Google's Selfish Ledger is an unsettling vision of Silicon Valley social engineering." The Verge. May 17, 2018. https://www.theverge.com/2018/5/17/17344250/google-x-selfish-ledger-video-data-privacy

13 Transcript of "The Selfish Ledger." VPN Reviews. May 27, 2018. https://vpnrevie.ws/selfish-ledger-transcript

Back to our three-legged (or two-legged) stool we go once more. Surprise: Where Google and Dataism are headed, there will be no need for a stool at all.

In 1944, C. S. Lewis had no inkling of Dataism, but he clearly envisioned the end result of man attempting to conquer nature:

> *It is not that they are bad men. They are not men at all. Stepping outside the Tao, they have stepped into the void. Nor are their subjects necessarily unhappy men. They are not men at all: they are artifacts. Man's final conquest has proved to be the abolition of Man.*[14] *[Emphasis added.]*

Where the evil twins of technocracy and transhumanism dare tread on Earth's soil, the abolition of man follows closely behind.

## Is Dataism the One World Religion?

There has been considerable speculation about how the various existing religious systems of the world might somehow morph together to create a unified global religion. We have already considered scientism, humanism, and transhumanism as religions.

The Catholic Church, under the leadership of Pope Francis, is in total agreement with the United Nations, advocating its Sustainable Development Goals (SDGs) and advancing a green economy (defined as low carbon, resource-efficient, and socially inclusive). Francis is also resolute on merging the Protestant church back into the Catholic Church from whence it came. Such a union would be a giant step toward one world religion.

Most mainline Protestant churches are compromised and follow hard after everything "green." Many of them openly promote far left dogma, including gender dysphoria and homosexuality.

Islam has nothing in common with either Catholicism or Protestantism, but it, too, supports the UN's SDGs. The Islamic leadership has set its sights on becoming the world's financial technology leader and has thus been working closely with Western institutions such as the World Bank, the International Monetary Fund, and the Bank for International Settlements.

---

14 Lewis. Page 64.

Odd as it sounds, the membership of some religions is being divided over the issue of transhumanism, with splinter groups going so far as to swallow aspects of the transhumanist agenda and even form associations to champion it.

For instance, the Mormon Transhumanist Association's website declares:

> *We believe that scientific knowledge and technological power are among the means ordained of God to enable such exaltation, including realization of diverse prophetic visions of transfiguration, immortality, resurrection, renewal of this world, and the discovery and creation of worlds without end.*[15]

The Christian Transhumanist Association says it is "using science and technology to participate in the work of God to cultivate life and renew creation."

A Muslim Transhumanist Association has been suggested; it has yet to be established.[16]

But no matter how many churches beat the drums for transhumanism, I believe the existing religious systems of the world are simply too diverse to merge together into a single, organically unified religion.

Not so with Dataism, though! Dataism is already an organic expression of both technocracy and transhumanism. It is a rapidly growing seedbed that is developing deep roots in and twisting tight tendrils around every culture and country. Dataism's encroachment does not depend upon whether or not you believe in it. For that matter, you don't even have to know it exists. As systems of data throughout the globe continue to expand and connect together, there will be a day in the not-too-distant future when Dataism is recognized and acknowledged as the all-encompassing world religion.

---

15 Mormon Transhumanist Association. https://transfigurism.org

16 Prisco, Giulio. "Muslim and Supermuslim: Toward Islamic transhumanism?" Turing Church. February 25, 2020. https://turingchurch.net/muslim-and-supermuslim-toward-islamic-transhumanism-e2583dbdd759

# CHAPTER 11

# Digitizing the World

*To digitize something is to record it, in a format that will last forever.* — *Edward Snowden*

The sole aim of those who seek to digitize the world can be summed up with two words: collect and control. That is, they collect data from objects in order to control them. Always. Never do they lose sight of or deviate from that single-minded goal.

When I say "objects," I mean both inanimate and animate objects. After all, they're one and the same in the mind of the technocrat, for whom collecting data about anything and anyone, about everything and everyone, is a habitual practice and a downright obsession.

In 2015, the total amount of digitized data in the world was about 5.5 zettabytes. By 2025, global storage will exceed 200 zettabytes. These calculations are based on anything and everything that can be digitized—from databases to audio and video—and that are stored on any platform—from personal computers to server farms to the "cloud."

How big is a zettabyte? See for yourself on this list of measurements (in ascending order):

| | | |
|---|---|---|
| Megabyte | MB | 1024[1] kilobytes |

1 What's with 1,024 instead of 1,000? Computer operation is based on binary, Base-2 math instead of Base-10. The progression of doubling, starting with 2, looks like this: 2, 4, 8, 16, 32, 64, 128, 256, 512, 1,024. There are 8 binary bits in one byte, each of which can be a "0" or a "1." One byte can express a maximum of 256 discrete values.

| | | |
|---|---|---|
| Gigabyte | GB | 1024 megabytes |
| Terabyte | TB | 1024 gigabytes |
| Petabyte | PB | 1024 terabytes |
| Exabyte | EB | 1024 petabytes |
| **Zettabyte** | **ZB** | **1024 exabytes** |
| Yottabyte | YB | 1024 zettabytes |

Most computer users today are comfortable talking in terms of gigabytes and terabytes of data, but any unit of measurement beyond that seems impossible to conceive.

Here are a few facts that might help put into perspective the race to digitize absolutely everything under the sun:

*— A fully digitized copy of only the printed documents housed in the Library of Congress, the largest library in the world, would require about 250 terabytes of data storage capacity. If video and audio and other normally digitized assets were added to those print materials, the Library of Congress would need an estimated 8 petabytes of data storage capacity. That's not a stretch, given that the Library of Congress is said to contain nearly 110 million items in almost every language and format—all stored on 532 miles of bookshelves.*

*— Compared to the 8 petabytes required to store everything in the Library of Congress, just one-half of one petabyte would store all the data owned by the academic libraries at all the universities in the US. (Note: Academic libraries, aka research libraries, are distinct from public libraries.)*

*— It took from the beginning of recorded history to the early 2000s to create the equivalent of only 5 exabytes of information. By comparison, now it takes a mere two days to generate 5 exabytes of data. And of course the pace of digitization is only speeding up.*[2]

For those of us who cannot comprehend the sizes of one zettabyte and one yottabyte, I'll spell them out in zeroes: The former is

2 Vance, Jeff. "Big Data Analytics Overview." Datamation. June 25, 2013. https://www.datamation.com/applications/big-data-analytics-overview.html

1,000,000,000,000,000,000,000 bytes (1021) and the latter is 1, 000,000,000,000,000,000,000,000 bytes (1024).

As if these numbers weren't mind-boggling enough, consider that the revolution of digitization didn't get underway until the early 2000s. Digitization has been exploding exponentially ever since. And as storage capacity grows, new possibilities open for even more digitization. Now that we have virtually unlimited storage space, there is a frenzied drive to digitize everything on earth. Limitless capacity was impossible to envision, much less achieve, at the *start* of the digital revolution.

There are two problems with all this digitized data.

First, there is no traditional type of software that would permit analysis of such large amounts of data. That problem has driven the market for artificial intelligence (AI) systems, which can consume enormous piles of data to find relevance, meaning, and outcomes.

The second problem is the limits to transmission speed. Data is useful only when it can be moved from one place to another. Speed of transmission has always been limited by technology, which has often not kept pace with the rate of increase in data storage. The term used for disk-bound data is "silo." Silos of data are everywhere, just waiting for a new transmission technology to set them free.

Note this differentiation: Data storage is measured in "bytes," as in megabytes and gigabytes. Transmission speeds are measured in "bits," as in megabits and gigabits. There are eight bits in one byte. Thus, if you have an Internet connection that can download 320 megabits per second, you are actually only getting 40 megabytes per second (320/8 = 40) worth of data. To its discredit, the computer hardware industry has intentionally made storage in bytes versus speed in bits confusing to consumers.

A new era of high-speed transmission has just arrived and will likely begin roll-out within twenty-four months. A group of researchers at Technical University of Denmark (DTU) has scored a major breakthrough that will theoretically allow Internet transfers of up to 100 petabits per second. I repeat: 100 petabits per second!

These researchers have already successfully tested their new optical chip at 1.8 petabits per second. That's less than two percent of the theoretical transfer speed of 100 Pbit/s. Yet, even at this relatively "slow" test speed, the entire data in the Library of Congress could be transferred *twice* in one second flat.

Needless to say, any technocrat who hears "big" and "fast" in the same sentence salivates over the possibility of new applications for big data collection combined with fast transmission. To a large extent, the blazingly fast wireless data transmission speed of 5G has already kick-started the digitization of everything—and by "everything" I mean *everything*! That said, 5G is still in its infancy.

## Digital Sequencing of DNA

One new initiative, mentioned in Chapter 6 as the Post-2020 Global Biodiversity Framework, proposes to digitize the DNA of all species on earth, under the label "Digital Sequence Information on Genetic Resources" (DSI). The resulting database is to be considered a global resource for researchers and genetic scientists to use in their gene editing projects. To gather the data, DNA profilers will be working in teams across all nations to catalog as many species as possible in the shortest amount of time possible.

The idea is to sequence DNA not just from a single representative of a particular species but from as many members of that species as can be found. Why? Because there are genetic variances within species, and comparisons of those differences are essential in determining traits and functions.

Scientists have estimated that there could be as many as 8.7 million species of animals and plants in existence but that only around 1.2 million have been discovered so far.[3]

Currently there are nearly 8 billion humans on earth. Yet, other species in the animal kingdom could easily surpass hundreds of billions of individuals. DNA sequencing of any single living crea-

3 National Geographic Resource Library. "Biodiversity." https://education.nationalgeographic.org/resource/biodiversity

ture, including a single human, creates a digitized file contained around seven gigabytes. Thus, sequencing the DNA of all humans on the planet would require at least one zettabyte. Add in other species in moderation and you are looking at the largest designation of data storage: the yottabyte. As the above chart shows, the yottabyte is 1,024 times larger than the zettabyte. (By the way, after the yottabyte—and off the chart!—comes the brontobyte and the gegobyte.) Thus, this single digitization project could easily stretch beyond the zettabyte range.

## Internet of Things

The Internet of Things (IoT) is like a man-made, digital version of a jungle. Just as wild animals and plants are all interconnected in one web of life in the jungle, so, in the IoT, are digital devices and cameras and machines of all kinds interconnected, both to one another and to the entire Internet. There are surveillance cameras and security cameras, street sensors and building sensors, smart health devices (including wearables and implantables) and smart city devices, smart meters and smart appliances, smart vehicles and drones, to name just a few things that constitute the IoT.

A prominent analytic and forecasting company, IDC Corporation (IDC), has predicted that by 2025 there will be 41.6 billion IoT devices connected to the Internet, generating a whopping 79.4 zettabytes of data per year. IDC contends the current compound annual growth of the IoT is close to 30 percent per year and is still accelerating.[4]

David Reinsel, senior vice president of IDC's Global DataSphere, agrees with my assessment that the technocrats' goal is to digitize the entire world. Reinsel observes:

> *Mankind is on a quest to digitize the world and a growing global DataSphere is the result. The world around us is becoming more "sensorized," bringing new levels of intelligence and order to personal and seemingly random environments,*

4 "41.6 billion IoT devices will be generating 79.4 zettabytes of data in 2025." Help Net Security. June 21, 2019. https://www.helpnetsecurity.com/2019/06/21/connected-iot-devices-forecast

*and Internet of Things devices are an integral part of this process.*[5]

I have written rather extensively about the IoT since its inception. I regard it as comparable to the network of the smallest blood vessels in your body. These capillaries, as they're called, deliver needed nutrients and oxygen to all the cells of the body and also transport CO2 to be eliminated through the lungs. Just as the body cannot live without this capillary system, so the digitized world cannot exist without the IoT.

The explosion in the number of devices connected to the IoT is largely enabled by 5G technology—in two ways. First, 5G, being wireless, has ridiculously fast transmission speeds. Second, 5G allows miniaturization of low-cost, low-energy transmitter circuits that permit the embedding of two-way communications in the smallest of devices. Examples include smart watches, smart meters, surveillance cameras, building sensors, and security alarms.

## Financial Transactions

In 2020, an estimated 726 billion individual financial transactions took place globally using digital payment technologies such as credit or debit cards and smart phones. I reckon that throughout 2022 there were approximately 20 billion financial transactions in just the global stock, bond, and commodities markets and other related contracts. These enormous volumes are growing well over 10 percent per year.

Each completed transaction typically involves multiple ledger entries. For instance, a credit card purchase at the store involves the customer's bank account, the store's bank account, and the bank system itself, which must trace the money from start to finish.

A department store, for instance, records detailed information on every customer purchase in order to conduct targeted marketing campaigns. Some big store chains already use facial recognition software to recognize customers as they walk in the door so that customized coupons can be instantly created to nudge them

5 Help Net Security.

toward certain additional purchases. Yes, the marketing pitch and the purchases are all recorded.

## Digital Twins

Now I'll talk about a fairly new concept, called digital twins. Digital twinning is made possible by a confluence of technological wonders—namely, the Internet of Things, massive storage availability, instantaneous collection of data, and advanced conceptualizing software that is based on artificial intelligence.

It's very important to understand digital twinning. Read the explanations below, carefully and slowly, in order to fully grasp the implications of this new technology.

Let's start with a definition of digital twinning. According to IBM:

> *A digital twin is a virtual representation of an object or system that spans its lifecycle, is updated from real-time data, and uses simulation, machine learning and reasoning to help decision-making.*[6]

Two pioneers of digital twinning, John Vickers of NASA and Michael Grieves of the Florida Institute of Technology, described digital twinning this way in their 2016 paper, "Origins of the Digital Twin Concept":

> *The premise driving the model was that each system consisted of two systems, the physical system that has always existed and a new virtual system that contained all of the information about the physical system. This meant that there was a mirroring or twinning of systems between what existed in real space to what existed in virtual space and vice versa.*[7]

A leading provider of digital twinning software and services, Resonai Inc., offers the easiest-to-grasp explanation in a blog post:

> *A digital twin is a virtual replica of a physical object or process that can update itself in real-time.*

---

6 Blog. "What Are Digital Twins?" Resonai Inc. December 21, 2021. https://www.resonai.com/blog/what-are-digital-twins#what-are-digital-twin-use-cases

7 Resonai blog.

*In other words, there's a real object, a virtual object, and data and information flow between them, allowing for constant updates and remote control.*[8]

Elsewhere in the same blog, Resonai makes these important clarifications:

*Just looking at the definitions of a digital twin, it can be easy to see how it might just seem like "digital twin" is another name for a simulation. But where they differ is that a simulation takes a set of data and extrapolates out from it, while a* ***digital twin uses a constant flow of information to update itself in real time.***

*Digital twins are also different from building information modeling (BIM), which are [sic] digital representations of facilities, installations, or other physical spaces. BIMs are usually 2D floor plans or 3D models and wireframes. These models are generated in order to assist designers, architects, and building managers to visualize what a space will look like either during design phases, or when not physically present onsite.*

***A digital twin similarly involves a model of a physical space, but it's not static. The data that comes from the physical location's sensors means that the model updates in real time, so it always has the most current information.***[9] *[Emphasis added.]*

So, summing up what we've learned thus far: A digital twin is a real-time visual rendering of an original physical building but updated continuously by data generated from the multitude of real-time sensors embedded in that building. Furthermore, the twin has a real-time reverse connection to the physical building, so if changes are made to the twin, the same changes are made to the original object.

You might imagine that when the modern elevator was invented, it was a luxury added to a few upscale multi-story buildings. But it didn't take long for elevators to become ubiquitous in

8 Resonai blog.
9 Resonai blog.

multi-story buildings. In fact, if there were a multi-story building today that had stairs but no elevator, it would be a candidate for demolition and replaced by a modern structure.

Well, in like manner, digital twinning for modern building management was once rare but has caught on and is now a necessity instead of a luxury.

If you have grasped the concept of a digital twin model for a physical building, you might surmise that digital twins for entire cities would be the next logical step. You would be right. The latest rage in smart city technology is digital twinning, and it is spreading throughout the world.

Las Vegas, for instance, is at the forefront of digital twin technology. According to the city's chief innovation officer, Michael Sherwood:

> *Digital Twins are rapidly becoming vital to how cities are run. Now in Las Vegas we will have a city-scale digital twin that is driven by the physical environment, and ultimately letting us control key systems through it. This will give us new levels of insights and control to benefit city planners, residents, and businesses. We're setting the benchmark for cities around the world to become smarter, efficient, safer, and more sustainable.*[10]

Other cities racing to implement digital twinning include Phoenix, New York City, and Chattanooga, Tennessee. In fact, hundreds of municipalities around the world are headed in that direction.

In a smart city setting, the grid of installed sensors that supplies data to the digital twin may be publicly or privately owned. Smart meters belong to either homeowners or the utility company of their choice. Building sensors belong to the building's owner. Traffic sensors and facial recognition cameras are owned by city governments. All of the data in a smart city can be fed from

---

10 "Las Vegas to accelerate urban transformation with first-ever IoT-enabled Digital Twin." Cityzenith press release. October 12, 2021. https://cityzenith.com/post/las-vegas-to-accelerate-urban-transformation-with-first-ever-iot-enabled-digital-twin

the physical buildings and sensor devices and camera systems into their digital twin on a real-time basis.

As has been made clear, the usefulness of a digital twin lies in its control over the physical twin. The digital counterpart can be used to simulate changes to the physical twin before they are rolled out to the real world.

Heat wave? The city's digital twin can be tinkered with to see what would happen if all air conditioning thermostats were raised by two degrees. Not a good outcome? Okay, then, let's experiment with raising temps only in houses with more than 1,800 square feet, but we'll leave commercial and apartment buildings alone. The point is: Whatever temperature the digital twin regulators decide is acceptable can be rolled out in selected physical structures within a city at the push of a button.

Not surprisingly, digital twinning is now being researched with the goal of using it not just in major cities but throughout entire nations. Data from cities and states and provinces are being fed into a giant model powered by a supercomputer and at the fastest available data transfer speeds.

I regret to say that digitization zealots are coming for the human body as well. Those handy dandy digital sensors we are "hooked on"—smart watches, smart phones, fitness trackers, and other gadgets—not to mention medical sensors like ingestible smart drugs and testing devices, all send data to digital twin technology that can model our bodies on a real-time basis. When analyzed by AI algorithms, our digital twin reveals more about us than we know about ourselves. The more we are "studied," if you will, in this invasive manner, the more we end up being nudged and prodded into treatments, lifestyle changes, behavioral modification, and so on.

All of this digital twin technology will require immense amounts of computing power as well as mountains of data storage that could easily exceed the zettabyte range. Without that power and storage, digital twinning would be impossible, left to the world of science fiction writers.

## Central Bank Digital Currency (CBDC)

Thanks to the age of digitization, a Central Bank Digital Currency (CBDC) is now possible. The worldwide central bank system, headed by the Bank for International Settlements located in Basel, Switzerland, is frantically developing a global system of currency based on blockchain technology. CBDC is intended to entirely replace our traditional system of digital fiat currency as well as cash.

Initially, only the banking infrastructure itself will adopt CBDCs. But eventually it will spread to consumer banking. Retail customers in the US, for instance, will be able to maintain a direct account with the Federal Reserve in order to store CBDCs and to purchase and sell items. With each transaction, a blockchain record will be created (including details such as customer names, account numbers, dollar amounts, etc.) and will then be transmitted back to the main CBDC database. Eventually, the issuing central banks will have knowledge of every transaction in the economic system, opening the door to their complete control over the system and over everyone who is tied to it, voluntarily or under protest.

The amount of data generated by CBDCs will be enormous, far exceeding any other kind of data discussed in this chapter.

## The Role of Data and AI

Much of the value of stored data is its use in training AI algorithms to see in real-time. The larger the data sets, it is reasoned, the better trained the AI program becomes. The primary role of AI is not to train on historical data. Rather, the Holy Grail of AI is its analysis of the actual incoming data flow in real-time to learn what it means before it even hits the storage device. The previous training gives context to the AI's analysis of this new data, and all in real-time.

As data collection and storage grows exponentially, it provides wide-open opportunities for new AI algorithms to jump in and learn ever more intelligently, thus speeding the development cycle by orders of magnitude.

## Sustainable Development and Digitization

The United Nations is worried about lack of success in implementing the seventeen Sustainable Development Goals (SDGs) it created in 2015. Indeed, nations of the world give lip service to the SDGs and then do little or nothing of what the UN wants them to do. How to overcome their intransigence? You guessed it: digitization.

An important UN agency, the United Nations Development Programme (UNDP), sponsors an online networking platform geared to the SDGs. In March 2021, UNDP, in cooperation with five other organizations—among them the UN Environment Programme (UNEP) and the German Environment Agency—initiated the Coalition for Digital Environmental Sustainability (CODES).

Although there is a considerable amount of written material on CODES that can be read online, I transcribed for you portions of a telling video in which several of its leaders describe the purpose and vision of the coalition.

The first speaker I quote is Dirk Messner of the German Environment Agency:

> ***There are two major transformations which are characterizing our age and our century —the sustainability transformation on the one hand side and on the other hand side the digital, AI-driven, machine-learning transformation towards a new technical infrastructure of all our societies.*** *If we look at the SDGs, we can see that in this system of sustainability goals, which we discussed and decided upon in 2015, only six years ago, there is no digital dynamic, there is no digital transformation, so* ***we have to learn to bring this together****. We, as CODES, as an alliance of stakeholders from the academic field, international organizations, actors from the private sector, non-governmental organizations—we are arguing that* ***if we don't bring these two megatrends together, we will not achieve sustainable development in the digital age.***[11] *[Emphasis added.]*

The other speaker I quote is the UNEP's David Jensen:

11 Transcribed from a YouTube video, "CODES." https://youtu.be/DGeYcSZqUSU

> *What is our vision? One of the big visions for CODES is to fully integrate environmental sustainability—data, values, and goals—directly into the codes of the digital economy. This means into the platforms,* ***the applications and the algorithms that currently underpin all of the digital transactions in the economy. If we can do this, we can potentially speed and scale environmentally sustainable products, behaviours and lifestyles to a level never before achieved in human history.*** *But this is going to require active collaboration and collective action at a planetary scale, and that's what CODES is hoping to broker: Collaboration across private sector, public sector, academia, civil society is going to be fundamentally necessary to take this big vision forward.*[12] *[Emphasis added.]*

CODES activities, if successful, will literally double all digital storage capacity on the planet.

## Conclusion

Read the above quote again carefully: CODES wants to incorporate "all of the digital transactions in the economy" in order to drive "behaviours and lifestyles to a level never before achieved in human history."

Again, this is always the sole aim of digitization: Data is collected in order to control the object from which the data was collected. *Always*. Those addicted to digitizing *never* lose sight of or deviate from that single-minded goal.

Yes, I said that in the opening of this chapter, and I repeat it in the closing. For, we *must* remember that, in the mind of the technocrat, collecting data about anything and anyone, about everything and everyone, is a habitual practice and a downright obsession.

The acceleration of digitization in the world and the magnitude of digitization of the world are stunning megatrends. Rapid advances in "good" technology—computing power, AI, and high-speed data transmission—have been utilized to generate a whole new "bad" paradigm of technocratic control. Because the techno-

12 CODES video.

logical advances show no signs of slowing, the technocratic control, sad to say, also shows no signs of slowing.

# CHAPTER 12

# The Battle for the World

*COME, LET US BUILD OURSELVES A CITY AND A TOWER WITH ITS TOP IN THE HEAVENS, AND LET US MAKE A NAME FOR OURSELVES. — GENESIS 11:4*

The original story of the tower of Babel cast all the people in the world as being in agreement about building a tower up to heaven, perhaps to drag God down out of heaven and deal with Him on earth. Whatever their intent, it turned out to be wishful thinking, as God Himself broke up the party and scattered the conspirators. The scene on modern earth is quite different, however. Today, a small group of elitists are in agreement with each other on how to reshape the world. If such a elitist group could now speak with a common language and purpose, it would be to say something like this:

> *We have dealt with God and he is dead. We run things now for our pleasure. We will reshape the structure and function of the world and then we will change you to fit into our new world. We will be immortal, omniscient, and omnipotent. You will not. You will be the resources we need to put our world in harmony. We don't care if you like it or not, because you are hopelessly trapped and are powerless to stop us.*

## Introduction

Thus far in this book, I have shown that technocracy and trans humanism are bound together by a common philosophical position known as scientism. They both make equal use of convergent science, or NBIC, to build a pseudoscience-based future. Technocracy deals with the transformation of society in a way that puts human consumption in balance with the perceived availability of resources. Transhumanism deals with the transformation of individual humans and their relationship to the technocratically run world.

We might say, then, that technocracy is the architecture; transhumanism is the compliance. Or, technocracy is the building; transhumanists are the tenants. Or, even more precisely, technocracy is the building code for the construction of the new world; transhumanism is the building code for the people who will live there.

Because much of the world's populace is resistant to, if not outright rebellious in the face of, these drastic changes—or would be, if they understood the plan—the technocrats and transhumanists have found it necessary to go to war with humanity and beat it into submission. This new "axis of evil," if you will, is collaborating to create a multifaceted winning strategy before the majority of people even know that an intentional war has been waged against them—and that they have already lost.

Wars throughout history have always been fought over territory, which has resulted in constantly fluctuating borders. This war is no different, except that it is orders of magnitude greater than any war preceding it. This war seeks to erase all national borders, gather up all public land and all private property and put it into a single global common trust operated (and preferably owned) by the elitists themselves.

We see this overarching aim as far back as 1970, when Zbigniew Brzezinski penned *Between Two Ages: America's Role in the Technetronic Era:*

> *The nation-state as a fundamental unit of man's organized life has ceased to be the principal creative force: International banks and multinational corporations are acting and planning in terms that are far in advance of the political concepts of the nation-state.*[1]

---

1 Brzezinski, Zbigniew. *Between Two Ages: America's Role in the Technetronic Era* (New York: Viking Press, 1973). Page 246.

## The Big Con

When elitist David Rockefeller invited Brzezinski to become a co-founder of the Trilateral Commission in 1973, *Between Two Ages* was the intellectual fodder that justified Rockefeller's monopolistic dream of the greatest land grab in history. Of course, Rockefeller was not alone in his quest to conquer the world, as evidenced by the like-minded cronies he invited to join the Trilateral Commission.

Nevertheless, the root of the Rockefeller family tree practically wrote the recipe for how to cook up a good con. As I said of the original Rockefeller in my book *Technocracy: The Hard Road to World Order*:

> *Dr. William Levingston was actually an itinerant salesman with a phony name who created a concoction of oil and laxative and branded it as a cure for cancer. Since cancer was a dreaded and usually fatal disease, people would buy and try literally anything for a cure. He would explain that if his miracle cure was strong enough to beat cancer, then it would most certainly take care of a whole lot of other diseases as well! When William came to a new town, he would mesmerize and trick people into buying his "miracle cure." As soon as anyone questioned his phony operation, he would ride out much faster than he had originally arrived. William was indeed a fraud and a con artist, but he somehow always managed to escape arrest or lynching. He died in 1906 at the ripe old age of 95. Earlier in life, he reportedly bragged, "I cheat my boys every chance I get. I want to make 'em sharp."*
>
> *However, Levingston's name was indeed a fraud. His real name was William Avery Rockefeller, Sr. and one of those "sharp" sons was John D. Rockefeller, who was soon to become the richest man in America and grandfather of David A. Rockefeller, founder of the Trilateral Commission in 1973.*[2]

This is the essence of a good con. Get a compelling-looking prop and make up claims about it that nobody can prove or dis-

---

2 Wood, Patrick. *Technocracy: The Hard Road To World Order*. (Coherent Publishing, 2018). Page 55.

prove. Match the prop to people's most compelling needs and charge them money for it. When the money starts to dry up, get a new prop.

Not surprisingly, William Avery Rockefeller, Sr.'s nickname was "Devil Bill."

The synthesis of science, scientism, and high-technology was a boon to the Rockefeller crowd, allowing them to "double-layer" the con. In other words, they could make science out to be god and then appoint themselves as the high priests. Thereafter, the god of scientism posing as science could be made to say anything they wanted, while, as high priests, they could dodge any pushback by simply saying, "Don't blame the messenger for the message." In any case, few common folk understood science, and even fewer knew how to recognize pseudoscience, much less challenge it.

Today, the god of scientism says that global warming is going to torch the earth, that traditional sources of energy must be destroyed, and that we must all convert our actions to conform to Sustainable Development, aka technocracy. The same god also says to curb our consumption of resources, to quit traveling beyond our national—or state, or even city—borders, to walk or bicycle to work, to live in tiny houses, and to eat bugs.

The god of scientism that produced SARS-CoV-2 said, "Wear a mask," "Social distance," "Isolate yourself," "Don't go to church," "Science takes precedence over the Constitution," and "Take an experimental mRNA-based injected therapy to save your neighbor."

Every con has a pitch, a transaction, and an outcome. We must not lose sight of the simplicity of the three-step move these con artists are making against us.

The pitch can take many forms. Positive pitches include the seventeen Sustainable Development Goals (SDGs)—eliminating poverty, education for all, jobs with dignity among them. Negative pitches include global warming that will scorch the earth and invisible viruses that will kill millions. Such fear-based pitches seduce us into listening to and accepting the con man's proposed transaction.

But what *is* that proposed transaction? Well, the only transaction we're being offered is to dutifully, unquestioningly accept the seventeen holy SDGs.

And what is the outcome of our accepting that offer? It's to turn over all our individual choices for producing and consuming goods and services to the United Nations. There is never a Plan B, only a Plan A.

So, has the con been consummated? Almost. We have now reached the end game of the con, and humanity is perilously close to accepting it without further questions.

## Polycrisis of Doom

In Chapter 9, "Who's Driving This Train?," I showed that "Corporate is the dominant group that controls Political and Academic and that *the white-hot core of Corporate is the central bankers.*" Indeed, it is Corporate that decides the end game. Then it showers Academic with grants to write white papers to justify that end game. Meanwhile, Political serves as the lapdog to Corporate. Politicians execute complementary policies that will lead to the end game.

The many hotspots in the war against humanity are not hard to identify. Viewed collectively, they describe a well-orchestrated strategy by the globalists to conquer the world and usher it into the Great Reset, aka technocracy.

## Energy Crisis

I have already discussed the war on traditional forms of energy, such as oil, gas, and coal. This long-term effort has worn down the global economic system to a point of extreme fragility. Alternative sources of energy, such as solar and wind turbines, are wholly inadequate to power the world in the manner that we in the West have become accustomed to.

Given that the purposeful, planned destruction of the energy system has been deliberately exacerbated by the war in Ukraine, it's no surprise that what threatened to be a full-blown global energy crisis has now worsened into a tectonic disaster. For one thing, shutting off Russia's natural gas supply in European countries triggered their instant regret over having become so dependent upon Russia at the expense of energy self-sufficiency. For another, Americans, too, are regretting the loss of energy independence, as gasoline prices have skyrocketed during the Biden Administration and a severe diesel shortage is emerging.

The war on traditional energy is actually decades old. In 1979, the now-late Professor Antony C. Sutton published *Energy: The Created Crisis*. His prescient research uncovered a root cause of the war on energy:

> *In the October 1976 issue of Foreign Affairs, that quarterly Establishment oracle which reflects elitist thinking and intended action, we find an article by Amory B. Lovins. Lovins is not a household word and has hardly made a scratch on the world of knowledge and ideas. However, merely because Foreign Affairs is his forum, Lovins' ideas became acceptable, are widely reported and taken seriously by high officials. Lovins is an instant engineer. His aim is to substitute "soft" technology for hard technology, that is,* ***windmills and solar panels for electric power stations and synthetic gas plants, all without a hint of economic or technical analysis.*** *In fact, Lovins writes as if analysis does not exist. On commentator summed it up very well:*
>
> *"Much of Mr. Lovins' theory is reminiscent of certain ideas utilized by the People's Republic of China during the years of the Great Leap Forward."*
>
> *A brief excerpt from Lovins will surface the approach:*
>
> ***"If you ask me, it'd be little short of disastrous for us to discover a source of clean, cheap, abundant energy because of what we would do with it..."***[3] *[emphasis added]*

What was physicist Amory B. Lovins talking about? *What* is it that "we would do with" clean, cheap, abundant energy? Horrors: We would actually *use* it abundantly! And that abundant use would, God forbid, allow for economic expansion, which in turn would lead to *more* resource consumption and a *larger* popula-

3 Sutton, Antony C. *Energy: The Created Crisis*. (Books In Focus, Inc., 1979). Page 150.

tion, both of which are anathema to faux environmentalists like Lovins, who push a fake decarbonization agenda and ignore real pollution.

In 2014, Lovins wrote a book called *Reinventing Fire*, which reflects not only his own philosophy but the underlying philosophy of the entire Sustainable Development community:

> *Just as whale-oil suppliers ran out of customers in the 1850s before they ran out of whales, oil and coal are becoming uncompetitive even at low prices before they become unavailable even at high prices.*[4]

Lovins' wife, Professor Hunter Lovins, is a member of the board of the Club of Rome and is internationally celebrated by the globalists for having pioneered Sustainable Development even before they hosted the Agenda 21 conference in 1992. *Time* magazine, for instance, declared her the Millennium Hero for the Planet in 2000.

The global economy has been at great risk of instability ever since the industrialized world began converting to unreliable and costly alternative energy. Nations and communities have been lured into a false sense of security. They were made to believe that all was well—that is, until this year, when the old-fashioned, reliable, abundant sources of energy were suddenly shut off.

## War in Ukraine

Prior to Russia's physical invasion of Ukraine On February 24, 2022, there was a long history of conflict and complexity between the two countries. During the lead-up, most anti-war analysts were scratching their heads, asking why Western politicians seemed to be egging Putin on, as if daring him to attack. Putin's initial and simple goal was to quickly take Kiev and effect a regime change in Ukraine. It appears he vastly underestimated the resistance he would face, and it now seems like he has buried Russia in a multi-year, protracted war reminiscent of its involvement with Afghanistan. There may be good reason for diplomacy via peace talks to stop the war, its cost, its killing, its long-term effects on innocent citizens and the world at large.

---

4 Lovins, Amory. *Reinventing Fire*. RMI. 2000.

So far, the effect of the war has been to put three key existential issues on the table. First, energy: Russia has an abundance of energy, while Europe has very little. Second, food: Russia, being the largest exporter of wheat in the world, has an abundance of food, while Europe has a dearth, to the point where a potential famine is now predicted for parts of that Eurasian subcontinent. Third, nuclear war: The West's serviceable nuclear weaponry pales in comparison to Russia's, and it is unlikely that Europe or the US could "win" in a nuclear conflict.

There is great fear throughout Europe that the Ukraine conflict will expand and literally spark WWIII. Whether or not that will happen is immaterial to the psychological impact the threat of it has on the citizens of many countries. Europeans have keen memories of WWI and WWII, both of which were fought on their own soil. They have good reason to be anxious.

## Global Food Crisis

Throughout history, famine has naturally followed war. But besides famine as a side effect of war, the intended destruction of food or limiting of food is an effective weapon of war.

Such is the case in Ukraine, where the war is being used as a weapon to disrupt the balance of global food production and distribution. Known as the "breadbasket of Europe," Ukraine is one of the top three exporters of grain in the world. More than seventy percent of its land mass is prime agricultural land particularly suited for grain production.[5] Because of the war with Russia, Ukraine's grain exports are down 41.5 percent in 2022.[6] And since Russia is a prime exporter of fertilizer, it is not surprising that Russia abruptly cut off Ukraine's supply of fertilizer, forcing farmers to purchase it elsewhere and sending prices skyward throughout Europe. The global supply chain that moved food and fertilizer around the world has had to make major adjustments

5 Knox, Joanne. "Why is Ukraine known as the 'breadbasket of Europe'? Here's what it produces and exports." Farming Life. February 24, 2022. https://www.farminglife.com/country-and-farming/why-is-ukraine-known-as-the-breadbasket-of-europe-heres-what-it-produces-and-exports-3584361

6 "Ukraine Grain Exports Down 41.5% So Far This Season, Ministry Says." Reuters via Successful Farming. September 28, 2022. https://www.agriculture.com/markets/newswire/ukraine-grain-exports-down-415-so-far-this-season-ministry-says

to restructure itself to make up for the shortfalls in various geographic areas, putting additional pressure on prices.

The war-related shock to food stability, however, was preceded by a broader and quieter attack on nitrogen-based fertilizers by "climate crisis" scientists, who have declared that a byproduct of such fertilizers—namely, nitrous oxide—is a destructive greenhouse gas. Therefore, they have asserted, governments must greatly restrict farmers' use of nitrogen-based fertilizers.

The atmosphere contains 78 percent nitrogen and is as essential to plant growth as is carbon dioxide. Since plants cannot absorb nitrogen directly from the atmosphere, it must be added to the soil in other ways, either by natural means or as fertilizer. Thus, crop yields are directly related to the amount of usable nitrogen in the soil.

The Netherlands is the second-largest exporter of food in the world, after the US.[7] In May 2022, climate activists associated with the United Nations and the European Union convinced the Dutch government to order its farmers to cut their use of nitrogen-based fertilizer up to 70 percent by 2030. If implemented and enforced, this ruling will have a devastating impact on food production and drive many Dutch livestock farmers out of business. As a result, they have been rebelling with tractorcades—blockades of roads, warehouses, and grocery stores. The government has openly revealed its disdain for farmers, as revealed by multiple press outlets:

> *This means many farms will have to radically change — or shut down altogether. The Hague has earmarked €25 billion to fund nitrogen-cutting techniques or to buy out certain farms. "The honest story is that not all farmers can continue with their business," the government said in June, prompting outrage.*[8]

---

7 McDonald, David. "How The Netherlands Has Become The World's Second-Largest Food Exporter." Medium via The Global Millennial. June 27, 2017. https://medium.com/the-global-millennial/how-the-netherlands-is-the-worlds-second-largest-food-exporter-c411b8fb14dd

8 Joyner, Ella. "Dutch farmers called upon to sort pollution or sell." Deutsche Welle. July 22, 2022. https://www.dw.com/en/dutch-farmers-feel-they-face-an-impossible-pollution-ultimatum-sort-it-or-sell-up/a-62460053

The Netherlands is not an isolated case.

Canada is following the same agenda:

*The Liberal government is pushing ahead with its goal, introduced in December 2020, to reduce absolute levels of greenhouse gas emissions arising from fertilizer use by 30 per cent below 2020 levels by 2030. Specifically, **it aims to reduce nitrous oxide emissions associated with synthetic nitrogen fertilizer use.**[9] [Emphasis added.]*

The Western Canadian Wheat Growers Association said in a press release:

*Over the past several years, farmers have been seriously harmed by the carbon tax, transportation stoppages, non-science-based decision making and now with the proposed 30 per cent reduction in [nitrogen] fertilizer emissions.[10]*

When and where did this war on nitrogen begin? In October 2019, the United Nations Environment Programme (UNEP) hosted a conference in Sri Lanka titled "Launch of United Nations Global Campaign on Sustainable Nitrogen Management." The conference declaration plainly states that its objective is to "develop national road-maps for sustainable nitrogen management, with an ambition to halve nitrogen waste by 2030."[11]

Apparently, Sri Lanka took a dose of its own medicine and implemented a ban on fertilizers. *The Guardian* reported on the resulting chaos:

*For the farmers of Sri Lanka, their problems began in April last year [2021] when President Gotabaya Rajapaksa, who now stands accused of pushing the country into financial ruin, **implemented a sudden ban on chemical fertilizers.**[12] [Emphasis added.]*

---

9 Hope, Legere. "Canada Issues Fertilizer Emission Restrictions." Vision Times. July 30, 2022. https://www.visiontimes.com/2022/07/30/canada-issues-fertilizer-emission-restrictions.html

10 Hope.

11 "Colombo Declaration on Sustainable Nitrogen Management." United Nations Environment Programme. October 24, 2019. Section 3. Paragraph 3.2. https://drive.google.com/file/d/15oxmxsoDSs8QCBFQbuWxugMfFdley_X6/view

12 Ellis-Petersen, Hannah. "'It will be hard to find a farmer left': Sri Lanka reels from rash fertilizer ban." The Guardian. April 20, 2022. https://www.theguard-

Food ran out. Riots ensued. Protestors beat police and burned down houses belonging to thirty-eight high-ranking politicians. President Rajapaksa was forced to flee in haste to Maldives.

Sri Lanka's troubles were just starting, it turned out. A year later, in 2022, the country "ran out of reserves, defaulted on its overseas bonds and couldn't afford to import essential items such as food and fuel."[13]

Because these draconian, yet totally unnecessary, restrictions on nitrogen fertilizers had been underway from 2019 to 2022, the global food supply was already weakened to the point where a food shock like the war in Ukraine would have a devastating effect. As a result, the ripples through the global agricultural food chain have turned into tsunamis, contributing significantly to the war on humanity.

## Financial Crisis

There are one hundred and one financial and economic indicators we could examine, all of which point to serious problems with the global economy and, in particular, with the financial system. I will save you a boring litany and cut to the chase. It's not slow-moving economic trends but a lack of liquidity that precipitates crises. Simply defined, liquidity refers to "how quickly an investment can be sold without negatively impacting its price."[14] Stocks and bonds are considered relatively liquid, while real estate, art, and private businesses are not.

As part of their monetary policy, central banks control liquidity by easing or restricting credit and the supply of money. When the Federal Reserve implemented quantitative easing (expanding liquidity) during the financial crisis of 2007–2008, it resulted in the Dow Jones Industrial Average increasing more than five times—from 6,450 in December 2008 to 36,679 in October 2021.

---

ian.com/world/2022/apr/20/sri-lanka-fertiliser-ban-president-rajapaksa-farmers-harvests-collapse

13 Durden, Tyler. "Global Food Import Bill Soars To 'Alarming Level' As Poor Countries On Brink Of Crisis." ZeroHedge. November 12, 2022. https://www.zerohedge.com/markets/global-food-import-bill-soars-alarming-level-poor-countries-brink-crisis

14 CFI Team. "What is Liquidity?" Corporate Finance Institute. November 1, 2022. https://corporatefinanceinstitute.com/resources/accounting/liquidity

But beginning in March 15, 2022, the Federal Reserve began to do the opposite, draining liquidity from the financial system with a monetary policy called quantitative tightening. Subsequently, the federal funds rate has been hiked six times, from 0.25 percent to 4 percent by November 2022. During this short time period, mortgage rates have risen to over 7 percent, sending the housing market into a virtual collapse as stocks entered into bear market territory. Bond prices have plunged more than 35 percent. One expected result: Consumer inflation has temporarily driven up prices on everything that supports human life, from food to utilities to household goods.

The Fed's finagling is destructive to wealth. It affects all Americans in real and tangible ways. Indeed, CNBC estimates that US consumers have lost between $9.5 trillion and $10 trillion in personal wealth.[15] The rich have been affected as well: Mark Zuckerberg's personal wealth dropped by over $87 billion during 2022. Elon Musk's fortune dipped by $66 billion. Jeff Bezos has waved goodbye to over $90 million since July 2021. The founders of Google, Sergey Brin and Larry Page, lost $71 billion between them.[16]

When liquidity is engineered to drop rapidly and severely, all sorts of potential crises can arise and cause hair-trigger reactions. Remember that liquidity is defined as "how quickly an investment can be sold without negatively impacting its price." Thus, as liquidity declines, the amount of time it takes to sell an asset increases. If you must sell something quickly, you may find there is no market for it until it is priced much lower.

In the US, this expression of financial warfare can only be laid at the feet of our own central bank, the Federal Reserve. And because other countries' central banks are following the same monetary policies, the result is a global shortage of liquidity. What will

15 Frank, Robert. "Stock market losses wipe out $9 trillion from Americans' wealth." CNBC. September 27, 2022. https://www.cnbc.com/2022/09/27/stock-market-losses-wipe-out-9-trillion-from-americans-wealth-.html
16 Carpio, Jillian. "10 billionaires who lost the most money in 2022, ranked." MSN via South China Morning Post. November 6, 2022. https://www.msn.com/en-xl/lifestyle/other/10-billionaires-who-lost-the-most-money-in-2022-ranked-from-elon-musk-s-twitter-buyout-and-bill-gates-philanthropy-to-jeff-bezos-falling-net-worth-from-amazon-and-mark-zuckerberg-s-meta-troubles/ar-AA13P6GY

trigger a global financial panic? Perhaps a stock market crash, a default on sovereign debt, or a major supply chain shock.

The ultimate outcome of a global financial panic is all but guaranteed: the destruction of the fiat currency system and the introduction of Central Bank Digital Currencies (CBDCs). This is a key objective of the World Economic Forum's so-called Great Reset.

## Currency Crisis

Make no mistake that the drive toward CDBCs is being orchestrated by the Bank for International Settlements (BIS) and its network of national central banks around the world. Three years ago, BIS Managing Director Agustín Carstens announced the establishment of an Innovation Hub,[17] which will allow central banks to study the technology needed to implement CBDCs and related technologies. The Innovation Hub is actually a network with centers located in Hong Kong, Singapore, Switzerland, London, Stockholm, Toronto, Frankfurt, Paris, and New York.[18] At the 2020 IMF Annual Meeting, Carstens revealed:

> *Our analysis on CBDC, in particular for the general use, we intend to establish the equivalence with cash, and there is a huge difference there. For example, in cash we don't know, for example, who is using a one-hundred-dollar bill. Today we don't know who is using a one-thousand-pesos bill. Today a key difference in the CBDC is that [the] central bank will have absolute control on the rules and regulations that will determine the use of that expression of central bank liability. And also we will have the technology to enforce that. Those two issues are extremely important, and that makes a huge difference with respect to what cash is.[19] [Emphasis added.]*

In a more recent presentation, at the World Government Summit 2022 in the UAE, Dr. Pippa Malmgren revealed the exact plan. (By the way, she is ranked in the top five of the Most Powerful

---

17 "BIS to set up Innovation Hub for central banks." BIS Press Release. June 30, 2019. https://www.bis.org/press/p190630a.htm

18 "BIS Innovation Hub Centres." BIS Hub Centres webpage. https://www.bis.org/about/bisih/locations.htm

19 Carstens, Agustín. "Cross-Border Payments—A Vision for the Future." IMF Annual Meeting. October 19, 2020.

Women in Finance and is based in the City of London.) Malmgren addressed the question, "Are we ready for a new world order?" Her statement builds on Carstens' comment:

> *We are on the brink of a dramatic change, where we are about to—and I'll say this boldly—***we are about to abandon the traditional system of money and accounting and introduce a new one.** *And the new one—the new accounting is what we call blockchain. [. . .]* **It means digital. It means having an almost perfect record of every single transaction that happens in the economy, which will give us far greater clarity over what's going on.**[20] *[Emphasis added.]*

Coupled with global implementation of CBDCs is the central banks' requirement for a universal ID system for everyone on earth. Such a system is the only possible way for them to know, as Carstens put it, "who is using a one-hundred-dollar bill."

Meanwhile, Klaus Schwab's World Economic Forum has weighed in on the subject, expressing alarm that "the COVID-19 pandemic has accelerated the need to identify and verify the identity of individuals and organizations across a wide range of sectors." Those sectors include health, employment, financial services, travel, government, e-commerce, and the gig economy.[21]

The BIS itself has confirmed that "the most promising CBDC design would be one tied to a digital identity."[22]

In the context of the current financial war on humankind, CBDCs, coupled with universal digital identity, are equivalent to the chains of slavery that conquering hordes placed upon their vanquished victims in wars of centuries past. CBDCs plus digital IDS will force every "enslaved" citizen of the world into spending

20 https://meetings.imf.org/en/2020/Annual/Schedule/2020/10/19/imf-cross-border-payments-a-vision-for-the-future
"World Government Summit 2022: Dr. Pippa Malmgren Talks About Blockchain & Digital Currencies." March 2022. YouTube. https://youtu.be/cvXdSvja-al

21 World Economic Forum Guide. "Digital Identity Ecosystems: Unlocking New Value." September 2021. Page 8. https://www3.weforum.org/docs/WEF_Guide_Digital_Identity_Ecosystems_2021.pdf

22 Bank for International Settlements Press Release. "Central bank digital currencies herald a new chapter for the monetary system." June 23, 2021. https://www.bis.org/press/p210623.htm

patterns that are in harmony with Sustainable Development, aka technocracy. The implication for the noncompliant is that there will be consequences. After all, this is war, wherein the aggressor tolerates no resistance.

## Health Crisis

The biological attack of SARS-CoV-2 is the most egregious attack on humanity in history. Not that the virus itself was so damaging, but the response to it was a crushing blow. A total of billions of citizens in almost every country were forced to submit to mandates that were not only useless, but destructive to health, wealth, and well-being. Face masks did nothing to stop contagion; if anything, they caused illness and emotional pain. Quarantine and isolation, also unnecessary for the most part, were comparable to martial law. In America, the Bill of Rights was virtually suspended—make that eviscerated. Churches were ordered closed. Public gatherings were forbidden. Governments ceased to respond to the pleas of citizens to stop issuing tyrannical dictates.

Then came the experimental mRNA injections that were rushed through without the rigorous and lengthy testing on humans that is traditionally required (actually, mandated) by the Food and Drug Administration. Of the billions who have been "vaccinated" worldwide, many millions have suffered adverse effects, some so severe as to cause death. Even those who have taken one or more injections but have so far suffered no side effects still face possible long-term health issues.

Legitimate doctors, scientists, and medical scholars have pleaded with government officials to halt these experimental drugs. But instead of being heeded, they are ignored, shunned, decertified, fired, and branded as conspiracy theorists or "vaccine" deniers. The manufacturers of mRNA injections are resolute in their quest to continue blanketing the global population with additional mRNA-based "therapies"—an oxymoron to end all oxymorons.

The effect of the pandemic crisis that started in early 2020 has been to demoralize, disrupt, and degrade the general mental, spiritual, and bodily health of individuals throughout the world.

Furthermore, it has caused major damage to the global economy, to the global supply chain, and to the global financial system. In sum, the crisis precipitated by the pandemic planners has been nothing short of an all-out war against mankind.

## Immigration Crisis

There are only two areas in the world where illegal immigration is a major problem: Europe and the United States. Strangely enough, no one is seeking a better job or more freedom by sneaking into China, Russia, or Argentina.

The immigration invasion policy is not random or helter-skelter. It is the result of a calculated, long-term plot originally set in motion by the United Nations.

Europe has been intentionally and substantially disrupted and transformed in recent years into a multicultural society.

America's southern border was thrown wide open after the November 2020 election of President Joe Biden. This premeditated plan was a continuation of the UN's agenda to weaken nation-states in general and the US in particular.

Throughout world history, immigration has been used to conquer and transform nations. It dilutes and breaks down culture, language, moral standards. It destroys the aggressed nation's rule of law as the invaders introduce their own laws and customs. Even the intermarriage that often results from immigration inevitably causes a loss of national identity.

In short, immigration is a time-tested and very successful element of war.

## Propaganda

Propaganda, censorship, and war go together. They are three peas in a pod. The globalist narrative, which promotes falsehoods and hides truth, is being broadcast day and night by a captured and controlled media complex. Alternative media is treated as illegitimate and is subject to being driven out of business with phony fact-checkers, disruptive infiltrators, and intelligence agents—often one and the same.

The world has never before experienced such sustained, intensive, deceptive propaganda. The problem, of course, is that many people believe the lies and become willing participants in their own capture by the forces of technocracy and transhumanism.

## Summary

In this chapter I have given a brief sketch of the multi-pronged attack on humanity by the evil twins of technocracy and transhumanism. I have covered the globalists' . . .

- War on Energy
- War in Ukraine
- War on Food
- War on Capitalism
- War on Currency
- War on Health
- War on Culture
- War on Media

The coup d'état that started in January 2020 with the advent of an engineered and orchestrated pandemic is far from over. In fact, the war on humanity is still in its infancy. If nothing is done to stop it, the attacks will increase in frequency and amplification.

Many will dismiss this assessment at their own peril. They will be astonished when the figurative knife suddenly plunges into them and severs their own freedoms, their own individual sovereignty. "We had no warning," they'll cry.

Or when a financial crisis turns the banking world upside down and quashes any semblance of financial privacy. "It was so sudden," they'll cry.

Or when their personal property is confiscated by the government without cause and they cannot retrieve it. "I didn't understand," they'll cry.

Perhaps then they'll remember having read this book or having heard an interview about it.

In the kind of wars I have described above, disasters and enemy breakthroughs always befall us suddenly, catching us unawares. By the time a cataclysm or enemy strikes, it is too late for us to combat it.

America is in the valley of decision. Americans must decide quickly if they will engage this enemy or not. For those who decide to remain silent, their silence becomes consent.

The words of Edmund Burke (1729–1797) are more prescient today than when they were first uttered: "When bad men combine, the good must associate; else they will fall, one by one, an unpitied sacrifice in a contemptible struggle."[23]

23 Burke, Edmund. "Thoughts on the Cause of the Present Discontents." (London: J. Dodsley in the Pall-Mall). April 23, 1770. Page 106.

# CHAPTER 13

# Conclusion

*LIBERTY, ONCE LOST, IS LOST FOREVER.*
*— JOHN ADAMS (1735–1826)*

This book intentionally presents a high-altitude view of many complex topics to give the reader an understanding of the forces shaping the world today. Getting unnecessarily bogged down in minutiae and running down rabbit trails would be counterproductive. The big takeaway is this: Those who claim to be the sole designers of our future will rob us of all our rights *to* that future and *in* that future. If we let them get away with this, their victory will be final and there will be no return.

When Aldous Huxley published *Brave New World* in 1932, he described a scientific dictatorship that resembled technocracy. In his book, all resources were carefully managed. There was no private property. Genetic engineering and conditioning produced just the right type and number of people to operate the system.

In 1958, Huxley wrote a follow-up called *Brave New World Revisited*. Even though he was an environmentalist and a globalist, he was disturbed by the prospect of a scientific dictatorship. He concluded *Revisited* by expressing his concerns in a backhanded way: "There seems to be no good reason why a thoroughly scientific dictatorship should ever be overthrown."[1]

In a scientific dictatorship like technocracy, there is no room for a political structure—say, a Constitution—that might allow citizens to change that structure, if they saw fit to do so. The early

1 Huxley, Aldous. *Brave New World Revisited.* (First published in 1958. The paperback was published in 2006 by Harper Perennial, under the name 1st Harper Perennial modern classics ed., New York.)

technocrats wanted to completely remove the political layer of society, opting to appoint technocrats, not politicians, to leadership positions.

Technocracy, as it was originally conceived, also dismissed ownership of private property. People who own nothing, whether land or cars or gold or guns, would have neither the means nor the might nor the right to defend themselves, should they choose to resist. Rather, under technocracy's universal basic income (UBI) system, they would be beholden to the technocracy and have no incentive or ability to better themselves or their position in life. They would be born into institutionalized slavery, and they would die in that same slavery.

We now know that technocracy and transhumanism are bound together like Siamese twins. They are joined at the hip—not to mention at the hand, the heart, and the head.

Transhumanism seeks to transform humanity in the same manner that technocracy seeks to transform society. They work as one, and neither can exist without the other.

If David Rockefeller had not started the Trilateral Commission in 1973 to promote the New International Economic Order, no Agenda 21 or Sustainable Development would have been created in 1992, nor would the 2030 Agenda, with its seventeen Sustainable Development Goals (SDGs), have been created by the United Nations in 2015. The 2016 Paris Agreement on global warming would not have been agreed to and signed by 195 nations.

Harking back to the early 1970s, we will recall that the Trilateral and United Nations globalists were just beginning to set up their confidence game, with the goal of grabbing for themselves the rich resources of the entire world. We had the impression they were lusting after land, timber, minerals, and wildlife alone. Only later did we discover that they considered *us humans* to be resources as well.

Since no nation or individual would ever wittingly and willingly give up their wealth to another, an elaborate scheme had to be devised to trick victims into voluntarily going along with the globalists' vision. Thus, a fake global warming scam was created by the UN to scare people into Sustainable Development, aka technocracy.

When that scam ran out of steam in 2019, the COVID scam came roaring down the tracks in 2020. Was it the scammers' intent that the overblown response to that contrived pandemic would kill millions and do untold damage to the global economy? If so, they succeeded. And, as they did with the global warming fraud, they made it appear that only Sustainable Development could save the world from what we now know to be a relatively harmless virus.

What can save us from a global financial crisis? Sustainable Development. What can save us from a global famine? Sustainable Development. What can save us from an energy crisis? Sustainable Development. What can save us from an ecological collapse? Sustainable Development. Are you seeing the picture the SDG-concocting con artists are shoving in your face?

Transhumanism officially joined forces with technocracy in 1992 at the first Earth Summit. Out of it came Agenda 21. The UN Summit on Biodiversity, which convened at the same time, had a related agenda: subject all living things to genetic modification. We did not know then, but *now* we know, that their plan for modifying the genetics of all living things includes human beings.

We also know that both technocracy and transhumanism are driven by scientism, which replaces God with the god of science—a twisted version of science. Scientism is an evil religion that C. S. Lewis predicted would ultimately result in the abolition of man. Once traditional values are completely discarded, he observed:

> *. . . we are mere nature to be kneaded and cut into new shapes for the pleasures of masters who must, by hypothesis, have no motive but their own 'natural' impulses.*[2]

Lewis came to essentially the same conclusion as Huxley did about the permanency of scientific dictatorship, but from a different angle: "If the eugenics are efficient enough," wrote Lewis, "there will be no second revolt [against nature], but all snug be-

2 Lewis, C. S. *The Abolition of Man*. (HarperCollins, 1944). Page 73.

neath the Conditioners, and the Conditioners beneath her, till the moon falls or the sun grows cold."[3]

Francis Schaeffer arrived at the same place as Lewis and Huxley, as I explained in Technocracy News & Trends in December 2021:

> *Dr. Francis Schaeffer was an historian, Christian philosopher and one of the greatest thinkers of the last century. In Episode X (the final segment) of his video series, How Should We Then Live?, he stated that society was falling into a moral abyss with no fixed absolutes to provide form and structure for living. To replace that necessary structure and thereby avoid utter societal chaos, he accurately and clearly recognized that such absolutes would be supplied by an increasingly authoritarian, technocratic elite.*[4]

Schaeffer's sentiment reminds me of a quote from Wesley J. Smith of Discovery Institute. Smith wrote in *The War on Humans*:

> *And then there is the attempt by some self-appointed "science advocates" to corrupt and co-opt the scientific method as a justification for a misguided philosophy known as scientism. Scientism mistakenly asserts that science can not only tell us the way things are and how things work, but also identify right from wrong.*[5]

Because scientism undergirds technocracy and transhumanism, both have been loosed from traditional moral and ethical values—from the "fixed absolutes" that Schaeffer spoke of. Both share a mechanistic worldview that envisions everything—man included—operating like a machine. Both believe that if enough is learned about that machine, it becomes the object of their control. Their absolute control.

## Ultimately to fail

In the end, there is no conceivable way that technocracy or transhumanism will survive or achieve their self-aggrandizing

3 Lewis. Page 68.

4 Wood, P. M. "Academic Backing of Technocracy." Technocracy News & Trends. December 22, 2021. https://www.technocracy.news/day-2-academic-backing-of-technocracy

5 Smith, Wesley J. *The War on Humans*. (Discovery Institute Press, 2014). Page 15.

goals. That might sound like good news, but it bears a warning. Every day that the evil twins have free rein to advance their Utopian agendas, the world will suffer increasingly harsh consequences. If and when the twins are stopped in their tracks, whether in the near or distant future, we will have to assess the cumulative damage they have caused and then look for *non*-authoritarian, *un*-tyrannical ways to set the world aright again—to set it and ourselves free.

If there is one thing both evil twins hate, it is noncompliance with their demands. A planned scientific dictatorship cannot tolerate outliers. That is why UN literature is riddled with sugar-coated phrases like "no person left behind" and seductive words like "inclusive." We see this mentality of pretending to care for humanity when we study the evil twins' drive for digital identity.

Digital ID isn't primarily for the industrialized world, which is already well-connected and mostly compliant. No, it is for all those who are not yet connected. This includes not only the unconnected in poor, rural areas of America but also the unconnected in African villages and in the Amazon rainforest.

To the evil twins, does unconnected mean non-compliant? One can't help but draw that conclusion. It is obvious they need to sweep all of humanity into their system if they are to be truly successful. Thus, to the extent outliers remain unconnected, they potentially pose a threat to the twins' new world order.

Understanding this gives us the first solid means of resistance: Don't comply. And the second solid means of resistance: Since silence is consent, don't consent.

This is not to imply that you must give up all of your electronic devices, bank accounts, and modern conveniences and go live under a bridge. That would be self-defeating. Let's consider a few examples of how to not comply and yet not renounce everything helpful to your life.

- Got a credit/debit card? The global banking establishment wants to create digital currencies to replace cash. What should you do? Use cash instead of plastic whenever possible; cash purchases are neither trackable nor traceable. To keep that cash in circulation, spend it daily. Use every opportunity to tell every cashier—what an appropriate word!—why you are giving them cash, and encourage them to do the same when they shop. Leave a cash tip for your waiters: They love not having to wait for days to get the tip electronically or for weeks to get it in a paycheck.

- Got a smart phone? Buy a Faraday bag for your phone, which will make you invisible to tracking or other surveillance. When inside the sealed bag, your phone cannot receive or send any signals. Faraday bags are inexpensive, and there are several manufacturers.
- Got a smart meter? Buy a Faraday cage that goes over the meter, blocking EMF and 5G radiation.
- Got other smart devices in your home? That is, things like Alexa, Siri, smart appliances, smart TVs, and security cameras. If they're hooked up to the Internet, disconnect them and stop the intrusion on your privacy. Remember, when connected, these devices can collect mountains of personal data from you every day.
- Got a Wi-Fi router at home or work? Hardwire your devices instead, and turn off the wireless portion of the router.
- Got email? Don't use any free email service like Gmail, which tracks everything you do. Instead, use ProtonMail, StartMail, Tutanota, or another secure email service. True, they charge a fee, because they don't collect and sell your data to the rest of the world—but it's a small price to pay for privacy. Tutanota is the least expensive of the three I cited.
- Told to wear a face mask or to take an EUA jab? Don't! Yes, it will cost you something—perhaps only convenience—to *not* go along with orders. But you'll feel so free when you calmly explain to the order-givers *why* you are not willing to comply.

- Do you buy stuff? Buy in locally owned shops. And, whenever possible, buy locally made or locally grown products. If not possible, then at least buy Made in America products.
- Live in a community? Get involved and take a stand. Civic involvement is the bedrock of a constitutional republic. There are boards, committees, and public forums where you can offer input and can influence local policies. Drive out technocrat and transhuman ideologies and policies, and educate others about the dangers the evil twins pose—dangers health-wise, money-wise, rights-wise.
- Like to be healthy? Take responsibility for your own health by demanding honest answers from any healthcare provider with whom you associate. Make your own informed decisions rather than accepting the propaganda.
- Like to watch TV? Consider dropping cable TV (which monitors everything you tune into) and instead install a TV antenna to get local channels. Many good alternative news organizations have free live and recorded channels on Rumble, Brighteon, and BitChute.
- Like to drive around town? If you have a smart phone but not a Faraday bag to block tracking, always at least turn off Wi-Fi so your phone doesn't harvest identities from surrounding Wi-Fi devices. If you don't need Bluetooth, turn it off, too.
- Like to attend church? Give your pastor a copy of this book and then discuss it with him in detail. Encourage your pastor to raise awareness in his congregation of the technocratic and transhuman agenda.

This is certainly not a definitive or exhaustive list of things you can do to become more of an outlier to the evil twins. But it should get you thinking in the right direction. Interfacing with the world is not an all-or-nothing proposition, either. Anything you can do to remain closer to outlier territory puts a wrench in their gears.

## Free Speech and the First Amendment

The Bill of Rights in the US Constitution starts with the First Amendment:

> *Congress shall make no law respecting an establishment of religion or prohibiting the free exercise thereof; or abridging the freedom of speech, or of the press; or the right of the people peaceably to assemble, and to petition the Government for a redress of grievances.*

The framers of the Bill of Rights understood these rights to be given by God to all men, rather than given by some men to other men—specifically, by some men called "public servants" to other men called "citizens." Thus, the First Amendment starts out by saying "Congress shall make no law . . . ."

The document's authors understood that the five elements enumerated in the First Amendment represent the bedrock of America:

1. Freedom to exercise religion
2. Freedom of speech
3. Freedom of the press
4. Freedom of assembly
5. Freedom to petition the government

In 2018, when social media sites like Twitter and Facebook began to de-platform individuals and organizations in a coordinated, colluding fashion, I knew that censorship was worsening and spreading like a gangrene infection. Prior to that, most censorship was in the form of so-called shadow banning, where a post would be prevented, by algorithms, from appearing in too many other news-feeds.

Sensing a very difficult time ahead, I started a nonprofit organization in 2018 called Citizens for Free Speech (CFFS)[6] to defend and support the First Amendment. Since then, CFFS has attracted tens of thousands of members. We have developed training programs to teach them how to engage locally in civil discourse

6 See https://www.CitizensForFreeSpeech.org.

so they can be heard and can bring about policy changes right where they live. The ability to properly engage in civil discourse is a learned skill that is quite easy to master, but it takes awareness and practice.

In the past four years, since founding CFFS, I have seen censors and fact checkers completely cave in to the cancel culture. Those who speak out against the globalist narrative are virtually wiped out of existence. Financial services like PayPal have ganged up to cancel fundraising and sales operations. Companies offering web support services like email and web hosting are canceling contracts with customers who hold an opinion they disagree with, even despise.

When the COVID-19 panic was purposely revved up in early 2020, the full assault on the First Amendment became painfully clear. Churches were shut down. Mouths were muzzled by masks. Journalists who actually did their jobs were censored for questioning tyrannical policies. Public gatherings were not permitted, except in very small groups.

By practicing *not* knuckling under, we at CFFS have learned an important and effective way to resist censorship: When you are told to not talk about certain things, talk about them even more. When you are told to shut up, talk even louder. When you are told to not attend church, hold services even more frequently. When you are ignored by your legislators or city councilors, protest even more vigorously.

Let me explain why. Our silence over the last forty years has given the evil twins the leeway to spread their propaganda and fulfill their agenda. Now it has reached the point where they are dominating and threatening the entire planet. The only way to take back our rights is to stop being silent. Speak up. Speak out. Speak authoritatively. Speak persuasively. Speak with fire in your belly. The spark of free speech in America must first become a din then turn into a rumble, then into an uproar.

Courage is contagious. But our courage has been intentionally suppressed by the constant onslaught of propaganda haranguing us to accept and obey the globalist narrative of the evil twins.

Famed composer Oscar Hammerstein II understood the importance of courage when he wrote the lyrics to *Stout-Hearted Men* with Sigmund Romberg in 1928:

*Give me some men*
*Who are stout-hearted men*
*Who will fight for the right they adore.*
*Start me with ten*
*Who are stout-hearted men*
*And I'll soon give you ten thousand more.*[7]

The final question is: Will we or won't we? If we fail, the road ahead leads to dystopia and scientific dictatorship. As Founding Father John Adams warned when the Constitution enshrined the God-given gift of liberty, "Liberty, once lost, is lost forever." John Adams knew whereof he spoke.

It is my hope that this book will not depress you but rather encourage you to take your proper place in the world by doing your part to put a stop to the "Evil Twins of Technocracy and Transhumanism."

7 Nelson Eddy singing Stout-Hearted Men. https://www.lyricsondemand.com/n/nelsoneddylyrics/stoutheartedmenlyrics.html

# Bibliography


Akin, William E., and William Ernest Akin. Technocracy and the American Dream: The Technocrat Movement, 1900-1941. Univ of California Press, 1977.

Arendt, Hannah. The Origins of Totalitarianism. 1968.

Arslanian, Henri, and Fabrice Fischer. The Future of Finance: The Impact of Fintech, Ai, and Crypto on Financial Services. Springer, 2019.

Baker, James Calvin. The Bank for International Settlements: Evolution and Evaluation. Greenwood Publishing Group, 2002.

Beck, Glenn. Agenda 21: Into the Shadows. Simon and Schuster, 2015.

Bell, Daniel. The Coming of Post-Industrial Society. Basic Books, 1976.

Blewitt, John. Understanding Sustainable Development. Routledge, 2017.

Bradley, Brendan. Esg Investing for Dummies. John Wiley & Sons, 2021.

Breggin, Peter, and Ginger Breggin. Covid-19 and the Global Predators: We Are the Prey. 2021.

Brzezinski, Zbigniew, and Zbigniew K. Brzezinski. Between Two Ages: America's Role in the Technetronic Era. Viking Press, 1976.

Burris, Beverly H. Technocracy At Work. SUNY Press, 1993.

Câmara, Paulo, and Filipe Morais. The Palgrave Handbook of Esg and Corporate Governance. Palgrave Macmillan, 2022.

Chishti, Susanne, and Janos Barberis. The Fintech Book: The Financial Technology Handbook for Investors, Entrepreneurs and Visionaries. John Wiley & Sons, 2016.

Cohen, Bonner. The Green Wave: Environmentalism and Its Consequences. 2006.

Coleman, Vernon. Endgame: The Hidden Agenda 21. Independently Published, 2021.

Collins, Paul David, and Phillip Darrell Collins. The Ascendancy of the Scientific Dictatorship: An Examination of Epistemic Autocracy, From the 19th to the 21st Century. Booksurge Llc, 2006.

Cowburn, John S J, and Tim Patrick. Scientism. Wipf & Stock Publishers, 2013.

Dargent, Eduardo. Technocracy and Democracy in Latin America. Cambridge University Press, 2015.

Desmet, Mattias. The Psychology of Totalitarianism. Chelsea Green Publishing, 2022.

DeWeese, Tom. Agenda 21: The Wrenching Transformation of America. 2018.

DeWeese, Tom. Agenda 21 and How to Stop it. 2019.

Dolan, Cristina, and Diana Barrero Zalles. Transparency in Esg and the Circular Economy: Capturing Opportunities Through Data. 2021.

Drexler, Eric. Engines of Creation: The Coming Era of Nanotechnology. Anchor, 1987.

Drucker, Peter. Post-Capitalist Society. Routledge, 2012.

Einzig, Paul. The Bank for International Settlements. London, Macmillan, 1930.

Esmark, Anders. The New Technocracy. Bristol University Press, 2020.

Fischer, Frank. Technocracy and the Politics of Expertise. SAGE Publications, Incorporated, 1990.

French, Duncan, and Louis J. Kotzé. Sustainable Development Goals: Law, Theory and Implementation. Edward Elgar Publishing, 2018.

Friedman, Jeffrey. Power Without Knowledge: A Critique of Technocracy. Oxford University Press, USA, 2020.

Frodeman, Robert. Transhumanism, Nature, and the Ends of Science: A Critique of Technoscience. Routledge, 2019.

Fuller, R. Buckminster. Operating Manual for Spaceship Earth. Estate of R. Buckminster Fuller, 2008.

Fuller, Richard Buckminster. Buckminster Fuller to Children of Earth. Doubleday Books, 1972.

Fuller, S. Humanity 2.0: What it Means to be Human Past, Present and Future. Springer, 2011.

Ganio-Mego, Joe. Artificial Intelligence and Religion: A Mathematical Approach, Religion, Ai and Evolution. Joe GANIO-MEGO, 101-01-01.

Geraci, Robert M. Apocalyptic Ai: Visions of Heaven in Robotics, Artificial Intelligence, and Virtual Reality. Oxford University Press, 2012.

Gupta, Pranay, and T. Mandy Tham. Fintech: The New DNA of Financial Services. Walter de Gruyter GmbH & Co KG, 2018.

Habermas, Jürgen. The Lure of Technocracy. John Wiley & Sons, 2015.

Harari, Yuval Noah. Sapiens: A Brief History of Humankind. Harper Collins, 2015.

Harari, Yuval Noah. Homo Deus: A Brief History of Tomorrow. HarperCollins, 2017.

Harari, Yuval Noah. Sapiens: A Graphic History: The Birth of Humankind (Vol. 1). HarperCollins, 2020.

Hawken, Paul, Amory Lovins, and L. Hunter Lovins. Natural Capitalism. Little, Brown, 2007.

Herbert, David. Becoming God: Transhumanism and the Quest for Cybernetic Immortality. Sola Scriptura Ministries International, 2014.

Hixson, J. B. Spirit of the Antichrist: The Gathering Cloud of Deception. 2022.

Huberman, Jennifer. Transhumanism: From Ancestors to Avatars. Cambridge University Press, 2020.

Huxley, Aldous. Brave New World. Harper Collins, 1998.

Huxley, Aldous. Brave New World Revisited: A Novel. Harper Collins, 2014.

inc, Technocracy. Technocracy Study Course. Lessons I. 1934.

Isely, Philip. A Constitution for the Federation of Earth. 1977.

Kennedy, Robert F. The Real Anthony Fauci: Bill Gates, Big Pharma, and the Global War on Democracy and Public Health. Skyhorse, 2021.

Khanna, Parag. How to Run the World: Charting a Course to the Next Renaissance. Random House Incorporated, 2011.

Khanna, Parag. Connectography: Mapping the Future of Global Civilization. Random House, 2016.

Khanna, Parag. Technocracy in America: Rise of the Info-State. 2017.

Kissinger, Henry A., Eric Schmidt, and Daniel Huttenlocher. The Age of a.I. 2021.

Kleinberg, Benjamin, and Benjamin S. Kleinberg. American Society in the Postindustrial Age: Technocracy, Power, and the End of Ideology. Merrill Publishing Company, 1973.

Klyczek, John Adam. School World Order: Skull and Bones, Technocracy, and the Corporate Globalization of Education. 2019.

Koire, Rosa. Behind the Green Mask: U.n. Agenda 21. 2011.

Kraay, Klaas. God and the Multiverse: Scientific, Philosophical, and Theological Perspectives. Routledge, 2014.

Kurzweil, Ray. The Age of Spiritual Machines: When Computers Exceed Human Intelligence. Penguin, 2000.

Kurzweil, Ray. The Singularity is Near: When Humans Transcend Biology. Penguin, 2005.

Kurzweil, Ray. How to Create a Mind: The Secret of Human Thought Revealed. Penguin, 2013.

Kurzweil, Ray. The Singularity is Nearer. Random House Large Print, 2022.

Laing, Graham Allan. Towards Technocracy. 1933.

Lane, Justin E. Understanding Religion Through Artificial Intelligence: Bonding and Belief. Bloomsbury Publishing, 2021.

Lewis, C. S. The Abolition of Man. Harper Collins, 2009.

Livingstone, David. Transhumanism: The History of a Dangerous Idea. David Livingstone, 2015.

Loeb, Harold. Life in a Technocracy: What it Might be Like. Syracuse University Press, 1996.

Lovins, L. Hunter, and Boyd Cohen. Climate Capitalism: Capitalism in the Age of Climate Change. Hill and Wang, 2011.

Lowrey, Annie. Give People Money: How a Universal Basic Income Would End Poverty, Revolutionize Work, and Remake the World. Crown, 2019.

Malleret, Thierry, and Klaus Schwab. Covid-19: The Great Reset. ISBN Agentur Schweiz, 2020.

Manzocco, Roberto. Transhumanism - Engineering the Human Condition: History, Philosophy and Current Status. Springer, 2019.

McDonough, Brian, and Jessie Bustillos Morales. Universal Basic Income. 2019.

Mercer, Calvin, and Tracy J. Trothen. Religion and the Technological Future: An Introduction to Biohacking, Artificial Intelligence, and Transhumanism. Springer Nature, 2021.

Mercola, Joseph, and Ronnie Cummins. The Truth About Covid-19: Exposing the Great Reset, Lockdowns, Vaccine Passports, and the New Normal. Chelsea Green Publishing, 2021.

Meynaud, Jean. Technocracy. New York : Free Press, 1969.

Mikovits, Judy, and Kent Heckenlively. Plague of Corruption: Restoring Faith in the Promise of Science. Simon and Schuster, 2021.

Morano, Marc. The Great Reset: Global Elites and the Permanent Lockdown. Simon and Schuster, 2022.

More, Max, and Natasha Vita-More. The Transhumanist Reader: Classical and Contemporary Essays on the Science, Technology, and Philosophy of the Human Future. John Wiley & Sons, 2013.

Moreland, J. P. Scientism and Secularism: Learning to Respond to a Dangerous Ideology. Crossway, 2018.

Musser, Mark. Nazi Ecology: The Oak Sacrifice of the Judeo-Christian Worldview in the Holocaust. 2018.

Nakajima, Tadahiro, Shigeyuki Hamori, Xie He, Guizhou Liu, Wenting Zhang, Yulian Zhang, and Tiantian Liu. Esg Investment in the Global Economy. Springer Nature, 2021.

Nations, United, and United Nations Division for Sustainable Development. Agenda 21: Earth Summit: The United Nations Programme of Action From Rio. Createspace Independent Pub, 2013.

Nordangard, Jacob. Rockfeller: Controlling the Game. Stiftelsen Pharos, 2019.

Olson, Richard. Science and Religion, 1450-1900: From Copernicus to Darwin. Greenwood Publishing Group, 2004.

Olson, Richard. Science and Scientism in Nineteenth-Century Europe. University of Illinois Press, 2008.

Olson, Richard G. Scientism and Technocracy in the Twentieth Century: The Legacy of Scientific Management. Lexington Books, 2015.

Our Common Future. 1992.

Porter, Henry Alfred. Roosevelt and Technocracy. 1932.

Postman, Neil. Technopoly: The Surrender of Culture to Technology. Vintage, 1993.

Putt, Archibald. Putt's Law and the Successful Technocrat. Smithtown, N.Y.: Exposition Press, 1981.

Putt, Archibald. Putt's Law and the Successful Technocrat: How to Win in the Information Age. John Wiley & Sons, 2006.

Radaelli, Claudio Maria. Technocracy in the European Union. Routledge, 1999.

Rana, Fazale R., and Kenneth Richard Samples. Humans 2.0: Scientific, Philosophical, and Theological Perspectives on Transhumanism. 2019.

Raymond, Allen. What is Technocracy. 1933.

Renneberg, Monika, and Mark Walker. Science, Technology, and National Socialism. Cambridge University Press, 2003.

Sachs, Jeffrey D. The Age of Sustainable Development. Columbia University Press, 2015.

Sanford, John C. Genetic Entropy & the Mystery of the Genome. Ivan Press, 2005.

Schneier, Bruce. Data and Goliath: The Hidden Battles to Collect Your Data and Control Your World. W. W. Norton & Company, 2015.

Schwab, Klaus. The Fourth Industrial Revolution. Currency, 2017.

Schwab, Klaus. Stakeholder Capitalism: A Global Economy That Works for Progress, People and Planet. John Wiley & Sons, 2021.

Schwab, Klaus, and Nicholas Davis. Shaping the Future of the Fourth Industrial Revolution. Currency, 2018.

Scott, Howard. Introduction to Technocracy. 1938.

Serap, Sisman-Ugur, and Gulsun, Kurubacak. Handbook of Research on Learning in the Age of Transhumanism. IGI Global, 2019.

Shatzer, Jacob. Transhumanism and thc Image of God: Today's Technology and the Future of Christian Discipleship. InterVarsity Press, 2019.

Singh, Rajesh. Human Species and Beyond. BookPros, LLC, 2006.

Sirius, R. U., and Jay Cornell. Transcendence: The Disinformation Encyclopedia of Transhumanism and the Singularity. Disinformation Company, 2015.

Smith, David Livingstone. On Inhumanity: Dehumanization and How to Resist it. Oxford University Press, 2020.

Smith, Wesley J. The Culture of Death: The Assault on Medical Ethics in America (Large Print 16pt). ReadHowYou-Want.com, 2010.

Smith, Wesley J. The War on Humans. Discovery Institute, 2014.

Smith, Wesley J. Culture of Death: The Age of Do Harm Medicine. Encounter Books, 2016.

Sorell, Tom. Scientism: Philosophy and the Infatuation With Science. Routledge, 2013.

Sorgner, Stefan Lorenz. On Transhumanism. Penn State Press, 2020.

Sutton & Wood. Trilaterals Over Washington, Volumes I and II. Coherent, 2015.

Taylor, Frederick Winslow. The Principles of Scientific Management. 1913.

Tegmark, Max. Life 3.0: Being Human in the Age of Artificial Intelligence. Vintage, 2017.

Teichrib, Carl. Game of Gods: The Temple of Man in the Age of Re-Enchantment. 2018.

Thacker, Jason. The Age of Ai: Artificial Intelligence and the Future of Humanity. Zondervan, 2020.

Williams, Richard N., and Daniel N. Robinson. Scientism: The New Orthodoxy. Bloomsbury Publishing, 2014.

Willis, Mikki. Plandemic: The Incredible True Story About the Most Banned Documentary in History. Skyhorse, 2021.

Wood, Patrick M. Technocracy: The Trojan Horse of Global Transformation. Coherent, 2015.

Wood, Patrick M. Technocracy: The Hard Road to World Order. Coherent, 2018.

Wyatt, John, and Stephen N. Williams. The Robot Will See You Now: Artificial Intelligence and the Christian Faith. SPCK, 2021.

Zuboff, Shoshana. In the Age of the Smart Machine: The Future of Work and Power. 1988.

Zuboff, Shoshana. The Age of Surveillance Capitalism: The Fight for a Human Future At the New Frontier of Power. PublicAffairs, 2019.

# Appendix I

# Key Transhumanist Documents

## *The Transhumanist Declaration (2012)*

*1. Humanity stands to be profoundly affected by science and technology in the future. We envision the possibility of broadening human potential by overcoming aging, cognitive shortcomings, involuntary suffering, and our confinement to planet Earth.*

*2. We believe that humanity's potential is still mostly unrealized. There are possible scenarios that lead to wonderful and exceedingly worthwhile enhanced human conditions.*

*3. We recognize that humanity faces serious risks, especially from the misuse of new technologies. There are possible realistic scenarios that lead to the loss of most, or even all, of what we hold valuable. Some of these scenarios are drastic, others are subtle. Although all progress is change, not all change is progress.*

*4. Research effort needs to be invested into understanding these prospects. We need to carefully deliberate how best to reduce risks and expedite beneficial applications. We also need forums where people can constructively discuss what could be done and a social order where responsible decisions can be implemented.*

*5. Reduction of risks of human extinction, and development of means for the preservation of life and health, the alleviation of grave suffering and the improvement of human foresight and wisdom, be pursued as urgent priorities and generously funded.*

*6. Policy making ought to be guided by responsible and inclusive moral vision, taking seriously both opportunities and risks, respecting autonomy and individual rights, and show-*

*ing solidarity with and concern for the interests and dignity of all people around the globe. We must also consider our moral responsibilities towards generations that will exist in the future.*

*7. We advocate the well-being of all sentience, including humans, non-human animals, and any future artificial intellects, modified life forms, or other intelligences to which technological and scientific advance may give rise.*

*8. We favor morphological freedom – the right to modify and enhance one's body, cognition, and emotions. This freedom includes the right to use or not to use techniques and technologies to extend life, preserve the self through cryonics, uploading, and other means, and to choose further modifications and enhancements.*[1]

1 The "Transhumanist Declaration" has been modified over the years by several organizations and individuals, although there is little record of the specific modifications and their respective authors. Nevertheless, the original "Transhumanist Declaration" was crafted in 1998 by, in alphabetical order: Alexander Sasha Chislenko, Anders Sandberg, Arjen Kamphuis, Bernie Staring, Bill Fantegrossi, Darren Reynolds, David Pearce, Den Otter, Doug Bailey, Eugene Leitl, Gustavo Alves, Holger Wagner, Kathryn Aegis, Keith Elis, Lee Daniel Crocker, Max More, Mikhail Sverdlov, Natasha Vita-More, Nick Bostrom, Ralf Fletcher, Shane Spaulding, T.O. Morrow, Thom Quinn. https://mxplx.com/meme/3743/

# Transhumanist Bill of Rights (Version 3)

### *Preamble*

*Whereas science and technology are now radically changing human beings and may also create future forms of advanced sapient and sentient life, transhumanists establish this TRANSHUMANIST BILL OF RIGHTS to help guide and enact sensible policies in the pursuit of life, liberty, security of person, and happiness.*

### *Articles*

***Article I.*** *All sentient entities are hereby entitled to pursue any and all rights within this document to the degree that they deem desirable – including not at all. All sentient entities are entitled, to the extent of their individual decisions, to all the rights and freedoms set forth in this TRANSHUMANIST BILL OF RIGHTS, without distinction of any kind, such as race, color, sex, gender, language, religion, political or other opinion, national, social, or planetary origin, property, birth (including manner of birth), biological or non-biological origins, or other status. Furthermore, no distinction shall be made on the basis of the political, jurisdictional, or international status of the country or territory to which a sentient entity belongs, whether it be independent, trust, non-self-governing, or under any other limitation of sovereignty. In the exercise of their rights and freedoms, all sentient entities shall be subject only to such limitations as are determined by law solely for the purpose of securing due recognition and respect for the rights and freedoms of others and of meeting the just requirements of morality, public order, and the general welfare in a democratic society, which may not undermine the peaceful prerogatives of any individual sentient entity. These rights and freedoms may in no case be exercised contrary to the purposes and principles of this TRANSHUMANIST BILL OF RIGHTS.*

***Article II.*** *The enumeration in this TRANSHUMANIST BILL OF RIGHTS of certain rights shall not be construed to deny or disparage any other rights retained by sentient entities.*

***Article III.*** *All sentient entities shall be granted equal and total access to any universal rights to life. All sentient entities are created free and equal in dignity and rights. They are endowed with reason and conscience and should act towards one another in a spirit of brotherhood (without necessitating any particular gender or implying any particular biological or non-biological origin or composition).*

***Article IV.*** *Sentient entities are entitled to universal rights of ending involuntary suffering, making personhood improvements, and achieving an indefinite lifespan via science and technology. The right of ending involuntary suffering does not refer to euthanasia but rather to the application of technology to eliminate involuntary suffering in still-living beings, while enabling their lives to continue with improved quality and length.*

***Article V.*** *No coercive legal restrictions should exist to bar access to life extension and life expansion for all sentient entities. Life expansion includes life extension, sensory improvements, and other technologically driven improvements of the human condition that might be achieved in the future.*

***Article VI.*** *Involuntary aging shall be classified as a disease. All nations and their governments will actively seek to dramatically extend the lives and improve the health of their citizens by offering them scientific and medical technologies to overcome involuntary aging.*

***Article VII.*** *All sentient entities should be the beneficiaries of a system of universal health care. A system of universal health care does not necessitate any particular means, policy framework, source, or method of payment for delivering health care. A system of universal health care may be provided privately, by governments, or by some combination thereof, as long as, in practice, health care is abundant, inex-*

*pensive, accessible, and effective in curing diseases, healing injuries, and lengthening lifespans.*

**Article VIII.** *Sentient entities are entitled to the freedom to conduct research, experiment, and explore life, science, technology, medicine, and extraterrestrial realms to overcome biological limitations of humanity. Such experimentation will not be carried out on any sapient being, without that being's informed consent. Sentient entities are also entitled to the freedom to create cybernetic artificial organs, bio-mechatronic parts, genetic modifications, systems, technologies, and enhancements to extend lifespan, eradicate illness, and improve all sentient life forms. Any such creations that demonstrate sapience cannot be considered property and are protected by the rights presented herein.*

**Article IX.** *Legal safeguards should be established to protect individual free choice in pursuing peaceful, consensual life-extension science, health improvements, body modification, and morphological enhancement. While all individuals should be free to formulate their independent opinions regarding the aforementioned pursuits, no hostile cultural, ethnic, or religious perspectives should be entitled to apply the force of law to erode the safeguards protecting peaceful, voluntary measures intended to maximize the number of life hours citizens possess.*

**Article X.** *Sentient entities agree to uphold morphological freedom—the right to do with one's physical attributes or intelligence whatever one wants so long as it does not harm others.*

*This right includes the prerogative for a sentient intelligence to set forth in advance provisions for how to handle its physical manifestation, should that intelligence enter into a vegetative, unconscious, or similarly inactive state, notwithstanding any legal definition of death. For instance, a cryonics patient has the right to determine in advance that the patient's body shall be cryopreserved and kept under specified conditions, in spite of any legal definition of death that might apply to that patient under cryopreservation.*

*Morphological freedom entails the duty to treat all sapiens as individuals instead of categorizing them into arbitrary subgroups or demographics, including as yet undefined subcategorizations that may arise as sapience evolves.*

*However, the proper exercise of morphological freedom must also ensure that any improvement of the self should not result in involuntary harms inflicted upon others. Furthermore, any sentient entity is also recognized to have the freedom not to modify itself without being subject to negative political repercussions, which include but are not limited to legal and/or socio-economic repercussions.*

**Article XI.** *An altered, augmented, cybernetic, transgenic, anthropomorphic, or avatar sentient entity, whether derived from or edited by science, comprised of or conjoined with technology, has the right to exist, form, and join the neo-civilization.*

**Article XII.** *All sentient entities are entitled to reproductive freedom, including through novel means such as the creation of mind clones, monoparent children, or benevolent artificial general intelligence. All sentient entities of full age and competency, without any limitation due to race, nationality, religion, or origin, have the right to marry and found a family or to found a family as single heads of household. They are entitled to equal rights as to marriage, during marriage, and at its dissolution. Marriage shall be entered into only with the free and full consent of the intending spouses. All families, including families formed through novel means, are entitled to protection by society and the State. All sentient entities also have the right to prevent unauthorized reproduction of themselves in both a physical and a digital context. Privacy and security legislation should be enacted to prevent any individual's DNA, data, or other information from being stolen and duplicated without that individual's authorization.*

***Article XIII.*** *No sentient entity shall be subjected to arbitrary interference with his, her, or its privacy, family, home, or correspondence, nor to attacks upon his, her, or its honor and reputation. Every sentient entity has the right to the protection of the law against such interference or attacks. All sentient entities have privacy rights to personal data, genetic material, digital, biographic, physical, and intellectual enhancements, and consciousness. Despite the differences between physical and virtual worlds, equal protections for privacy should apply to both physical and digital environments. Any data, such as footage from a public security camera, archived without the consent of the person(s) about whom the data were gathered and subject to legal retention, shall be removed after a period of seven (7) years, unless otherwise requested by said person(s).*

***Article XIV.*** *No sentient entity shall be subjected to arbitrary arrest, detention or exile. Sousveillance laws should be enacted to ensure that all members of peaceful communities feel safe, to achieve governmental transparency, and to provide counter-balances to any surveillance state. For instance, law-enforcement officials, when interacting with the public, should be required to wear body cameras or similar devices continuously monitoring their activities.*

***Article XV.*** *All sentient entities, with the exception only of those in legal detention, have the right to private internet access without such access being prohibited or circumvented by either private corporations or governmental bureaucracy.*

***Article XVI.*** *All sentient entities are equal before the law and are entitled without any discrimination to equal protection of the law. All sentient entities are entitled to equal protection against any discrimination in violation of this TRANSHUMANIST BILL OF RIGHTS and against any incitement to such discrimination. All sentient entities should be protected from discrimination based on their physical form in the context of business transactions and law enforcement.*

**Article XVII.** *All sentient entities have the right to life, liberty and security of person. All sentient entities have the right to defend themselves from attack, in both physical and virtual worlds.*

**Article XVIII.** *Societies of the present and future should afford all sentient entities sufficient basic access to wealth and resources to sustain the basic requirements of existence in a civilized society and function as the foundation for pursuits of self-improvement. This includes the right to a standard of living adequate for the health and well-being of oneself and one's family, including food or other necessary sources of energy, clothing, housing or other appropriate shelter, medical care or other necessary physical maintenance, necessary social services, and the right of security in the event of involuntary unemployment, sickness, disability, loss of family support, old age, or other lack of livelihood in circumstances beyond the sentient entity's control. Present and future societies should ensure that their members will not live in poverty solely for being born to the wrong parents. All children and other recently created sentient entities, irrespective of the manner or circumstances of their creation, shall enjoy the same social protection. Each sentient entity, as a member of society, has the right to social security and is entitled to realization, through national effort and international co-operation and in accordance with the organization and resources of each State, of the economic, social, and cultural rights indispensable for his, her, or its dignity and the free development of his, her, or its personality.*

**Article XIX.** *Irrespective of whether or not technology will eventually replace the need for the labor of sentient entities, all sentient entities should be the beneficiaries of an unconditional universal basic income, whereby the same minimum amount of money or other resources is provided irrespective of a sentient entity's life circumstances, occupations, or other income sources, so as to provide a means for the basic requirements of existence and liberty to be met.*

**Article XX.** *Present and future societies should provide education systems accessible and available to all in pursuit of factual knowledge to increase intellectual acuity; promote critical thinking and logic; foster creativity; form an enlightened collective; attain health; secure the bounty of liberty for all sentient entities for our posterity; and forge new ideas, meanings, and values. All sentient entities have the right to education. Education shall be free, at least in the elementary and fundamental stages. Technical and professional education shall be made generally available, and higher education shall be equally accessible to all on the basis of merit. Education shall be directed to the full development of the sentient entity's personality and to the strengthening of respect for all sentient entities' rights and fundamental freedoms. It shall promote understanding, tolerance, and friendship among all nations, racial, religious, and other sentient groups – whether biological, non-biological, or a combination thereof – and shall further the maintenance of peace. Parents and other creators of sentient entities have a prior right to choose the kind of education that shall be given to their children or other recently created sentient entities which have not yet developed sufficient maturity to select their own education.*

**Article XXI.** *All sentient entities are entitled to join their psyches to a collective noosphere in an effort to preserve self-consciousness in perpetuity. The noosphere is the sphere of human thought and includes, but is not limited to, intellectual systems in the realm of law, education, philosophy, technology, art, culture, and industry. All sentient entities have the right to participate in the noosphere using any level of technology that is conducive to constructive participation.*

**Article XXII.** *Sentient entities will take every reasonable precaution to prevent existential risks, including those of rogue artificial intelligence, asteroids, plagues, weapons of mass destruction, bioterrorism, war, and global warming, among others.*

**Article XXIII.** *All nations and their governments will take all reasonable measures to embrace and fund space travel,* *not only for the spirit of adventure and to gain knowledge by exploring the universe, but as an ultimate safeguard to its citizens and transhumanity should planet Earth become uninhabitable or be destroyed.*

**Article XXIV.** *Transhumanists stand opposed to the post-truth culture of deception. All governments should be required to make decisions and communicate information rationally and in accordance with facts. Lying for political gain or intentionally fomenting irrational fears among the general public should entail heavy political penalties for the officials who engage in such behaviors.*

**Article XXV.** *No sentient entity shall be held in slavery or involuntary servitude; slavery and the slave trade shall be prohibited in all their forms.*

**Article XXVI.** *No sentient entity shall be subjected to torture or to treatment or punishment that is cruel, degrading, inhuman, or otherwise unworthy of sentience or sapience.*

**Article XXVII.** *Each sentient entity has the right to recognition everywhere as a person before the law.*

**Article XXVIII.** *All individual sentient entities have the right to an effective remedy by the competent local, national, international, or interplanetary tribunals for acts violating the fundamental rights granted them by the constitution, by law, and/or by this TRANSHUMANIST BILL OF RIGHTS.*

**Article XXIX.** *All individual sentient entities are entitled in full equality to a fair and public hearing by an independent and impartial tribunal, in the determination of their individual rights and obligations and of any criminal charge against them.*

**Article XXX.** *All individual sentient entities charged with a penal offence have the right to be presumed innocent until proved guilty according to law in a public trial at which they individually have had all the guarantees necessary for their defense. No sentient entity shall be held guilty of any penal offence on account of any act or omission which did not constitute a penal offence, under national or international law,* *at the time when it was committed. Nor shall a heavier penalty be imposed than the one that was applicable at the time the penal offence was committed.*

**Article XXXI.** *All sentient entities have the right to freedom of movement and residence within the borders of each state. Each individual sentient entity has the right to leave any country, including his, her, or its own, and to return to his, her, or its country.*

**Article XXXII.** *All sentient entities have the right to seek and to enjoy in other countries asylum from persecution. This right may not be invoked in the case of prosecutions genuinely arising from non-political crimes or from acts contrary to the purposes and principles of this TRANSHUMANIST BILL OF RIGHTS.*

**Article XXXIII.** *All sentient entities have the right to a nationality. No sentient entity shall be arbitrarily deprived of his, her, or its nationality nor denied the right to change his, her, or its nationality.*

**Article XXXIV.** *All sentient entities have the right to own property alone as well as in association with others. No one shall be arbitrarily deprived of his, her, or its property.*

**Article XXXV.** *All sentient entities have the right to freedom of thought, conscience and religion; this right includes freedom to change one's religion or belief, and freedom, either alone or in community with others and in public or private, to manifest one's religion or belief in teaching, practice, worship, and observance. This right also includes freedom not to have a religion and to criticize or refuse to engage in any religious practice or belief without adverse legal consequences.*

**Article XXXVI.** *All sentient entities have the right to freedom of opinion and expression; this right includes freedom to hold opinions without interference and to seek, receive, and impart information and ideas through any media and regardless of frontiers.*

***Article XXXVII.*** *All sentient entities have the right to freedom of peaceful assembly and association. No sentient entity may be compelled to belong to an association.*

***Article XXXVIII.*** *All sentient entities have the right to take part in the government of their countries, directly or through freely chosen representatives. All sentient entities have the right of equal access to public service in their countries. The will of the constituent sentient entities shall be the basis of the authority of government; this will shall be expressed in periodic and genuine elections which shall be by universal and equal suffrage of sentient entities and shall be held by secret vote or by equivalent free voting procedures.*

***Article XXXIX.*** *All sentient entities have the right to work, to free choice of employment, and to just and favorable conditions of work, as long as employment is offered or considered economically necessary in the sentient entity's proximate society and contemporary epoch. All sentient entities who choose to work have the right to equal pay for equal work. All sentient entities who choose to work have the right to just and favorable remuneration, ensuring for themselves and their families an existence worthy of human dignity, and supplemented, if necessary, by other means of social protection, such as a universal basic income. All sentient entities have the right to form and join trade unions for the protection of their interests; however, no sentient entity may be compelled to join a trade union as a condition of employment.*

***Article XL.*** *All sentient entities have the right to rest and leisure commensurate with the physical requirements of those sentient entities for maintaining optimal physical and mental health, including reasonable limitation of working hours and periodic holidays with pay in societies where paid employment is considered economically necessary.*

***Article XLI.*** *All sentient entities have the right freely to participate in the cultural life of the community, to enjoy the arts, and to share in scientific advancement and its benefits. All sentient entities have the right to the protection of the moral* *and material interests resulting from any scientific, literary, or artistic production of which they are the authors.*

***Article XLII.*** *All sentient entities are entitled to a social and international order in which the rights and freedoms set forth in this TRANSHUMANIST BILL OF RIGHTS can be fully realized.*

***Article XLIII.*** *Nothing in this TRANSHUMANIST BILL OF RIGHTS may be interpreted as implying for any State, group, or sentient entity any right to engage in any activity or to perform any act aimed at the destruction of any of the rights and freedoms set forth herein.*[2]

---

2 Published by the U.S. Transhumanist Party and originally compiled by Zoltan Istvan. Version 1 (2015), version 2 (2016), version 3 (2018). https://transhumanist-party.org/tbr-3/.

# The Transhumanist Manifesto

The manifesto was originally authored by transhumanist pioneer Natasha Vita-More, PhD in 1983, but has been updated by the same author in 1998 and 2008. Vita-More is currently Executive Director and Chairman of Humanity+, a non-profit 501(c)(3) educational organization and a Professor of Graduate and Undergraduate Programs at the University of Advancing Technology. The Transhuman Manifesto is widely recognized as the authoritative and central document that guides the modern transhuman movement.[3]

The Transhumanist Manifesto asserts that both aging and death is a disease that can be overcome by the application of advanced technology, genetic engineering in particular, to the human condition. The text below represents the Version 4 that was released in 2020.

> ***A vision for shared appreciation of life and purpose***
>
> *People create theories and related opinions that can bring about discord and divisiveness by pitting one belief against another with false assumptions and suggest one group as being more or less worthy than another based on age, gender, race, appearance, religion, beliefs, and political and social status. This sentiment is not about biology or human evolution; it is about a human need to control that is triggered by fear, greed, and uncertainty. Humanity needs a change—a new outlook that helps us become more humane.*
>
> *This something new is transhumanism—a worldview that seeks a quality of life that brings about perpetual progress, self-transformation, practical optimism, visionary solutions, and critical thinking—the transhuman.*
>
> *The transhuman[ii] is a biological-technological organism, a transformation of the human species that continues to evolve with technology. This evolution is understood within the fields of paleontology, archaeology, evolutionary biolo-*

3 See curriculum vitae at: https://natashavita-more.com/wp-content/uploads/2022/04/CV-2022-1.pdf

*gy, and anthropology. It is further studied and understood in philosophical discourse and social and cultural studies. It is made aware and realized through advances in technology that bring about human-computer interaction, wearable devices, and computerized communication infrastructures. It is evidenced in medical science and scientific breakthroughs that identify genetic mutation and target disease as well as research and development of gene therapies that aim to reverse and restore cellular damage of biological system. On an environmental level, it is experienced in spaceflight by astronauts adapting to environments beyond earth. On an interactive level, it is experienced in the personalized avatar and character usage of virtual reality, augmented reality, video games, and other artificial environments.*

***Life Extension & Expansion***

*Life extension aims to increase the maximum human lifespan. Life expansion means increasing the length of time a person is alive and diversifying the matter in which increasing options and capabilities a person exists. For human life, the length of time is bounded by a single century and its matter is tied to biology.*

*To pursue longevity, it is crucial to uncover visible and invisible borders between interconnecting forces that disrupt health and well-being. It is also necessary to actively address ethical concerns about science and technology with reasonable defense, to protect human rights, including morphological freedom.[iii]*

*Transhumanism is the first philosophy and worldview to publicly proclaim the need to eradicate disease and to advocate for longevity and ageless thinking. Transhumanists have contributed toward the ideas, research, development, and education of longevity through science, technology and addressed governing bodies and groups on the ethical use of technology such as AI, nanotechnology, and genetic engineering.*

*Transhumanists are the world's strongest advocacy for a positive future of health, well-being, and prosperity for every human.*

***I would rather be a transhuman than a cyborg***

*The technology for transhuman transformation emerges from cybernetics. It is here where concepts of the human and machine integrate and the computer begins to interact (Wiener 1950:163)[iv] with the human body and its biology, bringing about the concept of the cyborg. Comparisons are often drawn between the cyborg and the transhuman deliberately and also unwittingly. A cyborg is positioned as an endpoint for the integration of human, machine, and computer; however, the transhuman is a continuous human evolution. This evolution includes a confluence of organic human, technological advances in AI, nanomedicine, and gene therapies that mitigate disease, the devices and prosthetics and enhance biology that append biology, and an awareness of personal identity, as a transformative, telematic, and expanded agency that expands through new tech-communication systems.*

*The cyborg, no matter how sophisticated the augmentations and implants or written essays on the topic, as articulated by Professors Steven Mann, Kevin Warwick, or Donna Haraway,[v] has yet to address issues of life extension. This area is most distinctly in concert with the transhuman as one obvious outcome of an enhanced person that seeks to life extension and to engage alternative options for perceptual, cognitive, and physical bodies.*

*A problem in the blurring of cyborg and transhuman (or future posthuman) proposes a tripartite delineation as follows:*

*"- the field of cybernetics parlayed the cyborg into existence through the relationship between the human and its man-machine augmentation (Clynes & Kline 1960)[vi]" [for the purposes of space exploration and did not foresee biotechnology, AI, or nanotechnology as bringing about an adaptive, evolutionary human—the transhuman];*

*"- the field of philosophy parlayed the transhuman into culture as a transitional stage of human transformation and regenerative processes and selective enhancement, more currently referred to as the activist and recipient of human enhancement ...(More 1990; Bostrom 2005)[vii];*

*"- the field of science fiction parlayed the posthuman into the arts (Pepperell 1995)[viii], now more currently aligned with artificial general intelligence and artificial platforms of the "upload" whole brain emulation and/or substrate-independent minds (Sandberg & Koene 2009)[ix]"*

*Simply adding gadgetry to our bodies will not make us modern or evolved, nor will designing new bodies and environment to inhabit without a transdisciplinary strategy. The human body and its diversification requires a cross-pollination of ideas to foster conjectural, multidimensional processes for addressing complex issues of machine and human. Human perception weaves cognition and bodily processes to transmit and translate information, which the patterns reflect an array of molecular activities of biology. Future human use of nano molecules of nanotechnology could work in concert with biology (Drexler 1987)[x]. The elements of molecular assembly will help to build new types of bodies, such as Platform Diverse Body (Vita-More, 1997) (2013)[xi].*

***Beyond: Social, Religious, Political Bias***

*Transhumanism offer a new philosophical approach to the human condition while simultaneously expanding upon antecedents, such as the Renaissance, Enlightenment, Modernism, and Postmodernism. Transhumanism values human potential but does not see the human as the final stage of existence.*

*Transhumanism accepts certain human enculturated behaviors as held between types of people but does not support the notions of a universal human nature. By this, transhumanism does not participate in social, religious, or political absolutes or biases that aim to constrain and curtail peoples' rights and freedoms. Rather than being divisive about religious and political views, transhumanism seeks a meta focus on healthy longevity as a positive end point rather than the path each person travels to get there. To support this end point, transhumanism advocates for legal wins within the medical, technological, and scientific domains that will help develop longevity research and development as well as personal freedoms for end of life choices. More awareness must be ignited for success in reaching the positive end point, which includes targeted global advocacy for education that focuses on humanity's future.*

*Transhumanism recognizes the uniqueness of people and the need to overcome irrelevant bias of age, race, gender, appearance, religion, beliefs, and political and social status, and supports gender diversity to include rather than exclude a heightened awareness of the potential multiplicities of gender and sexual options. In this transitional process, the transhuman sheds worn-out biases and integrates new values and methods for longevity—extending the maximum lifespan, improve biology, and increase mental acuity.*

1. *Beyond Mortality: The disease of aging leaves people helpless, locked in a system of sickness and death rather than a system of healthcare and life. We need new technology, science and social structures that promote positive conditions rather than negative conditions.*
2. *Beyond Scarcity: We must improve global quality of life. An economy of abundance is not about how much; it is about how good—a quality of life that provide basic human needs, freedom, well-being, and that advances opportunity and potential.*
3. *Beyond Cruelty: Discrimination of people because of sex, age, race, gender, appearance, religion, beliefs, and political and social status are global, verifiable, and prevalent. What would society need to overcome misperception and cognitive bias? With an abundance of compassion, discrimination has no place or purpose. [xii]*

*I am the architect of my existence. My life reflects my vision and represents my values. It conveys the very essence of my being—coalescing imagination and reason, challenging all limits.*

*Transhumanism calls upon a heightened sensibility to reveal the multiplicity of realms yet to be discovered, yet to be realized. We are exploring how current and future technologies affect our senses, our cognition, and our lives. Our attention to and comprehension of these relationships become fields of art as we participate in the most immediate and vital issues for transhumanity: extending life, augmenting intelligence, and creativity, exploring the universe.*

---

***Transhumanist Manifesto 1983***

*I am transhuman.*
*In an aim to integrate creativity and reason*
*for the purpose of self-awareness and longevitiy*
*—promoted by persistence*
*aware of odds, informed by risk,*
*alert to new discovery, welcoming challenge,*
*ever-changing—*
*I become.*

---

*Transhumanists invent and design with technology and collaborate with the cosmos, perform in multiple realities, automorph mind and body, conceive, innovate, and explore. We indelibly engrave longevity memes. We are the neo-cyberneticists utilizing high-end creativity, engineering skills, scientific data, and automated tools to author our visions.*

*Transhumanists encourage experimentation and attitudes of abundance and emphasizes the infinite possibilities of self-transformation as we seek new values indispensable to our self-creation. We have no interest in focusing on self-defeating thinking or entropy. We are achieving refined emotions through provocative forward thinking and analytical techniques.*

*Each person influences social and cultural change: how we live and who we are. Each person creates a sense of self, autonomous yet connected to culture's continuum. How we accomplish our intentions is a matter of selective individual choice—whether abstract or concrete, whether artifact or non-form. Our criteria for art remain open and we welcome cross-disciplinary innovations.*

*Our unique ingenuity will spread far out into the capillaries of society. We are active participants in our own evolution. We are shaping the image of whom we are becoming (1983 v.2; 1998 v.2.).*[4]

***Original references:***

*[i] More, Max (1990) Transhumanism: Toward a Futurist Philosophy. In Extropy Magazine. Vol. 4, No. 1.*

*[ii] Vita-More, N. (1986-1995). [Note: The research on the history of the term "transhuman" and "transhumanism" was completed by Natasha Vita-More and Winifred Drake Clark during the late 1980s to mid-1990s: "As an historical note, the Italian verb "transumanare" or "transumanar" was used for the first time by Dante Alighieri (1265-1321) in the Divine Comedy. It means "go outside the human condition and perception" and in English could be "to Transhumanate" or "to Transhumanize." T.S. Eliot wrote about the risks of the human journey in becoming illuminated as a "process by which the human is Transhumanised" (1950:147) in his play "The Cocktail Party" (1950). The actual concept of transhuman as an evolutionary transition was first expressed by FM-2030 (f/k/a FM Esfandiary). His trilogy, Optimism One (1970), Up-Wingers (1973)and Telespheres (1977) comprises his unique ideas about the transhuman, some of which were mentioned in the final chapter of Woman In The Year 2000 (1974). Ideas about humanity and evolution were explored by Julian Huxley in his writings on evolutionary humanism in the book Evolution: The Modern Synthesis (1942) and suggested the term transhuman for a "superior being aware of his potential and*

4 More, Natasha Vita-More, "Transhumanist Manifesto, Fourth Edition". https://natashavita-more.com/transhumanist-manifesto/.

*able to work toward it because of his knowledge" (Halacy 1965:11). Pierre Teilhard de Chardin referenced the transhuman in The Future of Man (2004) and, in 1966, FM-2030 (fka FM Esfandiary) outlined an evolutionary transhuman future while teaching "New Concepts of the Human" at the New School for Social Research in New York City. Abraham Maslow referred to transhumans in Toward a Psychology of Being (1968), Robert Ettinger also referred to transhumans in Man into Superman (1972), the author wrote the "Transhuman Manifesto" (1982), and Damien Broderick discusses the transhuman in the science fiction novel The Judas Mandala (1982), and by Natasha Vita-More in the "Transhuman Manifesto" (1983).[ii].*

*[iii] Wikipedia: https://en.wikipedia.org/wiki/Morphological_freedom.*

*[iv] Wiener, Norbert. (1950) The Human Use of Human Beings: Cybernetics. New York: Da Capo Press, pp. x, 58, 95, 103, 134-135, 163.*

*[v] Mann, Steve. (May 1998) WEARABLE COMPUTING as a means for PERSONAL EMPOWERMENT. Keynote address titled presented at the 1998 International Conference on Wearable Computing ICWC-98, Fairfax VA.*

*Warwick, Kevin. (2004) I, Cyborg. Champaign, IL: University of Illinois Press, p. 4.*

*Haraway, Donna. (1991) Simians, Cyborgs, and Women: The Reinvention of Nature. New York: Routledge, pp. 3-5, 149-181.*

*[vi] Clynes, Manfred E., and Kline, Nathan. S. (1960) Cyborgs and Space. In Astronautics, American Rocket Society Inc, New York, New York, pp. 26, 27, 29, 33.*

*[vii] Bostrom, Nick. (2005) A History of Transhumanist Thought. In Journal of Evolution and Technology, Vol. 14, No. 1.*

*[viii] Pepperell, Robert. (1995) The Post-Human Condition. Bristol, UK: Intellect.*

*[ix] Sandberg, Anders and Koene, Randal. (3 October 2009) Anders Sandberg and Randal Koene On Whole Brain Emulation. In H+ Magazine. See http://hplusmagazine.com/2009/10/03/singularity-summit-anders-sandberg-and-randal-keone-whole-brain-emulation/.*

*[x] Drexler, Eric. (1987) Engines of Creation. Harpswell, ME: Anchor, pp. v, 4, 213.*

*[xi] Vita-More, Natasha. (March 2012) Life Expansion. Plymouth, UK. University of Plymouth. https://pearl.plymouth.ac.uk/handle/10026.1/1182 [xi] . (2013) Body by Design. https://www.youtube.com/watch?v=vVG2MbpHd4o*

*[xii] Goertzel, B. and Vita-More, N. (2020). H+ Summit 2020. https://humanityplus.org/projects/humanity-conferences/*

# Appendix II

## Bible Questions & Answers

Because I frequently receive questions from readers relating to Bible prophecy, it is useful to relate not only the questions, but some answers as well.

Eschatology is a branch of theology that deals with future and final events concerning the world and humanity. The book of Revelation in the New Testament is one of the main texts of the Bible that deals almost exclusively with future things. As might be expected, there are many New and Old Testament passages that tie into Revelation. In this light, it is important to remember that the Bible is a single book with sixty-six chapters, written by 44 different authors over a period of 1,600 years.

Many Christians are sensing that the forces of evil seem to be rising all around the world. I have also heard this from non-Christians as well. Given the content of this book, there isn't much doubt that the world is in a very different state than it has ever been in the past.

When searching for answers in the Bible, it is most important to pay attention to every detail, carefully keeping each one in the context of the text as well as the entirety of scripture. The answers below are based on my own study and analysis of Bible Prophecy over 45 years. You may have different thoughts and conclusions.

### Question: Are we in the "end times"?

Acts 2:17a states, "And it shall come to pass in the **last days**, saith God, I will pour out of my spirit upon all flesh." However, the passage goes on to talk about signs in heaven and on earth that only match events that take place during the Tribulation - that is, the time of 7 years described in Revelation: blood and fire, sun turning to darkness and the moon turning red. All of this happens "before that great and notable day of the Lord come." (Acts 2:18). The "day of the Lord" is further described in 2 Peter 3:10:

*"But the day of the Lord will come as a thief in the night; in which the heavens shall pass away with a great noise, and the elements shall melt with fervent heat, the earth also and the works that are therein shall be burned up."*

It is self-evident that we have not reached this point, and that we are not in the 7-year tribulation period right before the second coming of Christ. Thus, the times we live in are not yet the "end times" spoken about in the Bible.

Are we close to the beginning of the 7-year tribulation period? Many Christians believe that we are very close. In that sense, it might better said that "We are close to the end times."

## Question: Are these as the "Days of Noah" ?

Matthew 24:36 states "But as the *days of Noah* were, so shall also the coming of the Son of man be." This question is closely related to the last one. The verse goes on to talk about the judgment of the world:

*Matthew 24:38 For as in the days that were before the flood they were eating and drinking, marrying and giving in marriage, until the day that Noah entered into the ark,*

*39 And knew not until the flood came, and took them all away; so shall also the coming of the Son of man be.*

The characteristics of the "days of Noah" seem familiar - eating, drinking, sexual immorality - but the worst is yet to come and will not happen until the world enters into the 7-year tribulation period. Then, social and societal structures will completely break down. That time will be marked by murders, stealing, drunkenness, abuse of drugs, sexual immorality, occultism and idol worship. We simply are not there yet.

However, are we getting close to that period? Again, many Christians believe so.

## Question: What is the "mark of the beast"?

Again, the "mark of the beast" is only seen in Revelation:

*Revelation 13:15 And he had power to give life unto the image of the beast, that the image of the beast should both speak, and cause that as many as would not worship the image of the beast should be killed.*

*16 And he causeth all, both small and great, -- rich and poor, free and bond, to receive a mark in their right hand, or in their foreheads:*

*17 And that no man might buy or sell, save he that had the mark, or the name of the beast, or the number of his name.*

This is the most frightening prospect because of what is stated in Revelation 14:11:

*And the smoke of their torment ascendeth up forever and ever: and they have no rest day nor night, who worship the beast and his image, and* **whosoever receiveth the mark of his name***.*

Even non-Christians are disturbed about the "mark of the beast", whatever it is, and rightly so because the consequences of receiving it are indeed horrifying.

This mark is identified in a lengthy passage in Revelation 13:

*11 And I beheld another beast coming up out of the earth; and he had two horns like a lamb, and he spake as a dragon.*

*12 And he exerciseth all the power of the first beast before him, and causeth the earth and them which dwell therein to worship the first beast, whose deadly wound was healed.*

*13 And he doeth great wonders, so that he maketh fire come down from heaven on the earth in the sight of men,*

*14 And deceiveth them that dwell on the earth by the means of those miracles which he had power to do in the sight of the beast; saying to them that dwell on the earth, that they should make an image to the beast, which had the wound by a sword, and did live.*

*15 And he had power to give life unto the image of the beast, that the image of the beast should both speak, and cause that as many as would not worship the image of the beast should be killed.*

*16* ***And he causeth all, both small and great, -- rich and poor, free and bond, to receive a mark in their right hand, or in their foreheads:***

*17 And that no man might buy or sell, save he that had the mark, or the name of the beast, or the number of his name.*

First, notice that there are three entities here: the "beast", the "image of the beast", and "another beast" with all the power of the first beast. Scholars identify the first beast as the Antichrist and the third one as the False Prophet. Thus, it is the False Prophet who creates the *image* of the Antichrist. This image, whatever it might be, is an object of worship for the followers of Antichrist. The proposition is clear: worship the image or die.

This is directly comparable to the story in chapter 3 of Daniel in the Old Testament. King Nebuchadnezzar ordered a 90 foot gold statue to be built on the plain of Dura near Babylon. He then called everyone to visit the statue. When the music played, the instructions were to "fall down and worship the gold statue" and if you refused, "you will be thrown into a blazing furnace right away." Thus, there were only two groups: those who worshiped and those who were killed.

In Revelation 13, those who are willing to worship the Antichrist will receive a special seal in their forehead or on their hand. Thereafter, since they are pledged to the Antichrist, they will be allowed to participate in his economic system to buy and sell to survive. For all who don't have the "mark", they will not be able buy or sell. Without the mark, they will be easily identified to receive the sword instead.

There are clear implications in the text:

- The entire issue of the mark is still future tense to this age, taking place midway through the Tribulation period. Thus, it is impossible to receive such a mark today because it is not available yet, nor has the Antichrist been revealed.
- No one can accidentally receive the mark. It is intentional based on worshiping the Antichrist.

- The mark is personally identifiable and allows worshipers to buy and sell freely.
- No one can go back once they "belong" to the Antichrist.
- The only ones who would refuse the mark at that time will be those already sealed by Christ Himself. They will quickly become martyrs as the Antichrist seeks to destroy all of God's people.

In any case, there is no reason to fear that some certain technology today is the "mark of the beast" and that if you touch or take it, you will be doomed.

## Question: Is it impossible to be saved during the Tribulation period?

This is an understandable question because many Christians have friends, family and loved ones who have not yet made a commitment to Christ. They are worried that when the 7-year Tribulation begins, the door to salvation will be closed forever.

This is not the case.

In Revelation chapter 7, God seals and sends out the 144,000 witnesses to the ends of the earth to proclaim the gospel to all who would receive salvation. Right after that, the fruit of their effort is seen in Heaven in verse 9:

> *9 After this I beheld, and, lo, a great multitude, which no man could number, of all nations, and kindreds, and people, and tongues, stood before the throne, and before the Lamb, clothed with white robes, and palms in their hands;*

To clear up any confusion as to who this large multitude is, one of the other saints in heaven made it plainly clear: **"These are they which came out of great tribulation, and have washed their robes, and made them white in the blood of the Lamb."** (Rev. 9:14)

When God takes over the primary task of witnessing during the Tribulation, He will leave no stone unturned. First, there is the 144,000 (chapter 7), then are the two witnesses in Jerusalem for 3 1/2 years, and finally, three angels are dispatched to circle the earth in mid-heaven to preach the "everlasting gospel" to all who remain. (Rev. 14:6-9)

Thus, in the midst of judgment on the earth and upon earth-dwellers, God's grace is extended to all who would believe, right up to the end.

## Question: My church is "woke". What can I do?

Sadly, many Christians have been compelled to leave churches that bowed to pandemic mandates such as wearing masks, social distancing, lockdowns, indefinite closures, and vaccination policies. Other churches have turned to "green" policies such as Sustainable Development, carbon reduction, Green New Deal, etc. Still other churches have slipped into beliefs and practices that are clearly not Biblical. One looks to church leadership for loving shepherding and sound teaching, not for the opposite.

I have talked with many in this position who have found church "online" and pastors who have stayed true to their calling. The problem with this is that in-person fellowship is not possible with a remote church.

Hebrews 10:24-25 reveals the importance of meeting regularly with other Christians:

> *24 And let us consider one another to provoke unto love and to good works:*
>
> *25 Not forsaking the assembling of ourselves together, as the manner of some is; but exhorting one another: and so much the more, as ye see the day approaching.*

Mutual consideration, exhortation, council, provoking to love and good works, etc., can only be done as an in-person experience.

If you are in this boat, consider starting a home fellowship or Bible study to meet other like-minded Christians. It doesn't have to be large or cost money. The important thing is just to start, even if with only three or four people.

## Question: Are Bible prophecies being fulfilled today?

This is a serious question but not satisfied with a simple "yes" or "no".

As you contemplate the events and conditions of the future 7-year Tribulation period, you can easily see how the building blocks of prophetical fulfillment are lining up. Here is a good example.

Revelation 13: 15 says, for instance, "And he had power to give life unto the image of the beast, that the image of the beast should both speak, and cause that as many as would not worship the image of the beast should be killed." An image that speaks and forces people into predetermined behavior sounds an awful lot like artificial intelligence (AI) coupled with facial recognition capabilities. It also apparently has the ability to cause the termination of people who do not have the "mark of the beast". Could this be facial recognition software? Or iris, heartbeat or embedded chip recognition? Could the image be a hologram or able to appear all over earth at the same time? Perhaps, but these could be also forerunners of future technology that will make these appear archaic. With technology currently advancing at an incredible rate of speed, we shouldn't be surprised at anything.

On the other hand, we have never seen so many things line up at once, and on a global scale.

If the Devil knows his "time" is at hand, I cannot imagine that he would want to waste even one minute, after the Tribulation starts, to build his infrastructure to control the earth. We might well figure that he would be doing everything in his power right now to create that infrastructure so that it is ready for him to take over on day one when the Tribulation starts.

The bottom line is this: could we say that AI and digital ID's are fulfillment of Bible prophecy? No. Could they play into an important role during the Tribulation, where prophecy is clearly fulfilled? Absolutely so!

As to "buying and selling", we could easily look to Central Bank Digital Currencies as a definitive means of controlling all economic activity. If the current monetary/currency system is scraped in favor of CBDCs, then all purchases and sales can be controlled down to the individuals involved. AI plays a prominent role to calculate consumer worthiness like China does with their Social Credit Score system. Again, such a financial system is not a direct fulfillment of prophecy, but it certainly could be a forerunner to that.

# INDEX

## T



## U



## W



## Z

## OTHER BOOKS BY PATRICK M. WOOD

*Trilaterals Over Washington, Volumes I and II* (Patrick M. Wood and Antony C. Sutton, 1978-1980, Coherent Publishing)

*Technocracy Rising: The Trojan Horse of Global Transformation* (2015, Coherent Publishing)

*Technocracy: The Hard Road to World Order* (2018, Coherent Publishing)

*Globalization and the Crucible of Global Banking* (Coherent Publishing, 2018)

For more information and updates, see:

**WWW.TECHNOCRACY.NEWS**

Coherent Publishing
P.O. Box 52247
Mesa, AZ 85208

Made in the USA
Thornton, CO
02/23/23 22:57:07

85f2cc7e-4962-40cc-9d80-448c595ab41eR01